ARMENIA
AND SURROUNDING
TERRITORIES ABOUT 1910

GURDJIEFF

Making a New World

Other books by J. G. BENNETT

The Crisis In Human Affairs

What Are We Living For?

The Dramatic Universe:

Concerning Subud

Christian Mysticism And Subud

Witness: The Story Of A Search

Values: An Anthology For Seekers

Energies: Material, Vital, Cosmic

A Spiritual Psychology

Long Pilgrimage

GURDJIEFF

MAKING A NEW WORLD

J. G. Bennett

Turnstone Books, London

© 1973 by John G. Bennett

published by
Turnstone Books Ltd.
37 Upper Addison Gardens
London W14 8AJ

ISBN: 0 85500 019 8

First published 1973

Set in Garamond type and printed in England by
The Anchor Press Ltd, and bound by Wm. Brendon & Son Ltd,
both of Tiptree, Essex

Contents

List of Illustrations

Endpaper Maps

Preface

GURDJIEFF died on the 29th of October 1949. He was an extraordinary man who made a profound impact upon those who met him even casually. He attracted widespread attention when he first came to Europe in the early 1920's. He founded a school in France, popularly known as the forest philosophers, and attracted a circle of remarkable men and women whose lives were changed by their contact with him. Through them his ideas have penetrated into the world, particularly among the English-speaking people, and they have had more influence than many suspect.

Nevertheless, after 1935, he almost disappeared from view and remained an enigma till the end of his life. He was surrounded by a small circle of devoted followers, the majority of whom after he died, pledged themselves to perpetuate his work and see to the publication of his books. Of his four books, only one, *The Herald of Coming Good*, was published during his lifetime and, within one year, repudiated and withdrawn from circulation. His great work consists of three books: the first, *Beelzebub's Tales to His Grandson*, was published a few months after his death, the second, *Meetings with Remarkable Men*, ten years later, and the third, now finally being published, *Life is Real Only Then, When "I Am."* These three were regarded by Gurdjieff as a single work with the title *All and Everything* but in practice this title was originally applied to the first.[a]

His books and books about him have been widely sold, but it is

---

[a] In this text, general reference is made to *Third Series*, but specific references use the bibliographic title: *Life is Real Only Then, When "I Am"*.

doubtful if they have been equally widely read. Many people have admitted to me that they had 'dipped into' Gurdjieff's *Beelzebub's Tales* without understanding what it was all about. Very few have read right through and fewer still have claimed to have understood his purpose in writing it. This may partly explain why it is that after his death, in spite of the publication of his books and the very wide circulation of Ouspensky's *In Search of the Miraculous*, which has come to be regarded as the most authoritative summary of Gurdjieff's ideas, he still remains an unknown quantity. His works are in libraries where they are usually classified under religion or occultism. They seldom appear under headings of philosophy or science, yet he claimed that his contribution was both scientific and philosophical. The truth is that it is a manifesto to humanity to which humanity is only now ready to listen.

This is indicated by the fact that now, nearly twenty-five years after his death, a new interest is being taken in him and his work. His books are being read and discussed differently. Appearing all over the world, especially in the English-speaking countries, are groups who set themselves to study his ideas and put them into practice. Many of those who are leading these groups have no acquaintance with his method except through what they have read. He himself asserted that it was not possible to transmit the essence of his teaching by books alone, which casts some doubt on the value of much that is going on.

We have here a not uncommon phenomenon: a strikingly original thinker, who is far ahead of his time, makes an impact upon his immediate followers, but is not understood or accepted by his contemporaries in general. A generation, or sometimes several, have to pass before an interest begins to awaken. This is what has happened with Gurdjieff. The resurgence has been most marked among the young people who are interested in his teaching, because they see in Gurdjieff a prophet of the New Age which they hope will come after the present crisis of mankind has passed. They see in him a break with the past and an understanding of the needs of the future. There is another side to this, which is the belief that in some way Gurdjieff is not a 'lone wolf', but that he belongs to a tradition that is timeless and is, therefore, unaffected by passing fashion and so capable of enlightening our changing world.

Scores of personal accounts of the impression made by Gurdjieff on those who worked with him for many years, or even met him only casually, have appeared in books and periodicals. Each is necessarily subjective, for Gurdjieff was an enigma presenting a different face to every person and to every occasion. His own account, that is to be found solely in the *Third Series* of his writings, *Life is Real Only Then, When "I Am"*, is more revealing than any other, and we are fortunate that this book is now to be published. The principal reason why personal impressions have so little value is that Gurdjieff was from start to finish a seeker experimenting with different ways of living and behaving and with different means for accomplishing his life's work. I can affirm that in me he always inspired love and complete confidence. I never doubted that he wished to help me to fulfil my own life's work, and that we were linked together in a common aim, which was to present to humanity a more acceptable account of 'Man, the World and God' than present-day psychology, science and religion could offer. He had devoted the first half of his life to this greatest of undertakings, and in the second he set himself to share with others the conclusions he had reached. In this he was not wholly successful because nearly all who met him were obsessed with their personal problems and needs and insisted upon looking at him as 'their' teacher. He had immense compassion and gave himself freely. Sometimes he revolted from the stupidity and narrowness of his own followers and shut himself away to find some better way of fulfilling his mission. It must be added that the impression he made upon people was usually needlessly distorted by the way of life he had deliberately set himself, of arousing hostility by 'treading heavily on the most sensitive corn of everyone he met'. What really mattered was Gurdjieff's message as it applies to the present-day world. It is also vital that we should form our own opinion as to whether his message was his own private affair or whether it was part of a greater message coming from a higher source.

In writing this book, I have set myself particularly to examine this aspect of Gurdjieff's life and work; to enquire whether Gurdjieff is to be regarded as an isolated phenomenon or whether he is a representative of a cultural tradition that has existed, does now exist, and is concerned with the present and future needs of mankind. Two chapters are devoted to the evidence that 'schools of wisdom' have existed in Central Asia and are likely, therefore, to exist in our day. In order to examine Gurdjieff's possible connection with 'schools of wisdom', it will be necessary to trace the course of his own searches, which forms a second thread that runs through the book.

The third thread is Gurdjieff's ideas in themselves and the methods that he used for transmitting them to his followers. The entire enterprise is held together by reference to 'Gurdjieff's Question' as I have called it in Chapter 8. This question and the answer he found to it leads to the conclusion that Gurdjieff has left a message of great importance in our day, and that we should set ourselves to decipher this message and put his advice into effect. The question is: "What is the sense and significance in general of life on the earth, and in particular of human life?"

This question does not arise explicitly in the first and second series of Gurdjieff's writings. This is no doubt one reason why few people have been able to look beyond Gurdjieff as man or Gurdjieff as teacher to Gurdjieff as precursor of the New Age. In the coming age, mankind will be compelled to face the question 'What are we here for?' Our grossly selfish and insensitive attitude towards life on the earth and indeed to the earth itself will have to break down before the overwhelming march of events, and the great question 'What are we here for?' will present itself in its stark realism as the central problem of our lives.

Notwithstanding this unifying question, it has not been easy to combine the three strands in the ravelled skein of Gurdjieff's life without some repetition and cross-reference. I have tried to achieve coherence in the context of the ideas rather than by the way of chronology or even the structure of Gurdjieff's 'system'. Gurdjieff himself seldom used the word 'system', and indeed insisted that the structure of our mental processes is inadequate for grasping the real world. He used the term "Objective Reason" to designate a property of the perfected man which combines the Beatific Vision of Religion with the Pure Reason of Kant and in addition implies the possession of imperishable Being. The aim of every individual must be to attain some degree of Objective Reason, for which he must be prepared to abandon reliance upon the usual processes of thought. The manner in which he presented his ideas was apparently chaotic and often contradictory, but on close study, discloses a deep underlying unity of purpose. It is this that I have tried to uncover.

This has necessitated the study of Gurdjieff's published works as well as the hitherto unpublished *Third Series* and many notes of lectures and conversations given between 1915 and the end of his life. I have also used my own diaries and letters that I wrote between 1923, when I first went to the Institute at Fontainebleau, and in

1948 and 1949, when I saw him frequently in Paris. I have been fortunate to use the very extensive notes and diaries given me by Miss Gladys Alexander who knew Gurdjieff from 1922 till the end of his life, and who spent many years in his Institute. She was one of his most successful pupils. And I have also used notes given to me by another English pupil, Miss Elinor Crowdy, who herself became a teacher of his ideas. I am very grateful to members of the group who worked with Gurdjieff in Paris during the war years for letting me have transcripts of meetings which give valuable insights into his final teaching period 1941–8. But most of all I am grateful to members of his own family who have allowed me to inspect his personal papers, passports and other official documents, thus enabling me to verify dates and places which would otherwise have remained conjectural. They have also given me permission to quote from his unpublished works in my possession.

The task would scarcely have been possible had I not been familiar with the countries of the Near East in which Gurdjieff lived and worked for more than half his life. Unfortunately, I have not fulfilled my ambition to travel extensively in Turkestan but I have met people from the region: Sarts and Uzbegs, Turkmen and Tartars, some of whom were dervishes well aware of the importance of their traditions. I have often remarked upon the strong feeling of 'growing warmer' that one experiences as one travels eastward from Istanbul towards Kars, and eastwards again across Persia towards the banks of the Amu Darya, the ancient Oxus, that wonderful river that for 10,000 years has seen the migrations of people, bringing together ancient cultures and enabling new ones to be established. The river is still a magnet to all who feel for the antiquity of man.

Alas, the time of greatness for *en-Nehir*, the River, as it is affectionately called, is closed. It is little more now than a frontier— a water curtain—that separates people who ought to be sharing their understanding, as they have done for thousands of years. Bokhara, Samarkand and Tashkent, names which evoke such wonderful images of past glories, have been converted into modern cities and centres of industry. The Ancient Wisdom is seeking fresh woods and new pastures in the West. One of the reasons why Gurdjieff and his life story have such a strong appeal for young people is the feeling that he has opened a channel to let the waters of life flow again. Others have claimed to have known the Masters of Wisdom, but

Gurdjieff brought their teaching and converted it into a practical way of life for the modern world, not only for individuals, but for the whole human family.

In terms of his hopes and aspirations, Gurdjieff's life may appear to have been a failure. His Institute collapsed; he left very few outstanding disciples behind him. His books have been read as curiosities rather than harbingers of the new world.

Gurdjieff took deliberate measures to ensure that he should not be made a 'cult-figure'. The very powerful effect on all who met him, he referred to as *Zvarnoharno*, which is incidentally the same as the Avestan *hvareno*, mark of a superior being or 'aura of kingship'. His outrageous behaviour was one means he adopted for deflecting incipient hero-worship. He followed this course until he finally abandoned, in 1935, the hope of establishing his Institute. After that time, until the end of his life, he was concerned primarily with individuals who could interpret his ideas. At first, he looked for writers whom he specially trained. These included many who did not become famous like Kathryn Hulme, and René Daumal, but who wrote notable books. He had some remarkable pupils in America, but he took steps to ensure that no organization should be created. Everyone who had capacity for initiative was encouraged to form his or her own group. If he required something done, he often entrusted the task to two, three or more people separately, thus causing confusion and jealousy.

Yet another precaution taken was to give out his ideas in many different forms, always incomplete and sometimes misleading. No one has the right to say: "This is the teaching which we had from Gurdjieff. It is complete, satisfactory and immutable. This is what we have to transmit." Yet, unfortunately, this is just what some of his followers have said. He did not leave behind him either an embryo organization, or a fixed teaching or a designated successor. He did leave a small group of loving and devoted pupils who have set themselves to keep his work in the form in which they received it, passing it on to those who are prepared to accept it without modifying it or adding anything from other sources.

I have followed a somewhat different line. I always have regarded Gurdjieff as my teacher and, a few days before he died, I promised that I would devote myself to making his ideas understood and accepted as far as it was in my power. I felt that, in order to do that, I had to work with it and make something of it for myself. I feel this has now been done, and I have now accepted the challenge to attempt to convey my own understanding to those who may be interested.

On the Saturday before he died, I had two hours alone with Gurdjieff sitting and talking at his café on the Avenue des Ternes. At one point I said that I could never repay him for all he had done for me and my wife. He was silent and then, looking very hard into my eyes, he said: "Only you. Only you can repay for all my labours." I did not and do not take this as an intimation that I was to be his successor: indeed, the very thought did not occur to me. But I was very clear that he was putting me under an immense obligation. Nearly thirty years had passed since I first met him in Constantinople in 1920. My whole life had been transformed by his ideas and his teaching. Since 1932, I had been engaged in working with groups, first under Ouspensky's direction and later on my own. I knew that I was bound to 'repay' by transmitting what I had received: but I did not understand this to mean that I must repeat like a parrot all that I had heard. Many years before, Mme Ouspensky had said to me: "Why do you imitate Mr. Ouspensky? You cannot do his work like he can. You must do your own work your own way." This wise advice had remained with me. We do not fulfil our destiny by imitating others, however superior they may be. Ouspensky himself was well aware of this. It happens that I have before me some pages of the first version of his *Fragments of an Unknown Teaching*, which was later published as *In Search of the Miraculous*. They are corrected in his own handwriting, but were not included in the final version. Nevertheless, they certainly represent Ouspensky's thinking at the time that the draft was written, that is about 1923. I quote because it throws so much light upon Ouspensky's relationship with his teacher. I am grateful to Madame Ouspensky's grand-daughter Tanya Nagro for permission to include it here.

"Gurdjieff's exposition differed so much from everything that we regard as good exposition that I want to say a little more about it. He never gave anything in a finished form. He always gave only the beginnings of ideas, leaving it to his pupils to work them out. He never bothered about terminology and nomenclature, taking the first words that occurred to him and fitting them to his purpose. Sometimes in this way he made definitions that were extraordinarily exact, but there was also such an accumulation of examples that it was necessary to know the subject very well in order to understand what it was about. But he always insisted on the necessity of understanding an idea on a large scale before one could pass to the details.

" 'You don't know how to speak', he used to say to men who were considered good lecturers according to European standards. 'One must speak "roughly". There is no need of detail, one must only indicate the centre of gravity.'

"But the chief thing about his method was the fact that in giving his listeners and his pupils only the beginning of ideas, he seemed to be always waiting to see what they would make of them. And if anyone could make something of what he had received, he could always count on obtaining more, while those who merely tried to remember what they had heard, and tried not to lose it, and, above all, not to show it to others, in the course of time inevitably lost all . . .

"It always reminded me of the parable of the talents. Gurdjieff invariably acted like

'a man travelling into a far country, who called his own servants and delivered unto them his goods. And unto one he gave five talents, to another two, and to another one; to every man according to his several ability; and straightway took his journey. Then he who had received the five talents went and traded with the same and made them other five talents. And likewise he that had received two, he also gained other two. But he that had received one went and digged in the earth and hid his lord's money.'

"It was exactly like this with Gurdjieff. One received more, another less, according to their power and training. The question was what each would make of it. If he tried to develop the ideas, to seek new correlations, to discover the meaning of the schemes in living facts and to pass the ideas on to others, the thought grew and after a while he himself wondered at the wealth of thought contained in two or three sentences dropped by Gurdjieff as though accidentally. But if he did not see the necessity for working upon the ideas, if he committed to memory literally what he had heard and decided that it was all that could be said on the subject, or, on the contrary thought that he had not been told all and that there was a secret he must wait to find out, he not only never found it, but gradually the idea, even in the form in which he first heard it, would begin to slip away from him and was very soon completely lost. But what happened to him often was useful to the former one, i.e., to him who tried to work out the idea.

'For whosoever hath, to him shall be given and he shall have more abundance; but whosoever hath not from him shall be taken away even that he hath.'

"As I watched all this and much else besides I came to the perfectly definite conclusion that Gurdjieff's ideas are 'living' ideas that grow and multiply if properly tended—that is, if they are in the right atmosphere. They never remain in their original form and either grow, or disappear, and in the man who has received the principles of them and accepted them rightly there begins a very interesting process of growth and combination of these ideas."

This is where the original version of Ouspensky's introduction ended.

When Ouspensky severed his connection with Gurdjieff in 1924 he took the view that the system itself should be separated from Gurdjieff, though he attached great importance to preserving it, as far as possible, in the form in which Gurdjieff had given it during the years from 1915 to 1918. He was well aware that Gurdjieff had changed his presentation considerably and he knew that Gurdjieff was writing, and he always received his mimeographed copies of the *Beelzebub's Tales* as and when they became available, but he never spoke to us about it. On the contrary, he said that we should take the ideas as they had been given and neither add nor remove anything. This has continued to be the programme which has been followed by the groups who were closest to Gurdjieff. I cannot find fault with this because it has the great advantage of ensuring that what was left by Gurdjieff will be available at all times, without encountering the difficulty of separating what has come from other sources. In the presentation that I make in this book, I have looked not to other materials so much as to the sources themselves from which Gurdjieff derived his ideas. I believe that it is only by connecting Gurdjieff with the sources—that I have called The Masters of Wisdom—that we can understand the ideas themselves. Their significance for the world turns to no small degree upon their being part of a great concerted action which I am sure is now proceeding to introduce mankind to a new way of thinking about man, the universe and God. It was no less a mission that Gurdjieff proposed for himself and I hope that I shall show in the book that he did a very great deal towards its accomplishment.

In conclusion, I want to make it clear that this book is not a biography of Gurdjieff, although I have been compelled as far as possible to reconstruct the story of the first thirty years of his life which is almost unknown in the West. It is not an exposition of his teaching, although I have felt it necessary to develop in detail some of his more important ideas. It is also not a personal record of my experiences as a pupil. I was tempted to write of some of the extraordinary events of the last two years of his life when I was seeing him very frequently, but I did not wish to give my subjective impressions. I have tried to be objective, making use of all the documentation available, but I have inevitably given my own interpretation. This will necessarily differ from that given by others, but at least it is based upon a long period—fifty-two years—of contact with Gurdjieff and his ideas and methods.

This book could not have reached the printer but for the intervention of Lord Thurlow who most generously devoted much of his first year of retirement from distinguished public service to undertake the editing and revision of my manuscript. He has not altered the sense which remains my responsibility, but he has eleiminated much that was superfluous and improved the sequence and presentation. Many defects remain but they are mine not his. In the later stages he was helped by Alick Bartholomew whom I am glad to have as my new publisher after 25 years of happy association with Hodder & Stoughton. It is no small praise to say that he has been as good to me as they were. I also want to thank Trilby Noon who as my secretary when the book was being written fended importunate visitors with tact and showed the clairvoyant powers to read my almost indecipherable manuscript.

1
Gurdjieff's Homeland

A WEST-BOUND traveller making his way a hundred years ago from Turkestan or Afghanistan would travel as far as he could on 'the river'—that is the Amu Darya, the ancient Oxus, which used to flow into the Caspian Sea and now runs north to the Sea of Aral. He would leave it where it turns near Merv and go south to enter the broad valleys of northern Iran. When he reached Hamadan, he could choose to go south-west through Kirmanshah or north-west through Tabriz. If he were a Muslim pilgrim on his way to the Hejaz, he would go through Baghdad and probably visit the dusty town of Kerbela to mourn with the Alevis the death of Hussein, the grandson of the Prophet. If he were a merchant, on his way to Constantinople, still the splendid capital of the fading Ottoman Empire, he would go north-west to Tabriz. He would be careful to avoid the regions of the Caspian Sea where the Russian secret police would be on the watch for any suspicious visitor who might be a Turkish spy: for war between Russia and Turkey was imminent. He would, therefore, keep to the broad valley bounded on his right hand by the Caucasus Mountains where majestic Mount Ararat, eternally snow-covered, would be visible after two or three days' journey. On his left, passing Lake Urmia, he would follow the interminable mountain ranges of Kurdistan. After several more days, he might discern a great barrier of mountains before him, with the Allahuekber Daglari, more than ten thousand feet above sea-level, between him and the Black Sea.

By now, he had entered the valley of Kars. His impression would depend very largely upon the season of the year. In the winter, the entire plain was snow-bound and little could be seen but flocks of sheep, barely keeping alive in the few sheltered valleys and villages mainly inhabited by Turks with a few scattered Armenians. In the summer, the valley would be scorched by a torrid sun that would leave little vegetation but for the innumerable streams that flow down from the mountains and irrigate the plain. In the spring, the snows thaw and there is heavy rainfall. There is more mud on every hand than one would imagine possible. In autumn, there is a rich harvest of cereals which keeps the population going through the succeeding months of snow and rain. It is a rich country with great pine forests covering the mountain slopes, non-ferrous minerals in the hills and abundant fish in the rivers. There was, at that time, a brisk trade between Persia and Turkey.

For thousands of years, this region has been the cockpit of the Levant. Between 1807 and 1877, four grim wars between Russia and Turkey made Kars itself a battleground. The city was four times besieged and successfully defended by the Turks until it fell at last to the Russians in 1877. At the time our traveller passed through Kars, a Turkish army fifty thousand strong was building up its defences. Forty miles to the east, the Russians were awaiting the signal to attack. Kars, where Gurdjieff grew up, used to be a famous city, the capital of the Armenian kings for five centuries. With its neighbour, Ani, it reached its greatest splendour in the ninth century AD under the Bagratid kings.

Century after century, waves of invasions from Central Asia have reached the corridor between the Kurdish Mountains and the Black Sea. Most had reached their limit and turned back. Between the Assyrians in 500 BC and the Seljuk Turks in AD 1000, the Armenian kingdoms dominated the region. Originally Greek-speaking and calling themselves Greeks, they were so strongly influenced by the Chaldean culture and Zoroastrian doctrine that they developed their own language, their own form of Christianity and an intense pride in their own identity as a people. From this race, came the family of Gurdjieff's mother and he was most at home in his mother's tongue.

Gurdjieff's father came from a family of Cappadocian Greeks. This is one of the oldest races in the world, known to have inhabited the same region for eight and perhaps ten thousand years. We do not know what language was spoken by the aboriginal inhabitants of Asia Minor, but we do know that they had a Great Mother culture, as is shown by the cult remains in the ancient cities that have recently been excavated at Catal Höyük and elsewhere. It is certain that they were among the first arable farmers of the world. There are evidences that they were successful in breeding a variety of grain crops eight or nine thousand years ago and that they had a settled agriculture earlier than any region except perhaps Central Asia. It was not until about the fourth millennium BC, five or six thousand years ago, that the Aryan culture penetrated into this region and blended with the indigenous tradition to produce one of the earliest examples of culture blending. Out of this there developed the powerful Greek language, which was the first language in which men developed abstract thought.

Asia Minor stood between the empires of Babylon and the Greco-Roman world and was influenced by these two great centres of civilization throughout the first millennium BC. After the time of Christ, it was one of the first regions to be converted to Christianity by St. Paul and his fellow missionaries. Cappadocia, which is at the centre of Asia Minor, was the place in which the Christian liturgy was created. This has considerable importance for our understanding of the sources of Gurdjieff's teaching.

During the first millennium of our era, there was a period of relative stability in Asia Minor as compared with the disturbances that were proceeding in Europe and this may be one reason why there was a greater continuity of development of Christian ideas here than in other parts of the world. Towards the end of the first millennium, the great invasions of the Turanian peoples began. The first and in some ways the greatest were the Seljuk Turks, who had already established a high prestige with their kingdoms in northern Persia. The Seljuks dominated Asia Minor for about two hundred years. They were succeeded by the Ottoman Turks, and gradually Asia Minor began to take the shape which it had when Gurdjieff's family were settled there. It was a mixed culture in which Christian and Muslim influences were almost equally powerful. Central Asia, which had possessed one of the highest cultures ever known, in Samarkand and Bokhara, had degenerated by the eighteenth century and fallen an easy prey to the Russian invaders from the west. Nevertheless, even as late as the end of the nineteenth century, the old Muslim influences were still powerful throughout Turkestan. The Caucasus, predominantly Christian, lay between Muslim cultures of the east, west and south. This was Gurdjieff's homeland.

Gurdjieff was born, like many of us, during a war. The country had scarcely recovered from the Crimean War of 1855 in which Kars was successfully defended by the Turks under the local hero,

Osman Agha, during a siege that lasted from 16th June to the 29th September, a fortnight after the fall of Sebastopol in the Crimea. The Treaty of Paris, March 30th, 1856, confirmed Turkish sovereignty over the region. Many Christians migrated across the frontier on the Arpa Chai River, among them Gurdjieff's father, who settled in Alexandropol, formerly Gumru, where Gurdjieff was born during the Russo-Turkish War of 1877. This was the war made famous by the defence of Plevna in Bulgaria, but the defence of Kars by the Turks was no less heroic. This time the city fell and, by the Treaty of St. Stephanos of the 3rd of March 1878, all the eastern provinces of Turkey—Erzurum, Batum, Ardahan and Kars —were ceded to Russia as war indemnity. It remained Russian until the 1917 Revolution when the Turks reoccupied the area up to the Arpa Chai, thus dividing old Armenia into Christian and non-Christian regions.

The date of Gurdjieff's birth, as shown on his passport, was on December 28th, 1877. He himself said that he was much older and also claimed that he was born on the 1st of January old style. I have found it hard to reconcile the chronology of his life with the date of 1877, but his family assert that this is correct. If it is so, he began his search at the early age of eleven because he refers to the year 1888 as a time when new vistas opened to him. He first went to Constantinople in 1891. He says he was a 'lad' at the time of this journey so that the dating is not obviously inconsistent. Nevertheless, it does seem strange that, if he was born in 1877, he should not have mentioned that this occurred during the Russo-Turkish War.

Gurdjieff's family was living in Russian territory at Gumru, only a few miles from the Arpa Chai River, which was then the Russo-Turkish frontier. The Russian army under General Loris Melikof crossed it on the 24th of April 1877. Bitter fighting continued right through the summer to gain possession of Kars, defended by the Turkish army under Gazi Mukhtar Pasha. In October the city was in the last throes and the Tsar sent his brother Grand Duke Nicholas to lead the final assault. With an overwhelming superiority in numbers and armaments the defences were overrun on the night of the 17th/18th November. Six weeks later Gurdjieff was born in Gumru, already renamed Alexandropol in honour of the Tsar's father.

The Russians dictated terms at San Stefano that would have destroyed the Ottoman power for good. Under pressure from Germany, Austria and England there were new negotiations leading to the Treaty of Berlin, 13th July 1878. The Russians kept all the Caucasian territories and the vilayet of Erzurum. Russian eyes were on the Balkans and the Dardanelles. The Caucasus was neglected with fearful consequences for the unfortunate populations.

The whole region was in a state of chaos. The Russian Government, in far away St. Petersburg, had little idea of the problems of the Caucasus and sent a succession of missions with conflicting orders to move and remove whole populations, to build railways and harbours and to enforce various arbitrary schemes of reunification. It is even probable that John Georgiades, later to take the Caucasian form Gurdjieff, did not wish to register the birth of his son George, not knowing where he would finally settle.

Between 1878 and 1893, there were disastrous forced migrations of population, including 80,000 Turks who fled westward to escape from the Russian army. Kars, formerly a prosperous city, had dwindled to a small frontier town with fewer than 10,000 inhabitants. The Russians, to replace more than a hundred thousand Turks who had emigrated into Anatolia, had invited groups of Greeks, Armenians, Yezidis and Assyrians to settle in the region. The population of the entire province consisted of 93,000 Muslims, 37,000 Armenians, 23,525 Greeks, 10,695 colonists from Russia, including Esthonians, Aisors and Romanys from Bessarabia and the Carpathians. There were 24,000 Russian soldiers and officials, but very few settlers from Russia. These figures are significant, because they explain why Gurdjieff grew up speaking Turkish as well as his mother tongue, Armenian, and also why he never really mastered the Russian language. All Greeks and Armenians could speak Turkish, which was the common language in which many races could share. Russian was almost unknown until draconian measures to enforce it were introduced in 1880. His knowledge of Turkish, and especially the dialect of the eastern provinces, was to stand him in good stead when he set out to travel in Central Asia. There were, at that time, many Turkish dialects spoken from Albania on the Adriatic to Chinese Turkestan, six thousand miles to the east. Unlike European languages, the Turkish dialects have remained so similar that it was possible for a Turk from Macedonia to converse without difficulty with an Uzbek or even a Buddhist Kalmuk or Tadjik. Gurdjieff's own writings betray the extent to which he relied upon his knowledge of Turkish. It is unlikely that he ever learned any true Persian dialect, though he no doubt achieved proficiency in the spoken Tibetan language. With the ability to copy the accent and use the idioms of Central Asian dialects, he could be at home anywhere from the Caspian Sea to the Gobi Desert.

We have only Gurdjieff's account, to some extent confirmed by his sister Sophie, who married a Georgian, Feodor Anastasieff, that his forbears were wealthy shepherds who emigrated from Cappadocia into the Trebizond area before the War of 1856. Having lost his fortune as a result of a cattle plague, his father moved on into Russia and became a carpenter. It must be understood that until Gurdjieff met Ouspensky in 1915, we have little information that did not come from his own books and conversations. His *Meetings with Remarkable Men* does not claim to be autobiographical in any strict sense. The purpose is to convey a picture of a value system different from that of modern man, rather than to give an account of Gurdjieff's own life.

Gurdjieff lived in Kars from early childhood to the age of fourteen and frequently returned until his family moved back to Alexandropol when he was over twenty. I visited Kars some years after his death and was able to identify many of the landmarks he describes. The Russian Military Cathedral, though derelict, still stands, as do the fortress, the Russian School and the town square. The old Greek quarter is close to the fortress. This does not explain how Gurdjieff, the son of a humble immigrant with no social status, was able to meet and make friends with priests and officers of the Russian garrison. He himself attributes this to the possession of a beautiful child's soprano voice, which gave him the entry to the cathedral choir and brought him under the influence of the dean who became his first tutor.

I found it hard to believe that one of the most remarkable men of the century could have grown up in that derelict frontier town, cut off from the mainstream of modern civilization. On deeper reflection, I began to see that no more propitious circumstances could have existed. Almost anywhere else Gurdjieff would have been under the conditioning pressure of a powerful culture. He had to meet an almost impossible challenge, but it was not the deadly embrace of a poisoned civilization or the stifling monotony of a culture that had lost its creativity. In 1952, I was shown the old Greek quarter and was astonished to see how the houses were in effect built under the ground with entry through the roofs, so that it was possible to walk over the tops of the houses without seeing what was underneath. It was not until I visited Catal Höyük many years later, that I realised that this was a mode of living that had persisted in Asia Minor for eight thousand years or more. Gurdjieff had his roots in the cradle of history unless we are to reserve that title for Turkestan. There are indeed many points of resemblance between Asia Minor and Turkestan. In both regions, the climatic conditions are very severe. The winters are bitterly cold. I have been there in temperatures as low as forty degrees below freezing. The summers are scorching hot and can go up to 110°F. in the shade. To live underground with a thick mud roof over one's head may very well be one of the most practical ways of meeting such conditions. This may explain why it is that houses of this type have persisted for many thousands of years. But there is also in this a valuable clue to understanding Gurdjieff's intense interest in the past.

He was born and passed his childhood in the midst of sharp historical events. The Russians, after the 1877 War, had stirred up all kinds of elements that had previously been more or less isolated from one another. By herding Yezidis and Assyrian Christians from the south, Armenians from the east, Greeks from the west, Romanys and Esthonians from the north into the valleys of Kars and Ardahan, the Russians created a peculiar cultural tension. The various groups could not avoid meeting and acting upon one another. An intelligent young man, curious to understand his world, could learn much in Kars about the peculiar customs of different peoples.

In his *Meetings with Remarkable Men*, Gurdjieff illustrates the polyethnic character of Kars. His friends included Russians, Aisors (Assyrian Christians), Armenians and Turks. A Tartar, a Gypsy and a Yezidi boy are mentioned in connection with strange events. There can be few places where such a strange collection could be found in one small town.

It is not easy for us to picture a mixed environment so suddenly brought into existence. The migrations of peoples from north, southeast and west were still going on when Gurdjieff was a boy. They had not had time to settle down to a stable symbiosis. The main concern was to create a home for one's family and to keep alive. The behaviour of groups living half a mile away was nobody's concern. The Assyrian Christians had totally different social customs from the Esthonians or the Romanys. The Yezidis were even more strange and unaccountable. Most of the groups kept their allegiance to the hereditary head of their community or church who might be living five hundred miles away. All this had the effect of loosening social constraints by which most people live and made it natural that Gurdjieff should begin to search away from his own home for answers to his questions. Another ethnic group that aroused Gurdjieff's interest were the Molokans, blond Caucasians, living a life apart with their own music and traditional dances. His contact with them may have started his lifelong interest in sacred gymnastics and contributed to this urge to travel.

Gurdjieff's father is presented to us as a man of the bardic tradition, which formerly was universally respected. Homer and the Nordic bards, the Avestan and Vedic poets have preserved for us traditions thousands of years old. Some of their sagas and hymns go back to the last ice age. We should not find it hard to believe that Gurdjieff's father could have known the Gilgamesh epic that was so widely sung in the valleys south of Kars three thousand years earlier. No doubt, Gurdjieff quotes the story at the beginning of his book in order to bring the reader into line with the theme of a continuing tradition as relevant today as it was hundreds or even thousands of years ago. Another significant story is of the conversations with Father Dean Borsh (probably a pseudonym) among which was the reference to Sarikamish where "God was making double ladders there and on the tops of them he was fastening happiness, so that individual people and whole nations might ascend and descend." (Sarikamish is twenty-five miles south-west of Kars in the steep narrow valley that leads to Erzurum. This is the only route into Asia Minor that does not rise above eight thousand feet.) The apparently senseless game of *kastousilia* played by the two 'old men' was to illustrate a form of communication that Gurdjieff used to the end of his life. He was always concerned to ensure that his intentions were understood by the right people and passed unnoticed by others. He was a past master of this art. It is not easy for those of us who are trained to believe that clarity and freedom from ambiguity have an absolute value in speech, to recognize the advantage of conveying meanings by veiled hints, allegories and even by contradictions.

When Gurdjieff asked his father to reveal the principle that had guided his life, he replied that it should be obvious to any man that one should live so as to assure oneself a happy old age. This reply might seem trivial to one who did not see that it implies freedom from the past, or in terms Gurdjieff used much later—"to have paid the debt of one's existence". Ouspensky describes the warm understanding that existed between him and his father and I myself can testify to the special place in his life occupied by his mother. He also referred very specially to his grandmother and the influence she had upon his attitude to life. He quotes in the first chapter of *Beelzebub's Tales*, her death-bed injunction: "In life, never do as others do. Either do nothing—just go to school—or do something nobody else does." We have to take into account in seeking to understand Gurdjieff, that this attitude was adopted by him as his own and gave many of his actions a colour that did not correspond to his deeper aims and purposes. He could be wilfully eccentric even where this was an obstacle to the attainment of objectives he had deeply at heart.

In all his writings, Gurdjieff emphasizes the importance of the family. This is natural enough for a Greek or an Armenian of Asia Minor, where family life in the nineteenth century was the only source of happiness and security. There was little social life, few chances of travelling and meeting knowledgeable people, but a strong feeling of the need to preserve the family culture and traditions. Gurdjieff was driven out to seek experience and knowledge, but he never lost his love of home. During the time that I knew him personally, I could see for myself that his family had a quite different significance for him from that of his pupils and friends. He did little to offer them opportunities to broaden their minds and gave then no encouragement to follow his teaching. The relationship was more than personal: his familp were part of himself and he treated them with the same ruthless disregard of comfort as he treated himself. He took pains to train them to be practical and especially to understand human nature, but appeared to withhold deliberately the kind of education that we value. Such an attitude was not peculiar to Gurdjieff. I have known Greek families from Cappadocia and Armenian families from the eastern vilayets who lived in much the same hard way. Centuries of precarious living under Turkish rule and exposure to the ruthless destructive raids of the mountain Kurds had made them cautious. When Gurdjieff was born, the 'Armenian massacres' were still unknown, but life for Christians in eastern Turkey was precarious. Russia had just liberated the serfs from effectual slavery but the condition of the landless peasants was harder than anything we know today. In the Caucasus and Armenia, the subject races were moving towards open revolt. Neither the Russian nor the Ottoman empires were loved and trusted and the State was very far from being a source of confidence and security. The secret police, which was growing in influence in both Russia and Turkey, was ruthless in its methods and cordially hated everywhere. All these circumstances contributed to the strengthening of family life and led to a feeling of belonging in a special way to one's own race. Round each individual, concentric circles of family, clan and nation presented barriers to intercourse. We must take this into account in considering the extraordinary openness that prevailed at Kars between 1880 and 1890, during Gurdjieff's boyhood. I believe that is partly attributable to the Russian policy of settling immigrants from many nations in Kars and the surrounding country.

In Asia Minor, when I travelled through the country early in 1919, before the Greek Army occupied Smyrna, the situation was much as it had been for the preceding fifty years. The different races or nations, Turks, Greeks, Armenians, Jews, Tatars, Lazes and Kurds, though fairly friendly, were enclosed in their own communities. Cities and even small towns were divided into 'quarters' within which each *raya*, the non-Muslim ethnic community, kept largely to itself. Kars was not like that after the Russian conquest. It was, therefore, not hard for Gurdjieff to meet and even become intimate with people from totally different cultural backgrounds, while, at the same time, maintaining a close family loyalty.

Gurdjieff often spoke of his interest in the gypsies, or more correctly, the Romanys who came to Kars from Bessarabia and resumed without difficulty their traditional mode of life. There were also Romanys in the Caucasus and even in Central Asia so that the migrations of the 1880's brought about a renewal of ancient bonds. I owe the following account to Miss Anna Durco, who first met Gurdjieff as a child of twelve at the Chicago World Fair in 1934 and made one of those friendships that Gurdjieff could make with children all his life. Her family background enabled her to talk with him in his favourite mixture of Russian, English and words from any language that happened to express what he wanted to say. He told her his name and made her repeat it several times. He said that in the early spring many tribes of nomads and semi-nomads would pass through Kars not far from where he lived and some would camp

near the Arpai Chai River. He said: "I go see and find these people.
I eat sometime and go together with the *chavale* (young boys). I go
for many days from home. We sleep out under heavens. Three times
almost caught for stealing, not valuable things, in bazaar. We ran
—not catch. Such people *see*, can *see*." She recounts: "He asked
me if I knew what *drikérin mehétne* means. I knew the term from
my father to mean foretelling the future and reading the past. He
then told me that he ran off with a tribe of semi-nomadic Romanys
who had come from the Carpathian Mountains and who were on the
road to horse markets. He was eleven years old when he went with
them. He added that although his father punished him severely, and
although he loved his father, he could not help going because he
learned many things from these people. Once they stopped in a
desert area near a large town—but in after life he could never find
that town again. In that town he saw a man walking with a snake
and followed him into an old crumbling mosque where he was living. He stayed with him five days and fell ill with fever. He did not
want to leave the man without learning all his secrets: but one day
he disappeared and Gurdjieff went back to his gypsy friends."

Such stories demonstrate that his search began at a very early age.
This would not be surprising in a society where schooling ended at
eleven years of age and a boy of fourteen would expect to be
independent of his family. It seems likely that Gurdjieff began to
take an interest in what he calls 'abstract' questions from the age of
eleven. He specifically mentions the year 1888 as a time when
he was already searching avidly for the explanation of unusual
phenomena. By the time he was fourteen, in 1891, he had already
visited Constantinople and many parts of Armenia.

At the end of the nineteenth century, the Black Sea was an
international highway which permitted free movement between
Russia, Turkey and the Balkans. Gurdjieff could find his way to
Constantinople by the sea route through Trebizond following the
valley of 365 churches that descends eight thousand feet in fifty
miles from Erzurum. In this valley there are many traces of ancient
cultures and, at that time, there were still Christian and Muslim communities which had preserved knowledge of the mysteries. If
Gurdjieff had taken this route, he would almost certainly have referred to it. It seems more likely that he travelled overland by the
railway which had been built only as far as Sivas. He indicates some
acquaintance with the sources of the Euphrates River, whose gorge

connects the highlands of Ezurum with the Central Anatolian
Steppe. He probably visited Caesarea—in Turkish Kayseri—the
home of his ancestors; but his destination was the Mediterranean.
His first long journey brought him a thousand miles from home to
the Turkish capital, then possessing a large and active Greek
population living on the eastern shore of the Golden Horn in Tatavla
and Galata. By his own account, the journey had no purpose beyond
'seeing the world', but it led to his friendship with Turks of very
different social rank, from porters and fishermen to pashas and
princes. When I first met him in Constantinople many years later,
in 1920, it was at Kuru Tcheshme Palace, the home of Prince
Sabaheddin, whom he had evidently known from the time when the
Prince's father Damad Mahmoud Pasha, had been Grand Vizir under
Sultan Abdul Hamid. He was thoroughly at home in Turkish and
spoke it like any other Armenian or Greek of the Levant, very
fluently but with an unmistakable accent.

I do not believe that Gurdjieff had intended to stay in Constantinople, but hoped to get to Crete and join 'the Greek guerillas'
who were harassing the Turkish rulers of the island. He must have
been too young, and it may be that he was already engaged in the
manœuvres with his passport which later were to make it so hard
to find his real age. He returned to Kars through Asia Minor, visit-
ing Konya, Hadji Bektash and other centres of Sufi activity. His
fascination with the legendary Turkish sage, Khwaja Nasruddin,
probably dates from this time. It is likely that there was an historical
character of this name, a contemporary of Tamerlane, with whom
many of his tales are associated.

Gurdjieff spoke more than once of a prolonged stay in Cappadocia,
where he seems to have made a special study of the origins of the
Christian liturgy as it was developed by St. Basil the Great and other
theologians of the third and fourth centuries who built a bridge between Christianity and the ancient religions without losing anything
of the purity of the Christian doctrine. At the end of the nineteenth
century there were still monasteries famous for their theological
learning. Gurdjieff regarded the Christian liturgy as a source of very
important knowledge. It is a 'legominism', as he called it, whereby
ancient wisdom is transmitted beneath a form ostensibly intended for
a quite different purpose.

If I am right in thinking that Gurdjieff intended to draw our
attention to the importance of Cappadocia, it is likely he himself

spent a certain amount of time there, investigating the sources and there is some confirmation of this in the account he gives in *Meetings with Remarkable Men*. After his adventures with Pogossian, he returned to the Caucasus, not by sea as most people would have done, but overland, through Asia Minor. It is very likely that he spent some considerable time among the Greek- and Turkish-speaking people of Asia Minor, who, after all, were of the same race as his own ancestors.

After his return to Kars, Gurdjieff threw himself wholeheartedly into the search for the 'ancient wisdom' in whose reality he was beginning to believe. Before we trace the course of his searches, we must examine the independent evidence for the belief that there have been brotherhoods in Asia who possess knowledge of a high order and able to exercise powers not accessible to ordinary people. I shall use the general term 'Masters of Wisdom' to designate the members of such brotherhoods.

2
The Masters of Wisdom

LEGENDS that have endured for centuries or even thousands of years have, nearly always, a foundation of historical fact. During the last hundred years, archaeological research has established the historical significance of many seemingly fanciful legends. The legend of Atlantis, which Plato reconstructed from fragments that reached him from Egyptian sources, was dismissed by Jowett as a moral fiction. Plato's story now turns out to be associated with the prodigious catastrophe that destroyed the early Minoan civilization about 1550 BC and was probably the origin also of the story of the exodus of the Israelites from Egypt at the same date. The reality is hardly less amazing than the legend, which is incredible only because Plato was out in his figuring by a factor of ten. The legend of the Tower of Babel is almost certainly associated with the destruction, about four thousand years ago, of the Ziggurat of Borsippa by an ironstone meteorite which carried such energy that thousands of tons of clay brick were turned into glass, and an intense magnetic field was generated that can to this day be detected at a distance of five miles. I visited the site in 1953 and brought home fragments of vitrified brick that our chemists reported must have been heated to 2700°F., an exceedingly rare occurrence in the open air on the surface of this planet. Not a soul could have been left alive for miles around and this may explain why no written record has been discovered. The legend, nevertheless, was created. It was transferred to Babylon by the Israelites and made the subject of the moral story of the men who tried to emulate God and perished in their sins.

A different kind of legend concerns human origins. There is, for example, in Genesis 7, 1–5, the story of a time when the 'sons of

God' walked on the earth and took the daughters of men to wife. Similar legends abound in almost every tradition. I believe that these strange stories refer to a remote period, perhaps forty thousand years ago, when modern man, *Homo sapiens sap.* appeared out of nowhere endowed with creative powers unlike any possessed by his predecessors. Recent researches in the anatomy of the vocal mechanism in man and the apes show that Neanderthal man could not articulate the range of sounds needed for speech as we know it today. This and other observations on the races of man strengthen the case for ascribing the appearance of modern man to just that kind of interbreeding with a different race of beings that is suggested by the story in Genesis. All races have preserved the tradition of a Golden Age, when men were happy and carefree, when 'the lion lay down with the lamb' and strife was unknown.

In this chapter and the next, I will examine the legend or tradition that there has been, since before the dawn of history, a group of wise men or 'Masters' who have watched over the destiny of mankind and have intervened from time to time to avert calamity or to change the course of events by injecting new modes of thought corresponding to the needs of a changing age. This legend is strongly established in Central Asia and the Near East. It is held in an obviously derived form by Buddhist communities of the great vehicle tradition associated with the belief in Bodhisattvas and Arahants. In Tibet, it is connected with the reincarnating Rim-po-ch'he Lamas. The Sufi schools, particularly those who trace their origin to Bactria and Sogdiana, assert that there is a perpetual hierarchy, headed by the *Kutb-i-Zaman* or Axis of the Age, who receives direct revelations of the Divine Purpose and transmits them to mankind through the Abdal or Transformed Ones and their followers. The tradition of a perpetual hierarchy is held by Sufi communities as remote in other respects as the Bektashis and the Naq'shbandis. These two trace their origin back to the city of Balkh, the former capital of the Bactrian Empire, but they are almost diametrically opposed in their teachings and methods. The Bektashis are mainly Turkish, they came to the fore during the time of troubles in the fourteenth century when the empire of the Seljuk Turks was falling apart and Asia Minor was in chaos. Hadji Bektash Veli (*veli* means saint) appealed directly to the people. He was a reformer who swept away many traditional practices. For example, he allowed women to become full members of the Bektashi communities and

B

encouraged free exchange with the Christian monks of Cappadocia. The Naq'shbandis were an aristocratic order who kept aloof from politics, insisted upon rigid observance of the Islamic code and exercised an extraordinary influence on the entire Islamic world on account of their reputed possession of secret wisdom and powers. Both Bektashis and Naq'shbandis teach that there is always a Kutb or supreme spiritual head. They believe in the hidden prophet Khidr who is mysteriously associated with the Archangel Gabriel and is perpetually seeking among the sons of men for those to whom he can transmit the secrets of salvation. These are the 'Masters of Wisdom' —the Khwajagān who appeared in history about a thousand years ago.

Strangely enough, the tradition of the Masters is almost unknown in India. When Helena Blavatsky published her books, *The Secret Doctrine* and *Isis Unveiled*, one of her chief claims was to have encountered in person some of the Masters in or beyond Tibet. The belief in Masters then became an integral part of the theosophical doctrine, but it acquired an occult character that weakened its credibility. Much of the mystery of the theosophical 'masters' derived from their supposed location in Tibet, though Helena Blavatsky herself asserted that their headquarters was beyond the mountains in the legendary 'Shamballa'. It never occurred to me that this was more than a pure invention until, quite recently, Idries Shah suggested to me that it could be derived from Shams-i-Balkh, the Bactrian Sun Temple, the ruins of which can still be seen at Balkh near the northern frontier of Afghanistan. Rudolph Steiner associated Balkh with Hraniratta, the centre of the Mithraic Sun worship. The point to be made here is that the belief in an ancient and continuing tradition is particularly strong in the regions of Central Asia in which Gurdjieff concentrated much of his search. In this chapter no attempt is made to settle the question whether or not a supreme spiritual hierarchy really does exist. I shall, however, carefully examine the suggestion that the name "Masters of Wisdom" comes from the Khwajagān who played such an extraordinary role in the heart of Asia between the eleventh and fifteenth centuries of the Christian Era. The word Khwaja means wise man or master, and is best rendered Master of Wisdom. Like our word Mister, it has lost its lofty significance and now means little more than teacher. I have little doubt that Gurdjieff had heard of these Masters in his youth, and that one of the principal objects of his travels in

Turkestan, Afghanistan and Tibet was to discover traces of their activity in order to reconstruct their teaching.

I owe most of my knowledge of the Khwajagān to the Turkish translations of a remarkable series of books written in Persian in the fifteenth and sixteenth centuries and especially to the admirable study made by Husan Lutfi Şuşud, himself an eminent Sufi, whose acquaintance I made years ago while travelling in Turkey. Hasan Şuşud's work called *Khwajagān Hanedani*, or the Dynasty of the Masters, was published in 1958 and has been partially translated into English. The most valuable Persian sources are the *Reshahat Ayn el Hayat*, the *Nefahat el Uns*, and the *Risalei Bahaiyye*. I have also made use of Wilhelm Bartold's *History of the Turks of Central Asia*, published in the *Welt des Islams* in 1926. The Khwajagān are referred to in many Russian studies of Turkestan and there is little doubt that Gurdjieff could have had access to these studies in his youth. By 1901, Gurdjieff himself was aware of the importance of this school; but so far as I can ascertain, he referred to it in writing only in the programme of his demonstration of Sacred Dances at the Théâtre des Champs-Élysées in Paris in December 1923.

The following study of the Khwajagān and their historical role may seem out of place in a book primarily devoted to Gurdjieff; but a true picture of his significance, can be formed only in the environment of his own searches. I became convinced from my own contacts with the successors of the Khwajagān, the Naq'shbandi Brotherhood, that he had adopted many of their ideas and techniques.

Before we turn to Central Asia, we should look at the corresponding sequence of events that had occurred in Europe a thousand years earlier. Between the third and seventh centuries after the time of Christ, Europe was convulsed by the hordes that erupted from Central Asia and destroyed the Roman Empire. In the midst of these upheavals, there arose the remarkable phenomenon of Christian monasticism ostensibly founded by St. Benedict and his successors. The monasteries of Europe restored stability and confidence, brought the land back into cultivation and created a new culture that endured for eight hundred years until it was superseded by the value system of the Renaissance. Few people would be prepared to associate these events with 'Masters' in the theosophical sense, with superhuman beings hidden from ordinary mortals. Nevertheless, the phenomenon is an historical fact that is not easily explained. The Gothic hordes were transformed from destroyers to creators in a manner that suggests that spiritual agencies were at work among them as well as in the European populations they conquered. It may be that these agencies originated in Central Asia.

There is a remarkable parallelism between the European events just described and the convulsions that shook most of Asia between the eleventh and sixteenth centuries. Hordes of Goths and Tartars, Turks and Mongols swept through the decaying empires of China and India. They destroyed the newly arisen kingdoms of the Khwarezm and Azerbaijan and the caliphates of Baghdad and Cairo. The climax came between 1220 and 1230 when Jenghis Khan and his Mongols broke down all resistance and devastated the ancient cultures. Jenghis Khan is one of the most important figures of history. From his time, there was a completely new situation that changed the world from China to Europe. The Mongols whom he led in his extraordinary career of conquest, between 1210 and 1225, were nomads who were strangers to the culture of the agricultural and urban communities and had no idea of the significance of a theistic religion. They worshipped the Great Spirit and they believed in possession by spiritual powers. The transformation that took place in the short period of twenty-five years could not have occurred without some special working of a kind not unlike that which had emerged with Christian monasticism about six hundred years earlier. We know that within twenty-five years the Mongols were converted to Islam and adopted the Persian language and culture. The parallelism with the Gothic adoption of European language and culture is probably more than a coincidence. By the beginning of the fourteenth century, the descendants of Jenghis Khan were the greatest patrons of art in the world, and Samarkand, the ancient Sogdiana, was known as the greatest centre of learning. Though equally spectacular transformations were occurring in China, the results were transient, and within a century the Mongol influence had virtually disappeared.

It is an historical fact that a major role in the transformation of Central Asia was played by the society or brotherhood of wise men known as the Khwajagān or Masters. Though they were Muslims and commonly known as Sufis, their doctrines and methods differed radically from those of the Sufi schools of Arabia, Africa and Spain.

The Khwajagān are seldom mentioned in books on Sufism, though their successors, the Naq'shbandi, are the most numerous and influential Sufi community in the world. The reason for this is that Sufism has been known in the West mainly from literary sources. Most people have heard of the great Sufi poets, Nizami, Hafiz, Jellalludin Rumi and Attar, and the names of the great philosophical writers, such as Muhyiddin ibn Arabi and Iman Gazali, are almost equally well known. The Khwajagān wrote very little except practical manuals until the fifteenth century. Fortunately these give detailed accounts of the life and works of many of the great Masters, and the rest can be filled in from contemporary documents. Some of these are provided by European travellers such as Guy de Ruysbrouck, a monk who travelled right across Turkestan into Mongolia in 1253, and the better-known Marco Polo who visited the Chinese court of Kublai Khan, the grandson of Jenghis Khan. The Arab explorer, Ibn Battuta, also refers to the influence of the Khwajagān in the regions of Sogdiana and Koreen Lin. The Persian historiographers, such as Ibn Rashid, who were bitterly hostile to the Mongols, refer indirectly to the Khwajagān and accept the fact that they established friendly relations with the Khans to the lasting benefit of the entire region.

Who then were these men, so little known in the West, and yet so influential over five centuries? The Masters did not spring from nowhere. Long before they appeared, a powerful stream of spirituality was flowing in Central Asia. When Zoroaster lived in Balkh, the 'Mother of Cities', in the sixth century before Christ, he inherited a still more ancient tradition. The earliest hymns of the Aryan people contain convincing evidence of having been composed in the far north ten thousand years ago. I believe that a continuous tradition can be traced back for more than thirty thousand years when Central Asia was a fertile region, the meeting ground of different cultures, far more ancient than those of Egypt, Mesopotamia and India which arose six or seven thousand years ago. We shall examine these ancient traditions in the next chapter.

We cannot hope to understand Gurdjieff unless we attempt to share his sense of the historical significance of spiritual traditions. He knew that periodic renewals are inevitable, but he was convinced that there is an eternal unchanging core of wisdom to which mankind has always had access. He frequently referred to traditions four or five thousand years old, that were still preserved when he travelled in Asia, as well as to more ancient teachings going back to human origins.

The Zoroastrian tradition gave way to the Christian and Manichean, and these in turn were absorbed by Islam. But Islam owes some of its most vital insights to its contacts with Persia and Central Asia. According to Muslim tradition, Selman the Persian, who was the first convert to Islam from the Magian religion and one of the close companions of the Prophet, belonged to the school of wisdom that flourished for nearly two thousand years at Balkh. This was the school of the Masters.

The title of Khwaja was first given to Yusuf of Hamadan in northwest Iran. Hamadan is on one of the main routes from Turkestan into Turkey and Mesopotamia and was certainly visited by Gurdjieff in one of his early journeys. Yusuf Hamadani was born in 1084 in the village of Bozenjird near Hamadan, which was then the capital of the first Seljuk Sultan Maghrib Beg. Yusuf grew up under his successor Malik Shah who was served by that most remarkable man, Nizam-ul-Mulk, the opponent of the notorious Assassins of Mount Elburz, who finally succeeded in having him murdered. About this time, Yusuf left Hamadan and went to Baghdad to train with a very famous teacher, Ibn Ishaq, one of the successors of Ibn Hanifa. Ishaq sent him to a succession of teachers from Ispahan to Bokhara and Samarkand, regions which were then still mainly Christian of the Nestorian or Unitarian tradition. It seems likely that he was given a special mission, because according to the *Fasl ul Hitab*, he was told to abandon all ordinary learning and enter the path of prayer, asceticism and self-purification. It is said in one account that he was initiated by Sheikh Ali Farmidi who was also the teacher of Imam Gazali, one of the greatest Islamic philosophers and mystics.

By the time he was thirty years old, Yusuf was already known as a Master and seekers (*salikin*) were coming to him from all parts of Asia. This was unusual, as few of the later Khwajas accepted pupils until they had served an apprenticeship of twenty or thirty years. He spent some time in Horasan, a much longer time in Bokhara and finally settled in Merv, where he was buried. Yusuf is described as tall, slender, with sandy hair and smiling brown eyes. He was gentle and compassionate and consorted freely with people of all religions. He is said to have been pock-marked. He always wore a patched woollen cloak. His principal spiritual exercise was the *zikr* with retention of breath, that he carried to such an extreme that while praying his whole body would be covered with sweat.

He was incessantly active. Hundreds of seekers came to visit him from distant places, but he worked with special intensity with a group of eleven men who accompanied him from Hamadan to Bokhara. In the year 1205, Sheikh Evhadduddin Kirmani reported to Muhyiddin ibn Arabi that Khwaja Yusuf had occupied the station of 'teacher of teachers' for sixty years. He died on his way from Herat to Merv in 1140 at the age of ninety-two.

Many details of his life and stories of wonders that he and his disciples performed are recorded in the literature of the Khwajagān. How are we to interpret all this? He was certainly known far and wide as the supreme spiritual leader of his time—the *Kutb-i-Zaman*. Several of the most important dervish brotherhoods trace their origin back to him. Although he avoided political life, the rulers of the age not only courted him, but followed his counsel. The title Khwaja or Master of Wisdom became the prerogative of a succession of remarkable men who had an enormous influence in Central Asia for five centuries. They present a very different picture from that of the hidden Masters given by the theosophists and in Alice Bailey's Tibetan books. The Khwajagān were practical men who accomplished practical tasks. Their mysticism was a means of fitting them for their task, never an end in itself.

We shall follow the history of some of the eleven disciples: The first successor of Yusuf Hamadani was Khwaja Hasan Abdullah of Berk, a native of Khwarezm. He was distinguished by remarkable spiritual powers and especially the gift of transmitting *Baraka* or effectual grace. This is a mark of a high degree of attainment and it was one of the gifts that was unmistakably present in Gurdjieff. Moreover, Gurdjieff told us that he had made a special search for men who still possessed the gift of *Baraka*. According to one legend, Khwaja Abdullah was so totally immersed in his spiritual exercises that he failed to provide for his wife and family. Yusuf Hamadani reproached him for this one day, but that night had a vision in which God told him: "I have bestowed on you the eye of the Intellect but to Hasan I have also given the eye of the Heart. Let him go his own way."

The third successor of Yusuf was Ahmed Yesevi, the first of the Turkish Khwajas. Ahmed Yesevi exercised an immense influence throughout the region of Ferghana that stretched for a thousand miles from what is now Tashkent to the Mongolian frontier with the ancient Jaxartes, now the Syr Darya, as its main east–west artery. Tashkent lies in the Syr Darya, almost in the centre of the great region known as Turkestan. Before the Muslim conquest, it was known as Binkath and is described as a great city surrounded by two lines of walls of which the outer had seven and the inner ten gates. The palace, the citadel and the bazaar were of great importance and known throughout Asia. Later the name of Binkath was replaced by that of Yesi. When Yesi became the capital of the Ferghanian Khanate, it was renamed Tashkent. It was in Yesi that Ahmed was born, reputedly in 1042, and he certainly died there in 1166, which would give him the exceptional age of 124. Ahmed Yesevi was the founder of Turkish spirituality. He was brought up in a Shamanist environment. He is said to have received his first training from a famous Shaman alchemist, but to have been guided in a vision to go to Hamadan and find Yusuf. He entered the small circle of eleven who went with Yusuf to Bokhara and after several years returned to Yesi (Tashkent) where he was very quickly recognized as a man of extraordinary spiritual powers. He was given the title Khwaja, but the Turks called him Bab-Arslan, or Lion Father.

Ahmed Yesevi set up his own school which continued after his death as the Yesevi Brotherhood. Gurdjieff was greatly interested in the Yesevis because they did more than any other Sufi community to develop music and exercises that act directly upon the physical body and emotions of man. In their *tekkiyas* or community centres, sacred dances and music were preserved from the earlier pre-Islamic period of Binkath and brought to new heights. Some of these sacred dances provide evidence of the high level of cosmological enquiry that obtained in Turkestan. The Yesevi Sufis also developed their own psychological techniques, which probably owe much to the Shamanist schools that still flourished in the region. We are accustomed to think of Shamans as magicians whose powers may have been genuine, but who did not possess any scientific knowledge of the world. We must not forget that the same Great Spirit culture of Central Asia gave birth to the profound Chinese doctrine of Tao and the doctrine of threefoldness which Gurdjieff described as one of the two fundamental cosmic laws.

Gurdjieff himself lived for some time in Tashkent while the Ferghanian Khanate was still to some degree independent of

Russian control. It seems probable that he found a Yesevi school that was connected with the Masters of Wisdom. He would certainly have been at home in the Turkish dialect spoken in the region. Although Tashkent is nearly two thousand miles from the borders of China, there was a very free movement of travellers and missionaries in the twelfth century when the declining Sung dynasty, still ruling in most of China, was no longer able to prevent the entry of foreigners. Indeed, Wang an Shih (1020–1086), the great social reformer, positively encouraged exchanges with the 'wise men of the West'. The religious reformer Chu Hsi (1120–1200), in his renewal of Confucianism, introduced cosmological concepts that were very similar to those that Gurdjieff found centuries later in Turkestan. The Chinese have always been unwilling to admit the part played in their culture by foreign ideas and so we cannot with confidence say whether developments such as Zen Buddhism owe their origin to Central Asian sources. One can only point to similarities of technique.

Unfortunately, none of Ahmed Yesevi's own teaching remains and we have only highly edited versions of his poetry in collections like the *Hazinei Jevahir ul Obrav* (The Treasury of Jewels of the Masters). He has always been recognized by the Turkish-speaking people as one of their greatest saints. He was still quoted in the nineteenth century among the Volga Tartars, and it is quite possible that his name was known to the Tartars with whom Gurdjieff became friendly in Kars.

The widespread influence wielded by Ahmed in his own time is shown by the fact that a special building was erected for him by the ruler of Yesi to enable pilgrims from east, west and south to be lodged and taught. Many cases are recorded of healing and spiritual conversions and even of miracles witnessed by outsiders. He was as ready to help those who opposed and rejected him as those who were his friends and pupils. The great Mogul conqueror, Tamerlane, who lived two centuries after him, records in his autobiography, *Wahiat-i-Timur*, that, when praying at the tomb of Ahmed Yesevi, he had a vision in which the saint taught him a *zikr* and told him to repeat it when in any difficulty. Years later, during his campaign in Asia Minor, he was in battle with the Turkish Sultan, Bayazid the Thunderer; while watching a cavalry charge, he repeated Ahmed's quatrain seventy times over, after which the enemy unexpectedly turned and fled.

Ahmed's successors, Mansur, Abdulmelik, Taj, Said and Suley-mann, were called Ata, meaning father. All these men belonged to the Khwajagān. One of the Yesevi Sheikhs, Hakim Ata, took a group of followers to the Volga and established there a Yesevi Community, which much later inspired the Bektashi Order. In the twentieth century Mustapha Kemal, the creator of modern Turkey, adopted the same title and gave himself the name of Ataturk. The Yesevis are regarded by the southern Sufis as unorthodox and have been ac-cused of magical practices learned from the Shamans. They had a centre at Kashgar.

We must now return to the mainstream of the Khwajagān activity. One of the eleven who went from Hamadan to Samarkand with Khwaja Yusuf was Abdulhalik Gujduvani. He is described in the history of the Khwajagān as the 'chief of the central circle of Masters'. His family was of Anatolian origin and came from the Byzantine province of Malatya. He was born at Gujduvan near Bok-hara, but was sent by his father to a succession of teachers and finally to Hamadan where he entered the service of Kawaja Yusuf. Accord-ing to his own account, he was directed to Hamadan by the 'hidden prophet' Khidr who appeared to him in a vision when he was twenty-two years old. Abdulhalik left a succinct account of the Sufi spiritual techniques that were taught on the Path of the Khwajagān. These are preserved in the *Essence of the Teaching of the Masters*.

1. *Hush der dem.* Be present at every breath. Do not let your attention wander for the duration of a single breath. Remember yourself always and in all situations.

2. *Nazar ber kadem.* Keep your intention before you at every step you take. You wish for freedom and you must never forget it.

3. *Safar der vatan.* Your journey is towards your homeland. Re-member that you are travelling from the world of appearances to the World of Reality.

4. *Halvat der endjuman.* Solitude in the crowd. In all your out-ward activity remain inwardly free. Learn not to identify yourself with anything whatsoever.

5. *Yad gerd.* Remember your Friend, i.e. God. Let the prayer (*zikr*) of your tongue be the prayer of your heart (*q'alb*).

6. *Baz gasht.* Return to God. No aim but to attain Reality.

7. *Nigah dasht.* Struggle with all alien thoughts. Keep your mind on what you are doing whether outwardly or inwardly.

8. *Yad dasht.* Be constantly aware of the quality of the Divine Presence. Become used to recognizing the Presence of God in your heart.

When Abdulhalik died in 1190, he was succeeded by Khwaja Ahmed Sadik of Bokhara. About this time it seems that the Inner Circle of the Masters was transferred to Bokhara, where according to Gurdjieff it remained for centuries. The storms were already gathering and the Mongols were uniting under Temurdjin who, at the great Kuriltay of 1206, took the name of Jenghis Khan and was proclaimed the Grand Khan of all the Mongols. His name already struck terror into the peoples of all the lands bordering on Mongolia. In the following year, an unheralded but scarcely less significant event occurred in Balkh, just across the Amu Darya (Oxus), which Jenghis Khan was to cross thirteen years later. This was the birth of Mēvlanā Djellaluddin Rumi, the greatest mystical poet of the Persian language whose name is associated with one of the great Sufi brotherhoods: the Mevlevis, or whirling dervishes. It is not strictly correct to refer to Djellaluddin as the founder of the Mevlevi Dervish Order, just as it is not correct to refer to Abdul Kadir Jilani as founder of the Kadiris or Khwaja Bektash Veli as the founder of the Bektashis. In each case, the great man filled a particular role and, after his mission was completed, left behind him a group of highly trained initiates who were able to pass on his teaching and his method. Usually a full generation later an organization came into being; and, in a remarkable way, it was nearly always the second successor who was the actual organizer and in the true sense the founder of the brotherhood. Gurdjieff refers to his peculiarity in his doctrine of 'Sacred Images' which we shall discuss in Chapter 10.

More than one stream of spiritual influences was flowing in the regions of what is now Iran, Afghanistan and Turkestan. One of these appears to have been centred in Balkh, the 'Mother of Cities', where Djellaluddin's father, Bahauddin Veled, was known as both theologian and mystic of the Western school and a follower of Ibn el Arabi.

Another stream was that of the Kubravi centred in north-west Persia and consisting of Shi'ites initiated into the ecstatic mysticism of the Alevis. They probably made use of hypnagogic drugs and other means of inducing mystical trance. The third stream was the Khwajagān centred in Bokhara, but dispersed over a wide area from the Kara Kum to the Gobi Desert.

Here we must pause to look at the total situation with which the appearance of the Masters was connected. Already in 1206, impending disaster could be foreseen even by eyes less discerning than those of the Khwajagān. Before the Mongol threat, three different lines of defence were prepared. Following a procedure well known to the Sufis, some emigrated beyond the danger zone. Some waited and deliberately allowed themselves to be assimilated into the new regime, even though it was completely alien. The third part remained and preserved their tradition intact by disguising its outward form. The most distinguished emigrant was Bahauddin Veled of Balkh, who moved west to Baghdad, then to Damascus, and finally to the Seljuk capital of Konya with his son, Djellaluddin, who was to receive the soubriquet Rumi because he lived in what the inhabitants of Central Asia regarded as part of the Roman dominion, the Anatolian peninsula. Another emigrant of the same school was Nije-meddin Daya, who also reached Konya, which was to become the centre of a powerful spiritual action that lasted until the end of the nineteenth century.

We are not concerned here with those who were assimilated to the Mongol conquerors. Some, such as Mahmud Yalavadj and his son, Mas'oud Yalavadji, became the trusted advisers of Jenghis Khan and were largely responsible for setting up the remarkably successful —though largely improvised—administration by which he governed his Muslim conquests. Others undertook to organize the guilds of craftsmen which were soon to produce such surpassing works of art, architecture, agriculture and metal-working. Others again introduced and surpassed Arab mathematics and astronomy.

Our present interest is with the third group, who maintained the traditional teachings secretly throughout all the convulsions of the period. Even before the Mongol invasion, all had not been peaceful in Transoxania. The Sultan of Harzem (Khwarezm), Muhammad Shah, conquered Eastern Afghanistan in 1202, Samarkand in 1212 and was generally recognized as the paramount ruler of the region by 1217. Within three years, his empire was in ruins. Bokhara was taken by Jenghis Khan in February 1220, and, in December, Muhammad, after fleeing across Asia to take refuge on an island in the Caspian Sea, died of grief and exhaustion.

Conflicting accounts of the Mongol conquest are given by the Arab and the Chinese historians. Yet another story appears in the *Secret History* compiled in 1240. Jenghis Khan was certainly a ruthless conqueror, but he had also a very superstitious nature, combined with an uncanny knowledge of men. The common stories of total destruction of cities and massacres of entire populations refer mainly to the acts of his generals, who, coming straight from the nomadic life of Siberia, regarded cities as unnatural and fit only to be destroyed. Even so, the pillage and the loss of life throughout Transoxania during the Mongol invasion were so frightful as to leave indelible marks. The administrative machinery collapsed and the Mongols, quite unprepared for the problems of an agricultural and urban population, lacked the experience needed to restore order. The wisdom and foresight of Jenghis Khan showed themselves in his pacification of the region with the help of well-chosen Muslim advisers. At that time, he ruled over the greatest empire the world has ever known, stretching from the Pacific Ocean to the boundaries of Europe. He was to live only seven years more, but his conquests were to be extended by his descendants to include most of India and China and reach as far as Russia in the west. The old world and the mutual isolation of its major regions had gone forever, and a new order was to come. The descendants of Jenghis Khan—if we included Tamerlane among them—were to keep the world in suspense for two hundred years: but out of this suspense a great vivifying action was generated.

In the midst of the convulsions, the Khwajagān continued, without interruption, their task of teaching the way of accelerated spiritual transformation and of preparing an élite who were to transmit and carry their influence far and wide through Asia, Europe and North Africa. Their secrets are known to us only up to a point. They were, essentially, men of a balanced life, fully engaged in practical matters, often craftsmen, faithful in their religious duties but very little interested in philosophy or theology. The contrast with the southern Sufis, such as the poets Attar and Hafiz and the philosopher Al Gazali, is shown in many anecdotes in which they are represented as cutting short any attempts at leading them into philosophical or theological discussions. Nor were they at all favourable to ecstasies and mystical raptures. One of the sayings of Khwaja

Azizan Ali illustrates this: "If at his time even one of Khwaja Abdulhalik's disciples had been on the spot, Hussein Mansur would not have got into trouble. He would have put Al Hallaj in his place and got rid of his nonsense." Mansur al Hallaj (AD 865–930) was the most famous of the mystical Sufis who affirmed total identification of the purified man with God. He was rejected and martyred in his lifetime, but became later a symbol of the perfect lover of God.

The distinction between the southern Sufis with their doctrine of Love and Union with God and the northern Sufis with their doctrine of Liberation from Selfhood is very important for understanding Gurdjieff's teaching. I think that there is little doubt that the northern Sufis were profoundly influenced by the Buddhist notion of liberation from the world of appearances. They were in close contact with the Buddhist schools of Tibet and Sinkiang and brought into their own Islamic beliefs the essentially Buddhist notion of attaining absolute freedom for the individual by the abandonment of selfhood.

This is a very different notion from that which we find in the mystical literature of the Arabs and even of the Indian Sufis. The Khwajagān were followers of the way of complete and final liberation. They used spiritual exercises, many of which were derived from Buddhist and Tantric sources, but they remained throughout Muslims presenting an orthodox exterior to the world. I think it is also probable that they were considerably influenced by the Nestorian Christians whose Unitarian concept of God was acceptable to Muslims. The so-called Nestorians were influenced by Buddhist and even Shamanist beliefs, all of which had their roots in the ancient Great Spirit culture.

The Masters were certainly not savants, nor were they theologians or ecstatic mystics. What then was their teaching and method? This will become clearer as we follow them through the next two centuries. From the start they based their teaching upon the *Khalka*, or group; upon companionship between master and disciple, *Sohbat*; upon spiritual exercise, *Zikr*; upon constant vigilance; and *Mujahede*, struggle with one's own weaknesses. They also used methods of awakening by means of shocks and surprises. Finally, and certainly not least in importance, was their engagement in practical enterprises. After the calamity of the Mongol invasion, they took the initiative in rebuilding mosques, schools and hospitals, working with their own hands and directing their *Khalkas*, which sometimes numbered several hundred members.

This brings us back to Jenghis Khan and the sack of Bokhara in February 1220. Jenghis Khan was a pagan in the full sense of the word. The Mongols were Shamanists and they had a deep respect for the powers of their Shamans. Jenghis Khan was no less convinced than his people that the Shamans could bring success or failure and even life or death to their people. He was for many years influenced, even at some moments dominated, by the Shaman Kokchu, who accompanied him on all his campaigns. We must take all this into account in our interpretation of the events of the years from 1210 to 1223, within which short time Jenghis Khan, from being a prodigiously successful leader of hordes of Mongolian nomads, became the no less successful ruler of the highly civilized agricultural and urban people of Transoxania and Persia.

The Muslim historian, Rashid-ed-din, makes no attempt to explain this or conceal his hatred of Jenghis Khan; but the Chinese biographer, Chang Chuen, has preserved an interesting story of Jenghis Khan on reaching a village two days' march from Bokhara, which may have been Ringerve, where Khwaja Arif passed most of his life, and saw a man of venerable appearance with an ox, irrigating the field of a village by means of an ingenious apparatus the like of which he had never seen. He was so impressed by what he saw that he gave the old man a guarantee of immunity from all requisitions. When Bokhara was taken a few days later, Jenghis Khan gave orders that all property could be pillaged, but only those who resisted were to be slaughtered. It may be true, as Djunaydi, the Persian historian, wrote in 1260, that he had the Muslims of Bokhara brought together in the Great Mosque and assured them that he had a mission to establish a new world. In fact, the mosques were not destroyed. The legend of wholesale massacre, in Bokhara at least, seems to be without foundation. Only some fanatical Ulemas who rallied groups of resistance were deliberately killed. Samarkand, taken a few weeks later, resisted stoutly and all who fought were ruthlessly slaughtered. By this time the religious authorities kept out of the battle and none of them was intentionally killed.

We can find a close connection between the story of Jenghis Khan, as told in Persian, Chinese and Mongol biographies, with that of the Khwajagān, preserved in their own records, especially the *Reshahat ayn-el-Hayat*. The rapid expansion of the circles affiliated to the

Masters within a generation of the Mongol invasions suggests that they succeeded in convincing the new rulers not only of their loyalty, but also of their value to the new society. It is more than likely that they were mainly responsible for one of the important events in history: the conversion of the Mongols from their ancestral Shamanism to Islam and the consequent establishment of Muslim power throughout south-west Asia, including India.

When, in 1273, Bokhara was again ravaged by the Mongols, this time their army came from the south, crossing the Amu Darya in the opposite direction from that taken by Jenghis Khan fifty years earlier. The links between China, Central Asia and south-west Asia had been well and truly forged and the great trade routes opened, making a real step toward the unification of the great society of peoples from the Atlantic to the Pacific Oceans that now comprises five-sixths of the human race. Thus what appeared to be un-mitigated disaster proved, in the greater perspective of world history, to have been a necessary element in the progress of humanity towards a single united society.

It would seem that Khwaja Arif Rivgerevi was the chief of the Masters during the period of the Mongol invasion of Trans-oxiana. Very little is known of Khwaja Arif and it is possible that the central group of Masters withdrew into the mountain passes where the Syr Darya falls into the plain of the Aral Sea. The great caverns of the Syr Darya have been occupied by little known cave-dwelling communities for a very long time—perhaps twelve thousand years according to some traditions. It is probable that these same caves were visited by Gurdjieff in the 1890's in an expedition that he mentions in *Meetings with Remarkable Men*.

Arif Rivgerevi was followed by Khwaja Mahmud Fagnevi who is best known as the teacher of Khwaja Azizan Ali of Ramiytin. By now, the worst of the crisis was over. Jenghis Khan had died in February 1227. His successor was his third son, Ogoday, but in accordance with Mongol custom the best of the Golden Horde was entrusted to his youngest son, Toulouy. The Mongols penetrated into Russia, but did not find a way through the Caucasian passes. It was at this time that Kars entered Turkish history, for the Turkish army, that was moving east to meet the Mongols under Hulagu, decided to remain on the defensive in the mountains to the west of Kars. The result was that Hulagu turned south and destroyed Baghdad in

February 1258, ending the five hundred years' rule of the Abbasid Caliphate and leaving only Turkey, Egypt and Spain as independent Muslim powers. Toulouy's second son, Qubilai (Kubla Khan of Marco Polo's story), conquered China and set up the Yuan dynasty. From the Atlantic to the Pacific Ocean, the Mongols were now known and dreaded : but their expansion had reached its limit.

The time had come for the Khwajagān to reappear in public. In their histories, there are many anecdotes portraying the shock of surprise caused to orthodox Sufis by the spiritual techniques brought to light by Khwaja Azizan Ali. He was the first of the Masters to be known by name during his lifetime far beyond the confines of Transoxiana. He was a contemporary of Mēvlanā Djellaluddin Rumi who wrote in one of his poems :

> If state (hal) were not preferred to speech (kal)
> Would the notables of Bokhara have
> made themselves the slaves of
> Khwaja Nessadj Azizan Ali?

An orthodox Sufi who became a pupil of Khwaja Azizan asked him three questions :

Q. Like you, we serve all who come and go. You don't offer them free meals whereas we do. And yet people love you and are suspicious of us. Why is this?

Azizan : Many people offer both generosity and service, but few understand how to serve generously. Set yourself to learn how to serve with generosity and people won't complain of you.

Q. It is said that you practise the *zikr-i-jerhi* (wounded *zikr*). What is this?

Azizan : We have heard that you practise the silent *zikr*. This means that your *zikr* will also become *jerhi*. The secret of effective *zikr* is to repeat each phrase as if it were your last breath, this is why it is called 'wounded'!

Q. It is said that you were initiated by Khidr, on whom be peace. What does this mean?

Azizan : Khidr loves those who are true lovers of God. His initiation is in the depth of the heart where there is no mind.

The reference to *Khidr* confirms the supposition that the

Khwajagān were accepted as an 'Inner Circle' of wise men receiving direct guidance from the spiritual *Khidr* which means—he who stands before the Face of God. The various 'Acts of the Masters' written about this time, contain many stories of miracles performed by Khwaja Azizan and his circle. He is reputed to have lived to the age of 130.

We must pass over the next generation of the Khwajas and come to Khwaja Muhammad Bahauddin of Bokhara. He was the great master of the fourteenth century. By this time the Khwajagān had completed the first stage of their task of self-development and training of an élite and were preparing to withdraw. At such a moment, a division takes place. There is a movement in, which is concentration, and a movement out, that is, manifestation. Between the fourteenth and fifteenth centuries, the Khwajagān, who had hitherto been without any name or external form, began to be known as Naq'shbandi or 'symbolists'. According to some accounts, Bahauddin was himself a noted painter of symbolic representations of the mysteries of the creation. Orthodox Muslims, who disapprove in principle of any kind of representative art, draw a veil over this side of Bahauddin's life and emphasize his capacity for conveying deep-truths by means of simple actions.

Several accounts of his life and achievements have been preserved from contemporary sources, all of which agree that from his earliest childhood he was recognized as an altogether exceptional being. He was born in January 1340 in the village of Kasri Arifan near Bokhara. He died in 1413 and was buried in the same village.

In his autobiographical work, *Hayat Name* (The Book of My Life), Bahauddin wrote: "As a young boy, my father took me to Samarkand, where we went to visit the great spiritual leaders in the city. I used to share in their prayers. After a time we returned to Bokhara and settled in Kasri. About this time, I was presented with the Dervish headpiece which had formerly been worn by that great saint Azizan Ali Ramiytani. As soon as I placed this cap on my head, my state was completely transformed. My heart was filled with the love of God and I have ever since carried this love with me wherever I went. Shortly after that, Seyyid Emir Kulal himself visited Kasri Arifan and showed me very special kindness. I spent some years under his training.

"One day as I was passing through the streets of Bokhara, I met

Khwaja Azizan who stopped me and said: 'Ey, Bahauddin I have seen you among the friends of God!' I replied, 'I hope that, if it is my Lord's will, I shall attain to that station.' He then asked me: 'When you have an impulse or feel a desire for something, what do you do?'

" 'If I get it, I give thanks, if I don't, I have patience.'

" 'That's easy, but its not the point. Now let me tell you what is really needed. Take yourself off to some deserted place for a week and decide to fast. Do not allow your body to get the upper hand, so that you can know the taste of freedom.' I did what he said.

"Soon after Azizan appeared in front of me and said: 'Your next task is to serve the people and do everything you can to make people happy. Always be on the watch to help the weak and poor.'

"I followed Azizan's instructions and this continued for some time. Once again, I went to visit him and he said: 'Hey, Bahauddin, it is now right for you to take care of animals. Do all you can to be kind to animals, remembering that, like you, they are God's creatures. They have their own secret prayer to God. If you see animals that are overloaded or suffering in any way, do what you can to lighten their burdens and help them.'

"I followed the orders of my sheikh. When I saw a heavy-laden horse, I took some of the burden off him. I cared for wounded and sick animals. Once in the height of summer, it was mid-August, I went out of Kasri Arifan and went into the desert, on the border of which I saw a wild boar looking fixedly into the sun. An extraordinary bliss came over me. The thought came into my mind that I should ask that wild boar to pray to God for me. As this thought came, I raised my hands and approached the wild boar with a salutation. In a state of ecstasy he threw himself down and rolled over and over in the dust. As soon as he stood again on his four feet, I said, 'Amen', and returned to my sheikh. Without letting me speak, he said: 'Very good, my boy. Now you go into the streets, wherever people are, and clean the streets and remove obstacles which get in people's way.' I did what he told me and, in this way, my soul made progress. Indeed, from this simple act of service, I became aware of some divine secrets."

He recounts a vision that he had as a boy in which a saintly Master enjoined him to follow two counsels.

" 'Bahauddin, the first counsel is represented by the burning candle

shown to you. This means that you have an aptitude for this path, but
your aptitude is like the wick of the candle. You have to keep it
trimmed. In order to reach the goal, the man with the necessary
aptitude has to work upon himself, according to his ability. The
second counsel is to hold fast to the right path as shown to us by the
Prophet, the bringer of grace. Various so-called "traditions" have
been given out since the time of our Prophet. Disregard them
all. Look for guidance to the acts of the Prophet and his companions.' "

Khwaja Naq'shbandi placed himself under the discipline of Mēvlanā Arif of Dikkeran and joined his Khalka.

Bahauddin wrote later: "When I began the repetition exercise
(*Zikr*), I became aware that a very great secret was close at hand.
I became a seeker after that secret. During my thirty years with Mēvlanā Arif, we were not idle. We wandered hither and thither in
search of the Guardians of the Truth (*Ahl-i-Haqq*). Twice we went
on the *hajj* together. We did not shut ourselves up in cells or caves;
whenever we heard of a man who might possess knowledge of the
Truth, we sought him out. If I had found another Master like Mēvlanā Arif, or even if I had found someone who had even a drop of
the Truth that Arif lacked, I would not have come to his side. Can
you imagine a man who will sit by you, knee to knee, and reveal
the loftiest heavenly mysteries and, what is more, convey to you their
inner and outer significance?"

After the death of Mēvlanā Arif, Bahauddin spent three months
with one of the Turkish sheikhs called Kasim, and subsequently
Bahauddin received a spiritual indication that he should go to the
noblest of the Turkish sheikhs Halil Ata.

When the Sultanate of Transoxania was established. Halil Ata accepted an invitation to go as Counsellor to the Sultan and remained
in his service six years. Bahauddin remained with him and, speaking
of that time, said: "He showed me great affection. Sometimes
gently, at other times brutally, he taught me the essential rules of
service. The experience I gained was of very great value to me, when
I came to undertake my own task. While Halil Ata was with the
Sultan, he often used to say in our group: 'Whoever, for the
love of God, serves me, will become great among the people.' He
often repeated this, and I well understood whom it was aimed
at."

Those were very troubled times. The Mongol power had broken into fragments and wars of succession, invasions, migrations were occurring throughout Turkestan, Persia and the Caucasus. It was a rare event for a sultan to take power without civil war, yet Halil was able to adminster his territory and open it freely to Muslims of the warring Shiah and Sunni sects and also to Christians and even Magians (Zoroastrians). Bahauddin remained with him all this time and reported afterwards on Halil's extraordinary power of bringing the best out of his people. He also taught Bahauddin the secrets of the Masters of Wisdom. Unfortunately, the last words of Jenghis Khan, "Never let Mongol fight with Mongol", were forgotten and the southern Mongols overran Turkestan and destroyed all that Halil had accomplished. Bahauddin in his autobiography writes:

"When I saw this state of affairs, all love of wordly power was wiped out of my heart and I wanted only to gain the treasure of the invisible world. In order to maintain myself in the midst of disaster, I took to commerce and returned to Bokhara."

Some of Bahauddin Naq'shbandi's talks to his *Khalka* have been preserved. A few extracts will give the best idea of his teaching:

"In my days of discipleship, according to the heritage of Khwaja Baba Semasi, I listened to many traditions and I talked with many learned men. But on my path, that which helped me the most was abasement and humiliation. I entered by that gate and whatever I may have found, that is how I found it."

"Our way is that of group discussion. In solitude, there is renown and in renown there is peril. Welfare is to be found in a group. Those who follow this way find great benefit and blessing in group-meetings."

"It is not possible for many to obtain the secret of Union (*tawhid*). To attain the secret of practical wisdom (*marifat*) is difficult but not impossible."

"We do not accept everyone, and if we do accept we do so with difficulty."

"A famous learned man asked what was the purpose of the way we follow. Khwaja Bahauddin answered: 'The clarification of practical wisdom.' 'And what is that?' asked his interlocutor. 'There are things to be believed that have been transmitted by reliable informants but only in a summary way. The clarification of practical wisdom consists in showing people how to discover them in their own personal experience.' "

The place of Khwaja Bahauddin Naq'shbandi in the tradition of the Masters is not, as often stated, that of the founder of a new dervish order, but rather as one who enriched the tradition by bringing into it much practical (*marifat*) wisdom that had been preserved by individual teachers and groups over a very wide area. This is the significance of his many years of travel with Mēvlanā Arif Dikkerani. He was concerned to consolidate and transmit the *marifat* he had brought together. Within two generations, his successors were to teach kings and guide nations, exercising an immense visible influence; but he avoided any such undertakings. When he was invited by the King of Herat, he said: "We have no business with kings and sultans; but if we don't go to them, they will come to us and that will be a nuisance to our dervishes and a burden upon the population, so we shall have to go and make this visit." When he did go, he seems to have shown reserve and even indifference. He refused to eat even a mouthful at the great banquet arranged in his honour or to accept the presents sent by the king; even a suit of clothes from his own wardrobe.

The history of the Masters divides into two periods at the time of Khwaja Bahauddin Naq'shbandi. After him, there were very great teachers, but the brotherhood was merged into recognized 'Orders' and was either disbanded or went into retirement. The Naq'shbandi Order claim that they are the true successors of the Khwajagān and have inherited their secrets.

One of the Khwajagān who lived at the time of Tamerlane gained a strange reputation and has become the subject of innumerable tales and legends. This was Khwaja Nasruddin whose reputed tomb is at Akshehir in Asia Minor about sixty miles from Konya. Gurdjieff professed unbounded admiration for Nasruddin, who also received the title Mēvlanā (our Lord), commonly shortened to Molla. Gurdjieff fastened many of his own aphorisms—sensible and nonsensical—upon Khwaja Nasruddin, whom most readers of his writings take to be a legendary character at best and, at worst, a recent invention. Neither version can be correct, for references to the Khwaja can be found in Turkish and Persian literature as far back as the sixteenth century. He is reputed to have gained the confidence of Tamerlane and to have saved the lives and property of many of his countrymen by his eloquent pleading. The traditional Khwaja Nasruddin stories contain very profound teaching which verifies his connection with the Masters of Wisdom. One I recently heard illustrates this: Nasruddin was one day in the bazaar and saw a man selling a parrot for which he asked five dirhem—a very large sum in those days. Saying nothing, the Khwaja went home and came back with a turkey which he offered at ten dirhem saying that he was a far greater bird than the parrot. The onlookers began to mock him, because he did not see that the value of the parrot lay in its ability to talk. Nasruddin was quite unperturbed and said: "The parrot may be able to talk but my turkey can think." This story contains no fewer than three distinct subleties not obvious to the careless listener. This concealment by subtlety is characteristic of the Khwajagān.

The Khwajagān remained strong and influential for two hundred years after the death of Bahauddin. As my object is not to write a history of the Masters of Wisdom, but to give an impression of the environment in which the greater part of Gurdjieff's training was accomplished, I shall pass over such great names as Khwajas Muhammed Parsa, Alaeddin Attar, who wrote a biography of Bahauddin Naq'shbandi; Saad'eddin of Kashgar, who founded a school that survived until the nineteenth century. But I shall give some account of the life and doings of Khwaja Ubeydullah Ahrar for whom I have a very special veneration. Although he lived five hundred years ago, I regard him as one of my teachers, and as a sheikh whose example is as valid today as it was in the aftermath of Tamerlane's world-shaking conquests.

Khwaja Ahrar was the most famous of the Khwajagān and the outstanding Sufi Master of the fifteenth century. He was born in Tashkent 1404 and died at Kemangiran, a village near Samarkand, at the age of eighty-five in the year 1490. His tomb is in Samarkand.

According to the compiler of the *Reshahat*, the fame of young Ubeydullah spread abroad and from early childhood, he was regarded as one specially favoured by God. Such radiance and intelligence shone upon his brow that whoever met his gaze, felt drawn to prayer and worship. The young Khwaja, for his part, was wholly free from guile and unaware that he was unlike other people imputing to them the same love, joy and faith that were in him.

At this time, he passed through the stage of loss of personal

identity, which occurs even in exeptional seekers only after many
years of search. He says: "At that time, my inner state was invaded
by such a flood of self-abasement, that I worshipped everyone I
met. It did not matter if they were slave or free, white or black,
lowly or great, master or servant, I would fall at their feet and beg
them to help my soul." By the time he was eighteen, his *Zikr* had become so strong, that like the followers of Abdullah Gujduvani, he
did not hear or see anything even in the tumult of a crowded
bazaar.

After two years in Samarkand, he went, at the age of twenty-
four, to Herat where he remained for five years, now as a pupil of
the leading Sufi Masters of the city. When he was twenty-nine, he
returned to Tashkent and took up farming. He began with a few
acres of pasture and a brace of oxen, but he was endowed with such
gifts and blessings in this calling that within a short time, he became the largest farmer in Tashkent and acquired vast domains.
He owned numerous farms and herds of cattle and was, above all,
an extraordinary successful cultivator of cereals—having an uncanny
knowledge of the crops that would succeed in a given place and time.
He used to say: "God Almighty bestowed such blessings on my
lands that every year I used to send to our suzerain Sultan Ahmed
Mirza in Samarkand from my own property, eight hundred thousand
bushels of grain, enough to feed the whole city."

In this connection, one day the Khwaja explained the phrase *Inna
a'tayna*—We have made you see—as signifying that those seekers
who are single-minded are given the power to testify to the Power of
God. "God does not show Himself to creatures directly, but He
can be known through His working by those who have been given
the gift of the inner vision. Their works become in themselves manifestations of God's power and bear witness to His presence in the
creation. Those who have this power must show it: there is no place
for shame or concealment."

Until the time of Masterhood arrived, Ubeydullah was constantly engaged in service. While in Herat, he used to go to the Ham-
man, known as the 'Old Man of Herat' and serve customers there
without pay. He used to say: "I did not learn the ways of Sufism
from books, but from service to people. God leads each soul to him
in His own way: I was led by the path of service. This is why I
love and treasure service so highly. If anyone comes to me whose
welfare I desire, I advise him to practise the art of service."

Ahrar met and was in constant communication with the noblest successors of Khwaja Bahauddin Naq'shbandi and the Masters of Wisdom in the principal centres of Turkestan, from the Gobi Desert and the Hindu Kush to the Caspian Sea and the Caucasus. He was the recognized *Kutb* (The Spiritual Axis) of his time and one of the very rare ones to play a public role. His initiator was Seyyid Kasim of Tabriz.

The *Reshahat* and other contemporary records are full of accounts of the supranormal powers and qualities manifested by Ubeydullah Ahrar. An eyewitness reported:

"We were at Firhet in the presence of Khwaja Ahrar. One day he asked for a scrap of paper and a pen. He wrote on the paper the name of Ibn Said Mirza and folding it tightly thrust it into the folds of his turban. At that time, no one had heard of Ibn Said Mirza. Some of the Khwaja's intimate friends begged him to tell them whose name he had written. The Khwaja said: 'It is the name of some one that should be ruling over you and me and all Tashkent and Samarkand and Horasan.' "

Very soon afterwards the fame of Sultan Ibn Said Mirza began to spread from Turkestan. Ibn Said saw Ahrar in a dream and went to find him. Soon after Mirza gained sovereignty over the whole of Turkestan.

He became completely captivated by the Khwaja's conversation and demeanour and throughout his reign constantly turned to him for advice and protection.

Ahrar never consented to be a teacher (sheikh). Once he said: "If I were to set up as a teacher, none of the sheikhs would be left with a single pupil. But my task is not teaching, but protecting innocent believers from oppression by tyrants and preventing wars and civil wars. On account of this, I have been obliged to consort with sovereigns and sultans and win their hearts."

Ahrar was regarded as a man possessing miraculous powers. His name appears in all histories of Central Asia of the fifteenth century. I shall suggest in the following chapter that he was the original of Gurdjieff's Olman Tabor, the head of the 'Assembly of the Enlightened', who succeeded in putting an end for two generations to the civil wars that were ravaging Asia.[a] Unlike many Sufis who were his contemporaries, Ahrar was an exponent of absolute liberation in a sense that would suggest a leaning towards Buddhism.

[a] *Beelzebub's Tales*, pp. 1001-3.

Within one generation after the death of Ahrar, the Khwajagān disappeared from view. An important part of their heritage passed to the Brotherhood known as the Naq'shbandis, but it is probable that the innermost core of the brotherhood returned to the society known for three thousand years as the Sarmān or Sarmoun. I shall next examine the evidence for the existence of such a fraternity and tradition.

3

Is There an 'Inner Circle' of Humanity?

REPORTS of brotherhoods who possess wisdom and powers—different from and more significant than those of ordinary people—suggest that there may be a foundation of fact that should be taken seriously. The supposition that such people have existed in the past, and that they decisively influenced human life in ways that ordinary people cannot understand, is the hypothesis that an 'Inner Circle' of Humanity existed in the past. If we extend the idea to include the present and the foreseeable future, we have the hypothesis in the form of a perpetual hierarchy. This tradition is common to most Sufi teachings and it was affirmed by Gurdjieff himself. He associates it with the idea of esoteric schools. He defined 'schools' as organizations that exist for the purpose of transmitting to the 'Outer Circle'—that is, ordinary people—the knowledge and powers that originate in the 'Inner Circle'.

The conclusion that schools do exist is by no means the same as acceptance of the belief in the existence of an 'Inner Circle' of Humanity. The latter can be regarded either as a dogma to be believed or as an hypothesis to be tested. We shall follow the second line. The hypothesis can be understood in a 'strong' sense or in a 'weak' one. The 'strong' sense holds that there are people who possess incomparably greater knowledge and powers than ordinary men and women, including those who occupy positions of authority in church, state and centres of learning. These people constitute a hierarchy at the head of which are superhuman beings who may or may not live in human form; but who, in any case, have a direct insight into cosmic purposes and processes and who can exercise powers that are entirely beyond the reach of ordinary mortals. Such are, for example, the Masters described by the theosophists, anthroposophists and other arcane schools. These are, as we saw in the last chapter, very different from the historical Masters in Central Asia: the Khwajagān who were not at all mysterious. In recent years, the 'strong' hypothesis has been extended to include visitors from extra-terrestrial regions, who visit the earth in 'flying saucers' as part of a plan to 'save' mankind.

The 'strong' view is very attractive to writers of fiction and it has been debased to such an extent that few people would be inclined to think it worth serious examination, unless they were already convinced that superhuman beings do exist and take an interest in our welfare. A trite objection to the belief in supernatural beings who are responsible for the welfare of humanity, is that they do not seem to be doing their job very well. A more serious difficulty is that we should expect such a significant factor in human history to be better known. There is no obvious reason why the 'Inner Circle' of Humanity—if it is as powerful as the 'strong' view suggests—should hide itself. Presumably, it requires co-operation from the uninitiated and one would expect that this co-operation would readily be forthcoming if only people were made aware of the help offered them and told what was required of them.

The objection 'if they existed, we should know them' conceals the fallacy that they must be 'knowable' to us. We can picture wise men exercising extraordinary powers and able to influence the immediate course of events. It must be conceded that human history as we know it during the past seven to ten thousand years is quite incompatible with this interpretation of the 'strong' view, which in any case would violate the law of probability which asserts that the time required for a change to occur is a parabolic function of the number of interacting factors that require to be changed. We cannot, however, exclude a different interpretation according to which the 'Inner Circle' is not concerned with short-term events, but surveys human affairs on a time scale of centuries or even millennia.

In several passages in *Beelzebub's Tales*, Gurdjieff made it clear that 'care for one's remote descendants' is one of the obligations of a man who has attained 'objective reason'. He also refers to the errors made by individuals of high reason that resulted in misfortunes that afflicted mankind for thousands of years. Nevertheless, it must be

said that there is no hint in *Beelzebub's Tales* of a permanent hierarchy that has influenced history. I myself have suggested in *The
Dramatic Universe* (Vol. IV, pp. 360 and 413) that the influences
guiding human affairs may intervene directly in the form of a Hidden
Directorate, surveying the human scene from epoch to epoch. Writing ten years later in the light of my subsequent work, I regard it as
more likely that the method of intervention is indirect. Though more
than ever convinced that there is a conscious guidance in human
affairs, I believe that this comes from a level of Being quite unlike
that of people as we know them. It does not seem at all probable
that there is a group of living people who have the power to influence human affairs on a grand scale. There is a certain naivete
in the 'strong' view that a higher level of being is describable in
the language that is appropriate to the every-day world. If we accept
Gurdjieff's dictum that ordinary man 'perceives reality in his
attention upside down', it may well be that the characteristics of a
true 'Inner Circle' would be exactly the opposite of what we should
expect. I will return to this suggestion after considering the 'weak'
view. We need not examine the 'strong' view of the 'Inner Circle' in
terms of visible history.

The 'weak' view attributes superior wisdom and powers to the
'Inner Circle' but does not regard it as all-powerful. This weaker
view might take various forms, ranging from simple confidence that
there are good and wise people who are working in some kind of
concert for the welfare of mankind, to belief in a traditional teaching transmitted by people who have attained a higher level of being
by their own effort, and who use their knowledge and powers to the
extent that world conditions permit. The second version corresponds to the picture of the Khwajagān as it emerged in the last
chapter. Virtually any form of belief in the possibility for man of
attaining higher levels of being implies acceptance that such men
have lived in the past and may be living in the present and have,
because of their transformation, a clearer understanding of human
destiny and a greater capacity for concerted action than ordinary
people. If there are people on a higher level of being, we could
reasonably expect that they would recognize one another and share
between them the burden of helping the world. The objection to this
supposition is that it appears to lead back to the 'strong' view that
we have rejected.

The objection rests on the assumption that the way in which

'higher beings' work can be deduced from the methods that are adopted by ordinary people and their societies. Now a most striking feature of all ordinary human activity is its shortsightedness. Crisis government—that is, stumbling from one awkward situation to another—characterizes all the political systems of the world. There are very few departments of human life in which decisions are made with regard to the foreseeable but remote future. It is the immediate present that dominates. We never catch up with ourselves, because our activity is so often directed towards targets that are no longer there when we reach them. Furthermore, our decision-making is always too narrowly based. We evaluate situations in terms of the factors which we believe that we understand, and disregard those that are outside our competence. We do not see that events are governed by laws that are quite different from 'causality' as we suppose it to operate. These observations will be examined in depth when we come to study Gurdjieff's cosmology. The point to be made here is that we have no means of evaluating an activity which uses techniques of which we are totally ignorant. We can 'judge by results' only if we know how to recognize what results were aimed at. A townsman sees a farmer ploughing a field and concludes that his aim is to destroy vegetation. Six months later he sees that the result is a crop of wheat. The next year he sees him leaving the field unploughed and accuses him of negligence, never having heard of the need from time to time to let land lie fallow. We suffer from a far deeper disability than the townsman on his first visit to the country. We look at events in the wrong time scale, but we do not even recognize the processes which must be set in motion if mankind is to go forward along the path of creative evolution.

In order to put the notion of an 'Inner Circle' into perspective, we need to introduce categories that are foreign to ordinary thinking. Three areas of human experience may be distinguished:

The Area of Fact: This comprises all that is in communication with our bodies by sense perception and mechanical interaction. This is pre-eminently the domain in which science, technology and economics operate. For materialistic and mechanistic theories of the world, it is the sole reality.

The Area of Value: This includes all those intangible influences that determine our judgments and our motives. This is pre-eminently the domain of morality, of aesthetics and of jurisprudence. Its content is all that ought to be. Usually 'values' are regarded as ideas or attitudes held by human beings. We should treat them as having their own reality, independent of our experience. The domain of value is the 'ideal world', and for the idealist who regards mere fact as illusion, the domain of values is the 'real' world.

The Area of Realization: The notion of a non-factual domain in which reality is constantly being created is foreign to ordinary thinking, but it is implicit in all Gurdjieff taught and did. It is indeed the central concept of all 'work' which, by definition, proceeds exclusively by creative activity that cannot be reduced to fact and value or even to a combination of the two.

Two great illusions by which mankind is enslaved are the belief that the domain of fact is real, and the belief that values can exist without being realized. We have sense experience and we have emotional impulses from which we construct in our 'minds' pictures of the world and we take these pictures for representations of reality. Gurdjieff was never tired of denouncing as self-deception such attitudes which effectively block the way to self-realization. 'Real' men are those who can create their own 'reality', but this takes them into a domain that is incomprehensible for those who believe in facts and values as 'real' in themselves.

The hypothesis of an 'Inner Circle' can now be stated as the supposition that there are people who have discovered the secret of realization. Since we do not look upon these as incarnations from another world, they must have attained their place by their own efforts. But, since they also have access to supernatural knowledge, they must have been chosen and given special help. They are the 'elect' upon whom the destiny of the world depends. Such people, if they do indeed exist, must be able to see more deeply into the way the world works than ordinary people. Among 'ordinary people' in this sense we include philosophers, scientists, sociologists, historians, economists and the leaders of church and state whose perceptions and powers have been exercised solely in the domains of fact and value. In principle, artists and religious people should be creating values, but for the most part, they are content to base their vocation upon an act of faith. Because they do not know how to change their perceptions, they are obliged in their conduct of practical affairs to rely upon the same methods as everyone else. They claim to rely upon the inspiration and guidance of the spirit, but seldom have the courage to throw away the calculations of human reason which cannot transcend the domain of fact.

By eliminating what would not qualify as the 'Inner Circle' of Humanity, we have come a little closer to answering the question whether such groups of people have existed and do exist today. A fairly strong version of the hypothesis must be considered, if we are to reach significant conclusions. This can now be expressed as the presence on earth of self-realized people who are working in the domain of realization in order to redeem humanity from the consequences of excessive reliance upon the power to manipulate 'facts'. Such people are 'strong', but not in the sense of 'powerful' or 'influential' and they are 'wise' but not in the sense of being learned. They are, therefore, likely to attract little attention from those who assess their fellow men in terms of their visible attainments.

It is probable that Gurdjieff's searches convinced him that people with such higher powers have lived on the earth and that they are active in our day, but apart from what he told Ouspensky in 1916, he does not seem to have made this a central feature of his teaching. Various explanations of this have been given. Some people say that he was never admitted to the innermost groups and was obliged to put together, as best he could, fragments collected from a variety of sources. Others believe that he was accepted as a missionary or messenger to prepare the way for a more decisive entry of the guardians of the tradition into the life of the West. We should certainly expect that he would have left sufficiently clear indications to enable us to reconstruct the true position. One purpose of the present book is to examine this expectation. We have already noted that in none of his own writings does Gurdjieff explicitly assert that there is an 'Inner Circle' or that he met with any evidence of it. It is true that he refers to 'World Brotherhoods' particularly in *Meetings with Remarkable Men*—but he presents them as closed orders withdrawn from the world, and concerned with the personal salvation of the few fortunate souls who happen to find their way to them. It is, however, possible to put together a more encouraging picture, if we follow some clues he left in various places.

One such clue given by Gurdjieff is the mention in several passages of the Sarmoun or Sarmān Society. The pronunciation is the same for either spelling and the word can be assigned to old Persian. It does, in fact, appear in some of the Pahlawi texts to designate those who preserved the doctrines of Zoroaster. The word can be interpreted in three ways. It is the word for bee, which has always been a symbol of those who collect the precious 'honey' of traditional wisdom and preserve it for future generations. A collection of legends, well known in Armenian and Syrian circles with the title *The Bees*, was revised by Mar Salamon,[a] a Nestorian Archimandrite in the thirteenth century, that is, about the time of Jenghis Khan. *The Bees*, refers to a mysterious power transmitted from the time of Zoroaster and made manifest in the time of Christ.

A more obvious rendering is to take the *mān* in its Persian meaning as the quality transmitted by heredity and hence a distinguished family or race. It can be the repository of an heirloom or tradition. The word *sar* means head, both literally and in the sense of principal or chief. The combination *sarmān* would thus mean the chief respository of the tradition, which has been called 'the perennial philosophy' passed down from generation to generation by 'iniatiated beings' to use Gurdjieff's description.

And still another possible meaning of the word Sarmān is 'those who have been enlightened'; literally, those whose heads have been purified. This gives us a possible clue to Gurdjieff's intention. In the chapter "Beelzebub's Opinion of War",[b] he refers to a fraternity existing in Central Asia under the name of the 'Assembly of the Enlightened'. He adds that in those days the brothers of this fraternity were very much venerated by other three-brained beings around them, and hence their brotherhood was sometimes called 'The Assembly-of-All-the-Living-Saints-of-the-Earth'. This is the nearest Gurdjieff comes to specific mention in his own writing of a group that could correspond to the 'Inner Circle' of Humanity.

He says that this brotherhood had already been formed long before by a group of beings who had noticed in themselves the properties of the Organ Kundabuffer[c] and had banded together to work collectively for their deliverance from these properties. The narrative goes on to describe the initiative taken by the Assembly to set up a society to prevent war. Gurdjieff carefully places this event by referring to the centre of the society as Mosul which is across the River Tigris from the ruins of Nimrud and Nineveh. He says it

---

[a] A Latin translation by Solomon, Bishop of Basra, is available in the British Museum Library.

[b] *Beelzebub's Tales*, p. 1091.

[c] See Chapter 11.

C

occurred several centuries ago, and fixes the date by saying that the society included the personal representatives of the famous conqueror Tamerlane. Tamerlane certainly passed through Mosul and, as we saw in the last chapter, he was a patron of the Sufis and a devotee of Khwaja Ahmed Yesevi of Tashkent.

It can reasonably be concluded that Gurdjieff intends the reader to infer that he is referring to historical events of special importance. This is confirmed by the surprising list of communities represented in the society: Mongols, Arabs, Kirghizes, Georgians, Little Russians and Tamils.[a] These cover most of the main religious groups: Shamans, Muslims, Buddhists, Christians and Hindus, but with the notable exception of Zoroastrians and Jews.

Now it is an historical fact that after two centuries of wars and civil wars, Asia had a period of relative peace in the fifteenth and sixteenth centuries and I have suggested in the last chapter that the Khwajagān may have played some part in this. It does not seem in the least likely that the 'Assembly-of-the-Enlightened' can be identified with the Khwajagān, for the simple reason that there is no evidence that the latter ever assembled to act in concert. The Masters were highly independent individuals who accepted and supported one another, but did not form a society until the Dervish brotherhoods, such as the Naq'shbandis, began to be organized in the sixteenth century.

Even if the Khwajagān and the Sarmān were not identical, it is possible that individual Khwajas were associated with the Sarmān Brotherhood. This is suggested by Gurdjieff, and by comparing dates and activities, we may identify his Brother Olmantaboor[b] with Ubeydullah Ahrar. Ahrar's biographer, Mēvlanā Djami, the greatest literary figure of Central Asia, was evidently aware that Ahrar's influence went far beyond his immediate environment. It will be remembered that he made a strong point of his concern with the prevention of war. This was something of a departure for the Sufis who had until that time tended to regard the world and its wickedness as an evil to be avoided rather than a field of beneficent activity.

It is likely that the original custodians of the traditions were the Sarmān Brotherhood and we must find out all that we can about their origins and activities. Gurdjieff provides here another astonishing

[a] Ibid., p. 1093.
[b] Ibid., p. 1092.

clue. He says that the society 'The Earth is Equally Free for All' set itself to establish in Asia a single religion, a single language and a single central authority. The religion they selected was "to be based in that of the Parsis, only changing it a little".*a* The language was to be Turkmen, the Turkish dialect spoken in Turkmenistan from Samarkand to Balkh. The central authority was to be established at Margelan, the capital of the Ferghanian Khanate. No reference to the Parsis, the religion founded by Zoroaster, appears elsewhere in Gurdjieff's writings. It is particularly remarkable that there is no reference to Zoroaster in the chapter on Religion, nor does his name appear among the wise men who assembled in Babylon and formed the society of adherents of legominism.*b* The date of the latter is easily fixed at 510 BC because Cambyses is known at that date to have brought learned men from Egypt to Babylon, and according to Iamblichus Pythagoras was one of them. This agrees with Beelzebub's tale.

Gurdjieff must have known the Greek traditions referring to Zoroaster or Zaratas. Apuleius refers to Zoroaster as the spiritual guide of Cyrus the Great and the teacher of Pythagoras, and there are many similar references in Greek literature. Iamblichus in his life of Pythagoras (Chapter Four) states that Pythagoras spent twelve years in Babylon consorting with the Magi. These are passages remarkably reminiscent of Gurdjieff's description of the Club of Adherent's of Legominism (*Beelzebub's Tales*, Chapter XXX). Gurdjieff certainly had read his Iamblichus and to some extent modelled his Institute upon the Pythagorean schools. Unless Zoroaster is to be identified with Ashiata Shiemash, he does not appear in Beelzebub's tales of the Babylonian period. Why then should his religion be referred to in a much later chapter describing events two thousand years after the time of Zoroaster, as the best foundation for a creed in which all Asiatic communities could share?

We should here note that Rudolf Steiner in 1911 wrote a book called *The Spiritual Guidance of Mankind* in which he claims that, by clairvoyant insight, he was able to reconstruct the history of the Zoroastrian influence in human life over a period of eight thousand years, or from the origins of the Aryan culture. As Gurdjieff makes several references to anthroposophy in *Beelzebub's Tales*, we may assume that he was aware of the importance that Steiner attached to

a Ibid., p. 1093.
b Ibid., p. 455.

the Zoroastrian traditions. He invariably refers to anthroposophy in slighting terms as an aberration of the same order as theosophy and spiritualism. It does not, by any means, follow that he rejected all the conclusions reached by Rudolf Steiner. From his attitude in conversation, I would surmise that he objected to the uncritical acceptance of statements which were unsupported by historical evidence.

It has been suggested that the 'Cosmic Individual incarnated from Above', who is called Ashiata Shiemash in *Beelzebub's Tales*,[a] is intended for Zarathustra (Zoroaster). Gurdjieff certainly spoke of Ashiata Shiemash in three different ways. He was an historical character who had really lived in Asia thousands of years ago. He was also the image of the prophet of the New Epoch who is still to come, and he was also Gurdjieff himself. He said more than once: "I am Ashiata Shiemash". It has also been asserted that these chapters are purely allegorical and refer to no historical situation past, present or future. In my opinion, all four interpretations are valid and we should therefore examine the first to see if it helps us with the search for an 'Inner Circle'.

After his enlightenment, Ashiata is said to have gone to "the capital city Djoolfapal of the country then called Kurlandtech which was situated in the middle of the continent of Asia". If this refers to Zarathustra's journey in his thirtieth year, after receiving enlightenment, the city must be Balkh where Kave Gushtaspa was king. Here Zarathustra found two men, counsellors of the king, Jamaspa and Frashaostra who were seeking for wisdom. He enlightened them and initiated the king. There is a remarkable verse in the Avesta fifth Gatha, verse 16) which says:

> "The leadership of the Maga mysteries has been bestowed on Kave Gushtaspa.
> At the same time he has been initiated into the path of Vohu Manah by inner-vision.
> This is the way that Ahura Mazda has decreed according to Asha."

In later Persian sacred literature, Asha becomes Ashtvahasht, which is strangely suggestive of Ashiata Shiemash.

According to the legend, Kave Gushtaspa placed himself entirely under the direction of Zarathustra and this inaugurated the reign of the Good Law.

[a] Ibid., Chapters XXVI and XXVII.

It is obviously possible that Gurdjieff has all this in mind, but he left no clear indication. The name Ashiata Shiemash can be derived from the Turkish word *Ash*, meaning food, and the words *iat* and *iem* which refer to eating. According to this interpretation, Ashiatashiemash personifies the principle of reciprocal feeding.[a] This is very interesting because of the conclusion I reach on other grounds that the principle has a Zoroastrian origin. (See Chapter 8 below.)

The nearest Gurdjieff comes anywhere to describing a society that influenced history is in the "Organization for Man's Existence Created by the Very Saintly Ashiata Shiemash".[b] The society, called the Brotherhood Heechtvori, developed from the society he found in Djoolfapal (Balkh?). He interprets the name to mean 'only he will be called and will become the Son of God who acquires in himself conscience.' This society was not occupied with social organization and reform nor with the exercise of power. It was a training establishment to which people went to have their 'reason enlightened'; first as to the real presence of conscience in man; and, secondly, as to the means whereby it can be 'manifested in order that a man may respond to the real sense and aim of his existence'.[c] The external, social consequences of the training are depicted as deep and far-reaching. New kinds of relationship came into being, men looked for guidance rather than for authority. Social and political conflicts disappeared. This was not the result of reform or reorganization, but solely of a change in people. I think Gurdjieff uses the story of Ashiata Shiemash not only to underline the central significance of conscience in his message to humanity, but also to suggest that he has no confidence in any kind of occult 'action at a distance'. People are to be helped by actions that they can understand and, in due course, produce for themselves.

Zoroaster was associated in the minds of Central Asian communities with the struggle that endured for thousands of years between the Turanian nomads and the Aryan settlers. The 'Avestan Gathas' often identify the Turanians with the evil spirits in spite of the fact that more than one Turanian prince became a follower of Zoroaster. Gurdjieff's society, 'The Earth is Equally Free for All', was to adopt the ancient Turanian language and combine it with the Aryan religion of Parsis and establish its main centre in Ferghana. The

[a] Ibid., Chapter XXXIX.
[b] Ibid., Chapter XXVII, p. 368.
[c] Ibid., p. 369.

only possible interpretation of such a combination is that it refers to a society that was on such a high level that the conflicts that divide religions and peoples did not touch it. No higher society could be imagined than the 'Assembly-of-All-the-Living-Saints-of-the-Earth'.

The connection between this society and the Sarmān Brotherhood is given both by the name and by the location, first in Mosul and then in Bokhara. In *Meetings with Remarkable Men*, Gurdjieff describes how he and his Armenian friend, Pogossian, found ancient Armenian texts, including the book *Merkhavat*, that referred to the 'Sarmoung' society as a famous esoteric school that according to tradition had been founded in Babylon as far back as 2500 BC and which was known to have existed in Mesopotamia up to the sixth or seventh century of the Christian era. The school was said to have possessed great knowledge containing the key to many secret mysteries.[a] The date of 2500 BC would put the founding of this school several centuries before the time of Hammurabi, the greatest lawgiver of antiquity, but it is not an impossible one. It is an interesting date, because it coincides with the migration that brought together a Semitic people, the Akkadians, and the older Indo-European race of the Sumerians. It is quite plausible to suppose that a school of wisdom could then have been established that guided the course of events towards the wonderful achievements of Sargon I and Hammurabi. If such a school existed, it would have abandoned Babylon after the time of Darius II, about 400 BC, and could very well have moved north into the upper valley of the Tigris where the Parthians were about to begin their long period of dominance in the mountains of Kurdistan and the Caucasus. The Parthians brought with them a pure Zoroastrian tradition. The Armenian hegemony bridged the gap until the arrival of the Seljuks at the end of the first millennium AD. This was a time when caravan routes in all directions passed through the upper valleys and it was possible to collect and concentrate traditions from China to Egypt.

This leads us to the next phase of Gurdjieff's contact with the Sarmān Brotherhood. He reports that in the course of a sojourn at Ani, one of the capitals of the Bagratid Armenian kingdom, he and Pogossian found a collection of letters written on parchment some time in the seventh century AD, one of which contained a reference

[a] *Meetings with Remarkable Men*, Chapter V, p. 90.

to the Sarmān Brotherhood as having one of their main centres near the town of Siranush. They had migrated to the north-east and settled in the valley of Izrumin, three days' journey from 'Nivssi'. Gurdjieff goes on to say that their further researches led them to identify Nivssi with Mosul which is already connected with the Society of the Enlightened. By the date mentioned, Nineveh had ceased to be inhabited but Nimrud, the ancient capital of the Assyrian king, Assurbanipal, was still a great trading centre on account of its location at a point where the Tigris begins to be navigable all the year round.

Three days' journey by camel from Nimrud through almost desert country leads to a valley green with trees, in the midst of which is Sheikh Adi—the chief sanctuary of the Yezidi Brotherhood. Now the Yezidis are certainly inheritors of the old Zoroastrian tradition and Gurdjieff specifically refers to them among the groups of Assyrians he found in the region surrounding Mosul which was the heart of the old Assyrian Empire. I visited Sheikh Adi in 1952 and was convinced that the Yezidis possessed secrets unsuspected by orientalists who classify their faith as a relic of paganism. Their connection with the Mithraic tradition is generally accepted because of their chief festival of the white bull which takes place at Sheikh Adi in October every year. They are even more directly descended from the followers of Manes whose influence spread very widely all through Asia in the third and fourth centuries of our era, only two hundred years before the Sarmān Brotherhood was reported as having its headquarters at Izrumin.

It seems probable that a very strong tradition did exist in Chaldaea from very early times. Gurdjieff, both in his writings and in his conversations with his pupils, constantly referred to this ancient tradition. We can assume that, during the great upheavals of history, the guardians of the tradition responded in the way described in the last chapter: dividing into three branches, one of which migrated, one was assimilated into the new regime and the third went into hiding.

At the time of the Muslim conquests in the seventh and eighth centuries, groups like the Yezidis and the Ahl-i-Haqq were formed. They presented more or less acceptable doctrines to the Arabs, who could not understand the subtleties of Persian spirituality. There was relatively little forced conversion of Nestorian Christians, whose beliefs were substantially compatible with the teaching of the

Qur'an. Our main concern is with the third group who withdrew into Central Asia. This is the group that corresponds to Gurdjieff's account of the Sarmān Brotherhood.

Gurdjieff himself makes no attempt to explain the migration. In his adventures with Pogossian, the 'Sarmoung' Brotherhood is located in Chaldaea. In the story of Prince Yuri Lubovedsky,[a] they have moved to Central Asia, twenty days' journey from Kabul and twelve days' journey from Bokhara. He refers to the valleys of the Pyandje and the Syr Darya, which suggest an area in the mountains south-east of Tashkent. He discloses at the end of this chapter that this particular brotherhood had another centre in the 'Olman' monastery on the northern slopes of the Himalayas. The word 'Olman' is a link with Olmantaboor who was the head of the 'Assembly-of-the-Enlightened'. The northern slopes of the Himalayas connect with the Amu Darya and Syr Darya rivers.

We must now closely examine the slender clues that Gurdjieff has left us to reconstruct the teaching he found at the monastery between the Amu and Syr Darya rivers, and described both directly and obliquely in *Meetings with Remarkable Men*.

Gurdjieff provides us with no direct information about what he learned during his three-month stay at the Sarmān monastery. For a man so quick in perception as Gurdjieff, three months is a long time and he could have acquired all that the Sheikh chose to make available, once he was accepted there. He does not make it clear, by the way, how long he remained after the departure of Prince Yuri. Reference in another place to a two years' stay at a sanctuary in Central Asia may refer to the same place.[b] In any case, he leaves the reader in no doubt that this contact was of the greatest importance to him and that he learned secrets of a different order of significance from those he found in the various Sufi communities he visited.

By drawing attention to the 'apparatuses' used to train priestesses, Gurdjieff fixes in the mind of the reader the central importance occupied by the 'Law of Sevenfoldness'. These apparatuses were of very ancient workmanship, made of ebony, inlaid with ivory and mother-of-pearl. Since ebony was brought from Africa and mother-of-pearl from India, this suggests that the apparatus represents a synthesis of Semitic and Aryan teachings. Associated with the

[a] *Meetings with Remarkable Men*, Chapter VII, p. 149.
[b] *Herald of Coming Good*, p. 20.

apparatus were places carrying the pattern of the message to be conveyed. The plates were of gold and they and the apparatus were of great antiquity. They had a vertical column to which were fitted seven movable arms and each of these arms provided with seven universal joints similar to those of the human shoulder. Each of the forty-nine joints and the ends carried a sign. The positions were read from the plates and were interpreted in the postures and gestures of the dancers. The dance thus became an utterance, the language of which was known to the brethren, and enabled them to read truths placed there thousands of years before. There is no indication that the dances served any other purpose than the transmission of 'truths' and Gurdjieff underlines this by comparing them to our books. According to him, experts had determined that the plates were at least four thousand five hundred years old. This corresponds to the date— 2600 BC—given in the Pogassian chapter for the founding of the Sarmān Brotherhood in Babylon. It also agrees with the date given in *Beelzebub's Tales* for the 'Tikliamishian Civilization' which refers to the kingdoms of Sumer and Akkad in Mesopotamia prior to the Hittite invasions at the end of the second millennium BC. The dating would suggest the time of Sargon I, the first Semitic ruler. He did much to promote intercourse with other countries and, in his time, Kish, only thirty miles from Babylon, became one of the first centres of culture. Although Gurdjieff specifically associates Tikliamish with the Sumerians, he distinguishes between a legendary period before the destruction of cultures by the dry sandstorms of the fourth millennium BC and the historical period of the third and second millennia. The word 'Tikliamish', as so many others in *Beelzebub's Tales*, must be read both in an allegorical and in an historical sense. When definite dates are given and means of relating to known historical events are inserted, I assume that Gurdjieff intends the reader to undertake the historical research needed to elaborate the meagre details he provides.

I asked him in 1949 whether some of the stories in *Beelzebub's Tales* were to be taken in a strict historical sense. He was most emphatic in his affirmation, saying: "Everything in *Beelzebub* is historical." He added that it is indispensable to seek for reliable knowledge of long-past events not only to help us to undertand the present, but because we are connected with the past and must learn to make use of this connection.

In all his descriptions of what he found in this and other

monasteries, Gurdjieff makes no reference to any higher 'powers' or to the control of energies that could produce external results in the world. It seems likely that if Gurdjieff had regarded the Sarmān Brotherhood as the 'Inner Circle' in the 'strong' sense discussed at the beginning of this chapter, he would have said so or at least left some hint to this effect.

The episode that suggests a widely spread influence is the story of Prince Yuri's invitation. He meets an old man in the house of the Aga Khan whom he suspects of being connected with a visitor who came to him in Russia many years earlier and set him upon the path of his subsequent search. The Ishmailis, of whom the Aga Khan is the hereditary spiritual leader, were then a widely spread brotherhood with remarkable influence in all parts of the world. Gurdjieff never mentions them by name, but must certainly have met many Ishmailis in the course of his travels.

It seems to me that we reach the conclusion that Gurdjieff neither expected to find nor looked for an 'Inner Circle' of Humanity in the 'strong' sense. He did, however, unquestionably believe in a traditional wisdom that is not preserved in books but in the experience of people. Indeed, the collection, preservation and transmission of 'Higher Knowledge' occupies such a central position in all Gurdjieff's writings and in his conversations with his pupils and friends that it would be absurd to suggest that he did not take it seriously.

What did Gurdjieff mean by 'truths' transmitted from the past? He sometimes refers to true information about past events and the difficulty of finding it except through legominisms,[a] to be interpreted by initiates. This information is necessary for subsequent generations to enable them to meet the difficulties that arise in the rise and fall of cultures, difficulties that people never believe will occur again because 'the world is now different'. Gurdjieff, on the contrary, believed that there is a pattern of events that is destined to lead man along the path of evolution, but is constantly disrupted by our own egoistic foolishness and "unbecoming conditions of existence".

In order to understand what is required of us, we must not only know ourselves, but also the 'laws of World Creation and World Maintenance'. Ashiata Shiemash is said to have given his disciples five principles of Right Life. They should strive:

[a] *Beelzebub's Tales*, Chapter I, p. 16.

to have in their ordinary being-existence everything satisfying and really necessary for their planetary body.

to have a constant and unflagging instinctive need for self-perfection in the sense of being.

to know ever more and more concerning the laws of World-creation and World-maintenance.

to pay for their arising and their individuality as quickly as possible, in order afterwards to be free to lighten as much as possible the Sorrow of our *Common Father*.

always to assist the most rapid perfecting of other beings, up to the degree of self-individuality.

The third principle was certainly manifested in Gurdjieff's own life's search. From childhood he had reached the conviction that, at different times in the past, men had made significant discoveries about the way the world works, and that these discoveries were subsequently, for the most part, lost or distorted. Since knowledge of man and the world is necessary for right living, a part of our own effort should be directed to rediscovering these laws.

I think it is fair to suppose that during his stay at the Sarmān monastery, Gurdjieff was brought into contact with the extraordinary system of thought that he represents with the aid of the enneagram symbol.[a] I shall discuss the symbol and its significance in a later chapter, but here would only say that it makes use of the properties of the numbers 3, 7 and 10 in a way that makes its Chaldean origin almost certain. The Sumerians, or possibly their Semitic neighbours, the Akkadians, were the first to use an arithmetic based on the first six numbers with 60 as the base and to observe that the number 7 would not fit into it. We are then taken back to the period four thousand five hundred years before the present to which Gurdjieff attributes the formation of the Sarmān Society. The science of numbers, in the widest sense, originated in Mesopotamia and developed over a period of four thousand years from 2500 BC to AD 1500, by which time, it had moved north into Sogdiana; that is, the region of Samarkand and Bokhara. We should have no difficulty in accepting the suggestion that the Sarmān were founded in Kish by agreement between the guardians of the Aryan (Sumerian) and Semitic (Akkadian) traditions about 2400 BC, at the time of Sargon I. They moved to Babylon a few centuries later

[a] *In Search of the Miraculous*, pp. 285–94.

and became active during the most glorious, if not the most magnificent period of Babylonian history, which was crowned by the reign of Hammurabi.

This period has remained in Middle Eastern tradition as the Golden Age of peace and justice. When it ended, the Sarmān Brotherhood moved north to Khorsabad and only later returned to Babylon. The strange powers exercised by Nebuchadnezzar and his final breakdown may have been associated with a period of contact with the Brotherhood broken by the jealousy of the regular priests of Ishtar. The sarmāni may, during this time, have retired into the mountains and come forward much later when Cyrus the Great destroyed the Assyrian power and inaugurated a rare period of spiritual activity which included the return of the Israelites from the Babylonian captivity and the promulgation of the 'New Law' (Deuteronomy) and probably the incorporation into the beliefs of the Israelites of the Babylonian account of the Creation of the World and Man. It included the time which Pythagoras and Epaminondas, two of the founders of Greek philosophy, spent in Babylon. The Achemenenan Dynasty, founded by Cyrus, was the first since Hammurabi, 1,300 years earlier, to have a genuine spiritual basis, although unfortunately after a few generations very little remained. When Cyrus's grandson Cambyses, conquered Egypt in 524 BC and destroyed the centre of culture that had existed there for thousands of years, he took into captivity all the technicians and artists who could serve to enrich and beautify Babylon.

He also took the priests and scientists—in those days the two were the same—whom Gurdjieff describes in Chapters XXIV and XXX of *Beelzebub's Tales*. One very significant hint is dropped where it is said that "the highest school existing on Earth at that time was found in Egypt and was called the 'School of Materializing Thought'."[a] Materializing of thought or the creation of thought forms is one of the principal techniques whereby events can be influenced and forces transmitted from one place and time to another. Gurdjieff refers to it in an earlier chapter in connection with the Society Akhaldan which migrated to Egypt. The 'sympathetic Assyrian', Hamolinadir,[b] who discourses on the instability of human reason, was trained in the 'School of Materializing Thought', but

[a] *Beelzebub's Tales*, p. 232.
[b] Ibid., pp. 235-7.

evidently recognized the uselessness of the acquisition of mental powers in the absence of an established set of convictions. This indirectly suggests that the Sarmān Brotherhood had a more practical understanding of human needs than the Egyptian sages. This agrees with an often-quoted statement of Gurdjieff's that different kinds of schools have, from very early times, existed in different regions. "In India, philosophy; in Egypt, theory; in Central Asia and the Middle East, practice."[a]

This is not to say that the interaction of different cultural streams in Babylon, in the middle of the first millennium BC, was not highly significant. On the contrary, it was one of the turning points of human history and its effects are still with us. Babylon continued to be the headquarters of the Sarmān Brotherhood until the dispersal of 320 BC. They then moved north again to avoid contact with Alexander of Macedon—that 'vainglorious Greek' as Gurdjieff calls him —and the degrading Hellenistic period that preceded the time of Christ. Their role in the Gospel Drama is an unrevealed mystery, unless we associate them with the 'wise men from the East' of St. Matthew's Gospel.

It seems that Manes, that remarkable prophet of the third century AD (born 216, martyred 276), was in some way associated with the Sarmān Brotherhood, for, at that time, according to Gurdjieff's account, the Brotherhood was at 'Nivssi' which corresponds roughly to the ancient Nimrud, the modern Mosul. Manes was such an important figure in the transmission of the traditional wisdom that we must ask why Gurdjieff never mentions him by name. The Manichean Teaching was upon all levels. Manes was the first to bring art and music fully into the service of sacramental religion. The liturgy of the Christian Church created by Gregory and his school in Cappadocia was taken directly from the form of worship which comes from the Aryan tradition and is found with its fourfold ritual in the Avestar Gathas. It is probable that Manes drew upon Mithraic and Christian sources for his own liturgy. His ideas had a powerful influence in spite of his premature death.

All over Europe, including Britain, we can find evidence of the widespread penetration of Manichean ideas between the third and fifth centuries of our era. His influence spread northwards across the Oxus into Central Asia. When Gurdjieff was travelling in those

[a] *In Search of the Miraculous*, p. 15.

regions, in 1907, a Russian expedition to the centre of the Gobi Desert discovered at Turfan a collection of manuscripts attributed to Manes himself and certainly emanating directly from his school. I have not been able to trace the translation of these manuscripts which were published in Russia, but they must have been known to Gurdjieff as they were highly relevant to his own researches. According to the extracts I have seen, they contain teachings about world creation that have significant points in common with what we find in *Beelzebub's Tales*, particularly the doctrine of reciprocal maintenance. Now Gurdjieff writes that this latter doctrine was re-discovered by a Kurdish philosopher in the fifteenth century in an ancient manuscript, written by 'some ancient learned being', which contained the hypothesis "In all probability there exists in the world some law of the reciprocal maintenance of all that exists"[a] Since this discovery is directly connected with the 'Assembly of the Enlightened', which I have suggested may stand for the Sarmān Brotherhood, we have a possible link with Manes, who had lived twelve hundred years earlier in the region of the upper Tigris where Kurd Atarnakh is said to have been born. One could follow up such clues by the legion; they cannot be called evidence and it was not Gurdjieff's purpose to 'prove' anything, but rather to make the reader search and think for himself.

The conundrum he sets before us here is to account for the place of Manes in the esoteric tradition and to see if he was likely to be connected with the Sarmān Brotherhood. Manes declared that in two spiritual experiences at the ages of sixteen and thirty, he had been called to be the prophet of Christ sent into the world to bring about the unity of religions. He accepted the Pauline doctrine of the redemption, but he saw that much that was of vital importance to mankind in the teaching of Zoroaster had been left out of Christianity. In particular, the dualism of worlds of matter and spirit having nothing in common, that had entered Greek thought and has been taken over by Christian theologians, was evidently leading to the eventual collapse of religion. Manes saw that the Israelites, in taking over the doctrine of the Saoshyant or Divine Saviour, had converted it into a quasi-political expectation of the Messiah who was to restore the kingdom of Judah. The more serious error is that of dividing man on the same dualistic basis into an immortal, spiritual soul and a mortal, physical body. This false dualism, in spite of its

[a] *Beelzebub's Tales*, p. 1096.

obvious absurdity, has never been eradicated from Christian doctrine.

All this was clear to Manes, who seized the essence of the Zoroastrian and Mithraic psychology and succeeded in converting a very large following. Gurdjieff castigates the 'Babylonian dualism' in terms reminiscent of Manes.[a] An even closer correspondence is to be found between Gurdjieff's teaching of Conscience and Manes's 'Call from Above', described in a manuscript discovered in Egypt and reputedly from his own hand. The 'Call of Conscience' is the message sent by the good spirit, Ahura Mazda, to awaken man from his prevailing state of delusion.

Some connection between Manes and the Sarmān is suggested by his life story, his teaching, and the geographical location, and by the indication given by Gurdjieff that the society existed in 'Nivssi' from the fourth to the tenth century. During the early period, Manicheanism continued to be the accepted religion of the region between Mesopotamia, Iran and the Caucasus until the rise of the Armenian power that dominated from the eighth to the twelfth century. Once again, we have the phenomenon of threefold preservation. One part of the Manichean heritage was directly assimilated into Armenian Christianity and makes it so distinctively different from that of the west. A second part migrated to the north. The third part went underground and reappeared later in the form of the Yezidi community and other sects which persist to this day as a spiritual force in the region. The interest taken in the Brotherhood by the Armenian monk whose letters were discovered by Gurdjieff and Pogossian in the ruins of Ani is a good indication that the Sarmāni were not regarded as alien by the Armenian Christians as late as the twelfth or thirteenth century. They were, however, driven out by the 'Byzantines' who, during the time of Paleologue II, erupted into Assyria and drove Assyrian Christianity into the mountains.

It is probable that the Sarmān Brotherhood went across the Amu Darya in the twelfth century, at the time of the rise of the Khwajagān with whom they must have had some link. They are not likely to have settled in the troubled region of Transoxania, which was for two centuries to be ravaged by war, but further north on the Syr Darya, where the almost limitless limestone caverns have been inhabited for the past ten thousand years. It is quite possible that the

[a] Ibid., pp. 338–45.

legend brought back by Helen Blavatsky of the hidden Masters living in the great caves of Central Asia may have originated in stories of the Sarmān Brotherhood. Gurdjieff (*Meetings with Remarkable Men*, p. 148) says that the Brotherhood was "known among the dervishes by the name of Sarmoun". I should here mention a clue given in the name of the dervish 'Bogga Eddin', through whom Gurdjieff learned in Bokhara of the Sarmān Monastery. Gurdjieff invariably rendered the letter *h* by a *g*, as there is no appropriate *h* in Russian, Armenian or Greek. Bogga Eddin would, therefore, be 'Bahauddin' : and the founder of the Naq'shbandi dervishes was also a native of Bokhara. In *Beelzebub's Tales*, another dervish with the name Hodje Zaphir Bogga Eddin appears. Hence the name is evidently derived from familiar Muslim names and should read Hodje Zafer Bahauddin. The combination of Hodje, which derives from Khwaja, and Zafer, which means conqueror, suggests that Gurdjieff wishes to contrast the outwardly successful Khwajagān with the hidden Sarmān. The 'caves' in which Beelzebub meets the 'last really great terrestrial Sage', Khwaja Asvatz Troov, are probably the caves of the Syr Darya, which runs about two hundred miles to the north of the Amu Darya and is a part of Turkestan with which Gurdjieff was personally familiar. They were accessible, as he describes it himself, by horse from Bokhara.

I think that we should accept that Gurdjieff himself does wish to convey in his chapter "The Bokharian Dervish" something of his own personal experience of contact with a source of knowledge. He disguises this source in various ways. First of all, in this Bokharian Dervish chapter, by making it an individual who was living in caves to the north-west of Bokhara; and, in the chapter on Prince Lubovedsky in *Meetings with Remarkable Men*, where he makes it a monastery to the south-east of Bokhara in the regions of the Pyandje River, which is one of the tributaries of the Amu Darya. The whole of that extraordinary country, which lies above the central plateau where Bokhara, Samarkand, and Tashkent are situated, is and has been for a very long time the home of a number of remarkable communities. There was a town called Sarmanjan or Sarmanjin, between Tirmidh and Balkh, which flourished from the eighth to the fourteenth centuries AD. This is the only reference I have been able to find to a place containing the name Sarmān. It was visited by Chinese and Indian travellers and it is just possible that it was the place of one of the Sarmān monasteries at that time (W. Barthold, *Turkestan down to the Mongol Invasion,* 1958, pp. 73–4). In the midst of these communities, there are also monasteries or brotherhoods who occupy favourable situations so remote from the general movement of trade and travel that they may very well have remained undisturbed to this day. Reviewing the evidence I have been able to collect, I must admit that the very existence of a brotherhood with the name Sarmān or Sarmoun remains speculative; but this does not invalidate the belief that there has been a very ancient tradition linking many different teachings and that this tradition has, for more than a thousand years, been situated in Turkestan.

If we now proceed on the assumption that there has been a tradition which was for a very long time associated with Central Asia, which from time to time has spread outwards into different parts of the world—north, south, east and west—and that, at other times, has drawn back again towards the source, we have to ask ourselves the questions, "What is this tradition?" "What part has this tradition played in the general history of mankind?" There are two points to be made: there is, first, the generation of ideas; and, second, the generation of energy.

I will illustrate the generation of ideas by looking at the period about 500 or 600 BC, when there was a profound change introduced into the thinking of people about the significance of the human individual. It has previously been held that immortality, giving unique significance to the individual human soul, was the privilege of the few, and that the many did not participate in this. This was clearly held in Egypt; it belonged also to the earlier Sumerian teachings. This is what I call the Heroic or Hemitheandric Age, when it was believed that there were beings on earth who were already half-divine, whose destiny was totally different from that of ordinary people. This, on the one hand, created a sense of security that there were such people who had higher powers, who had the ability to communicate directly with the gods, and that this was their chief privilege. In that sense, they were the descendants of the magicians or the shamans who were able right through that period to communicate with the higher or spiritual powers. But this idea was capable of terrible abuse, as occurred when the privileged spiritual position was associated with despotic political power in the external sense. It reached the height of its wickedness with the Assyrian kings who dominated south-west Asia and finally with

Nebuchadnezzar and his immediate successors until they were over-thrown by the Persians when a different regime was inaugurated.

It is true that in much earlier periods, for example in the time of Hammurabi the lawgiver, in Sumeria, or in the time of the great Egyptian reformers, there were edicts protecting and safeguarding the welfare of the individual; but it still remained true that these privileges were conceded by the favour of the king or pharaoh or the representative of the gods, who alone had rights. No rights inhered in the people: but, chiefly because they were helpless, because they were an inferior race, there was an obligation to protect them and see that they were not unjustly treated. So long, however, as it was be-lieved that this was a grace conceded by the semi-divine rulers, there was always the possibility of its being revoked; the semi-divine ruler himself could then become a ruthless despot, as happened a number of times in all parts of the world.

The new idea referred to arose in China, India, Mesopotamia, Egypt, Greece, and Rome about the sixth century BC, with such names as Lao Tzu. Confucius, Gautama the Buddha, the Mahavira the Jain, Zoroaster, the Hebrew prophets of the Exile, Solon, Pythagoras and other Greek philosophers. This extraordinary set of men preached the right of every man to find his own salvation, to look directly for his own completion. It was implied that the possibility of completion and liberation was inherent in every human soul. Hence, arose the idea of the sacredness of the individual, which gradually emerged and has dominated the last two thousand years. However often we depart from it and however much brutality and savagery there is in the world, we now have an attitude which is totally different from that which existed before about 600 BC.

We saw earlier there is the tradition that there was a contact be-tween all these prophets and founders of the new religions, taking place, according to some, in Babylon, according to others, in the city of Balkh in northern Afghanistan. At any rate, there was some kind of concerted action by men of wisdom and foresight to introduce a new mode of thinking into the world. Whether or not we accept this as an historical fact, it does represent a way in which we can look at the working of the 'Inner Circle' of Humanity. If there is an 'Inner Circle' of Humanity, this is how we should expect it to operate. The point here is that at the time these events occurred, they were insignificant as compared with the greater political events that were taking place in the realms of conquest, of opening up of trade routes, of the scientific and technical progress which so marked the period between the twelfth and seventh centuries BC. These new ideas that were injected into the world were, at first, accepted only by small groups, but they gradually began to spread, partly by force of the ideas themselves and partly by the strength which was conveyed by the transformation of the people who were responsible for spreading them. This is why the entry of new ideas has always been accompanied by a religious and spiritual revival.

Those who study the origins of the great religions generally direct their attention primarily to the message and manifestation of the founder, to the activity of the apostles who were left behind to spread the message, and to the subsequent social and political activities that made the message effective. Conventional history regards the takeover of Christianity by the Roman Empire, the launching of Buddhism by King Asoka in India, and the success of the Abassid caliphs in establishing Islam as a world power with its centre in Baghdad as the important milestones in religious thought.

But these accounts of the origin of religions miss out one essential point, that the transition from the activity of a small, esoteric group to a great public organization, a Church, is made possible because a certain kind of energy is at work. This energy requires to be concentrated, and must be controlled by those who understand how it is to be channelled. This we dimly suspect when we see the martyrs and the early apostles of the great religions, when we see what they were able to do, and how they were ready to suffer for the cause for which they stood. However we tend to regard this as a personal matter, something which they did because of their own faith and integrity. There was more to it than this, for they became centres for the production of energy of a very high level—which Gurdjieff understood very well. It is inherent in his approach to the problem of human transformation and of human history that there is an invisible action of the higher energies that makes the work of evolution possible.

Here we have to look again at this concept of an 'Inner Circle', not only as a source of new and powerful ideas that will eventually change the course of human thinking, but also as the generator of high-level energy. Gurdjieff, in his *Beelzebub's Tales*, and particularly in the first book, says categorically that the role of man on earth is to be an apparatus for transformation of energy; that certain energies which man has to produce are required for cosmic purposes, and that those who understand how these energies are produced are the ones who truly fulfil the purpose of human life.

This brings us back again to the question whether Gurdjieff himself was in contact with people who not only understood energy transformation, but practised it at a high intensity. Everything that he has written in his books indicates that he not only believed this to be man's destiny but also that he had learned a great deal about the practical methods and the practical significance of this energy transformation. If this is so, it is probably the most convincing evidence that Gurdjieff did come, during his travels in the East, in contact with a higher source. We can identify this source with what we may call either the Masters of Wisdom or the 'Inner Circle' of Humanity. It does not mean, of course, that he reached the innermost circle of this source; but it shows that he had access to the essential teaching and was able to draw upon the methods emanating from it. We must ask whether the belief in energy transformation is something characteristic of Gurdjieff's system or whether it has a wider range, for example, in the great religions of the world.

There is an old Christian doctrine of the transfer of merits. According to this, an individual who has already reached a certain degree of sanctification can by his or her prayers and austerities, by the purity of his or her life, be a means for helping those who cannot help themselves. In the first place, the monk or nun can help sinners toward repentance even without their knowledge and perhaps without their own wish. In the second, it is a means of transferring effectual grace, by which the wark of sanctification is possible, to those who are at an earlier stage in their spiritual evolution. Similar beliefs are held in India and in Buddhism, where it is particularly taught that it is sufficient to enter into the *darshan* of a sanctified individual, to receive a permanent and enduring help in one's own spiritual progress. Similarly, in Islam, there is the doctrine that the simple contact, *sohbat*, with a man of high level of spiritual development is sufficient to bring about a transformation of the fortunate person.

These doctrines, however, do not give the same interpretation as Gurdjieff gives to the mechanism by which this help is transferred. As taught by Gurdjieff, the transfer is by a particular substance or combination of substances which are generated by the being who is already more fully developed and can be transmitted to others. In *Beelzebub's Tales to his Grandson*, this substance is liberated by the work of conscious labour and intentional suffering; these are the same as is taught in religion: work, austerity, sacrifice, and prayer.

The question is whether Gurdjieff himself had access to a source or generating centre for such energies. About this he says nothing very specific, but he told me in 1923 about those who were able to produce a certain substance that could help individuals to accomplish in their work what they could never accomplish by their own un-aided efforts. He said that those who had this power were regarded as "a special caste of the 'Inner Circle' of Humanity". It is interest-ing to compare this with the beliefs of Christian Monasticism, that it is possible under certain circumstances for this transfer of merits to take place. Again particular monasteries or orders exist whose work is directed specially to praying for others and particularly for those who recognize and know themselves to be sinners.

Similar doctrines are present in different traditions throughout the world. The difference is that Gurdjieff appears to have come across some concrete evidence of the way in which this process works, and even to have learned himself how to generate such energy. He used to speak himself, for example, about what he called *Hanbledzoin*, or the life energy of the second body, the *Kesdjan*[a] body of man. He also called it the blood of the *Kesdjan* body. He referred to himself as being able to produce this *Hanbledzoin* in quantities that were in excess of his own needs for his own spiritual development and could, therefore, lend it to others. Sometimes, when the people could not perform the difficult tasks which he set them, he would tell them to "draw on my *Hanbledzoin* and you will be able to do this work". In that sense, Gurdjieff held himself out to be a source of higher energy upon which people could draw. He also, though not so specifically, referred to himself as being in contact with a higher source, and said that by drawing upon this higher source, the work for which he was responsible would be able to spread and gain strength in the world.

In one very remarkable conversation, a few months before he died, he referred to this, in a cryptic but unmistakable manner. He said that at this time an organization of a higher order was being established in the world which would be able to accept only those who had reached such a stage of spiritual development that they were

[a] Ibid., Chapter IV, p. 23, for usage to denote the astral body.

able to generate higher energies. Those who were able to communicate with and draw upon this organization would themselves have to be able to participate in this work of generating and transmitting higher energies. He certainly did not refer to this organization as being of his own creation. He spoke of it in an objective way, as something which was being done of which he was aware and with which he was associated, but not in a central capacity—not as the leader or originator. I think he wished to convey to us that we should, after his death, have the opportunity, if we were prepared and able to work as required, to become connected ourselves with this source, and in turn to become a means for the transmission of this higher energy to those who require it.

I have left to the end of this survey the most significant reference to the way in which the 'Inner Circle' is said to operate. This is by the Fourth Way mentioned many times in Ouspensky's book, but not once in any of Gurdjieff's own writings. Gurdjieff gave a special meaning to the word 'way'; namely, the transformation that leads a man from the 'outer circle' to the 'Inner Circle'. Most people are familiar with the Buddhist *marga* which is the path of liberation, but the Noble Eightfold Path is entirely different from Gurdjieff's Fourth Way and the contrast lies precisely in the absence in Buddhism of an 'Inner Circle of Humanity' doctrine. The Fourth Way would have no meaning if there were not an 'Inner Circle' to which it leads. Even more important is the reverse notion that the Fourth Way alternates between activity and repose according to the decision of the 'Inner Circle' as to the needs of mankind. If this is accepted, we are involved in a fairly 'strong' version of the 'Inner Circle' hypothesis. Those of us who in the early 1920's accepted Gurdjieff and Ouspensky as our teachers had no doubt that we were entering a 'Fourth Way School'. Our only doubt was whether we were sufficiently prepared for the opportunity.

Looking back after nearly fifty years, the issue does not look so clean cut. We can see that our work did correspond to the methods ascribed by Gurdjieff to Fourth Way schools. What is not so clear is the chain of transmission. Without examining the arguments for and against the validity of Gurdjieff's mission—which I shall have to do in a later chapter—I think it can safely be said that there is evidence that Gurdjieff did believe that there is, in a fairly strong sense, an 'Inner Circle'.

I made a search in 1953 for such organizations unconnected with Gurdjieff when I travelled in the Near and Middle East. I met several schools of the Naq'shbandi dervishes and found that organization and methods corresponded to a remarkable degree with Gurdjieff's description. Gurdjieff himself only once mentioned the Naq'shis in the programme of the demonstration of movements in 1923 and 1924. The Naq'shbandis are known to be the successors of the Khwajagān and they are similarly engaged in practical undertakings for the good of society. This is said to be a mark of a Fourth Way school. They also attach importance to balanced development of all sides of man's nature. An even more important clue appeared when I found that each of the Naq'shbandi Sufis I met, spoke to me about a 'higher teacher' whom I could hope to meet if I persisted in my search. It is well-known that although the Naq'shbandis are the most numerous and widely distributed of Sufi orders, no one knows or will reveal anything about their hierarchy or their central groups. This leaves us with the possibility that the Naq'shbandis are in some way connected with a real 'Inner Circle'.

My own conclusion is that the matter is not so simple. If there is an 'Inner Circle', it cannot be exclusively Islamic. The true significance of such a group must lie in its mission. The more that one becomes aware of the spiritual realities, the more convinced does one become that a very great action is now proceeding in the world. The task before us is to help mankind to make the difficult and dangerous transition to a new epoch. If we find evidence that Gurdjieff was concerned in this task and moreover that he opened the way for us to participate in it; we shall have gone a long way to connecting him with the 'Inner Circle'.

4
Gurdjieff's Search

No one who met Gurdjieff face to face doubted that he was an extraordinary man. Those who knew him best were convinced that he was a very great man and many believed that he had a very great mission. I have been struck, however, both in reading books about Gurdjieff and in hearing people who knew him, speak about him, by the tendency to treat him as an isolated phenomenon, unique and self-sufficient. He himself emphatically refuted such suggestions. I have more than once heard him say: "Every man must have a teacher. Even I, Gurdjieff, have my teacher." He would sometimes add, "I am never separated from my teacher, even now I am communicating with him." Unlike almost all others who have written about Gurdjieff, P. D. Ouspensky was greatly concerned to find out more about his background and the sources of his teaching. Ouspensky was convinced that in some way Gurdjieff had found the sources of an ancient school of wisdom and had collected scraps of its teaching and welded them into the 'system' that he used as the basis of his own teaching.

After his death in 1949, some of Gurdjieff's nearest followers made various journeys to the East in the hope of making a fresh contact with the sources of his teaching. Mme de Salzmann told me that he had given her an address in Kabul and, at one time, she suggested that I might go there with her son Michel, but nothing came of it. So far as I know, none of the journeys has led to anything positive.

In a book recently published,[a] the pseudonymous author states that he succeeded in tracing the sources of Gurdjieff's teaching and even

[a] *The Teachers of Gurdjieff*, by Rafael Lefort: Gollancz, London 1966.

to have met some of his teachers in person. As the journeys purport to have taken place in the 1960's, that is, seventy years after Gurdjieff set out upon his travels, it is very unlikely that any 'teacher' would still be alive. The book is recognizable as a set of fables written to express a point of view and not in any sense a factual account. Some of the episodes cited are borrowed from other sources and others are amusing inventions. It is unfortunate that some readers, unacquainted with the customs of Asiatic peoples, have taken the book literally and have been confused by the suggestion that Gurdjieff left little of value behind him. The currency of such a suggestion makes it all the more important to re-examine the whole story in the light of what Gurdjieff himself had to say and of any information we can collect and verify about the state of affairs in the Near East and Central Asia at the end of the nineteenth century and the first decade of the twentieth.

If we are to accept the warning given by Gurdjieff and reported by Ouspensky, that no teacher can be authentic unless he is in contact, albeit indirectly, with the source of his teaching, we must not abandon but intensify the search. In the previous chapters, I have given my reasons for believing that the schools of wisdom of Central Asia were not so occult or inaccessible as is suggested in theosophical writings. For the purpose of the present chapter, I shall put aside the hypothesis of an 'Inner Circle' and look only for the verifiable sources of Gurdjieff's life and teaching. His search was for 'hidden knowledge' and not for 'occult power'. I am satisfied from my own limited experience that it is still possible to find both individuals and groups who possess knowledge and powers that originated from schools of wisdom. It happens that most of those I have met personally were from the Naq'shbandi or other Sufi *tarikats* directly affiliated with the Khwajagān. When Gurdjieff was searching, there were certainly more opportunities than there are now. He spent at least twenty years in his travels, and he had an incomparable capacity, as he himself put it, "of gaining access to the so-called holy-of-holies of nearly all hermetic organizations such as religious, philosophical, occult, political and mystic societies, congregations, parties, unions, etc., which were inaccessible to the ordinary man, and of discussing and exchanging views with innumerable people who, in comparison with others, are real authorities."[a]

Even with all these advantages, it is a source of amazement to any-

[a] *The Herald of Coming Good*, p. 17.

one who has deeply studied Gurdjieff's views on man, the universe and God (as he put it), that he should have been able to bring together so many new and revolutionary concepts. In 1950, that remarkable scholar and author, Denis Saurat, the Director of the French Institute in London, wrote to me that he had reached the conclusion that some parts of Gurdjieff's teaching "could not be of terrestial origin. Either Gurdjieff had revelations vouchsafed only to prophets or he had access to a school on a supernatural level".

Attitudes towards Gurdjieff are divided between the two hypotheses. Most of those who have written books based on their personal experiences as pupils have looked at Gurdjieff the man and have not looked beyond him. They implicitly assume that his extraordinary teaching was his own achievement; using, it is true, materials from traditional sources, but so transforming them as to make it, in effect, a new creation. With such an attitude, research into sources could only be an academic exercise of minor importance. The essential for them was to preserve all that Gurdjieff taught unchanged and unspoiled and not to look further.

The second attitude is much more challenging. If Gurdjieff found a school or even more than one school on a supernatural level, then there are such schools, always have been and always will be. If there are, then we too can hope to be connected with them. Gurdjieff becomes a way and not an end: a *murshid*—that is one who shows the way and not an *avatar* who incarnates the Goal.

Gurdjieff spoke ambiguously about himself. Sometimes he came very near to claiming that he was an *avatar*, a Cosmic individual incarnated to help mankind. Some of his pupils believed this and read perhaps too much into his utterances which may have been intended to shock rather than to inform. If we put this interpretation aside, Gurdjieff's role still remains extraordinary. He brought the notion of Masters into focus as a tangible element in human history. This notion is in no way strange for dwellers in Asia where the belief in men transformed into supermen is almost universally held. In the West, it is revolutionary and has been accepted only by those with an irresistible thirst for miracles and wonders. Gurdjieff succeeded in preserving the central belief, but stripped it of its occult or sentimental trappings.

He achieved this partly through his book *Meetings with Remarkable Men*, but mainly through his practical teaching which showed us that the attainment of higher levels of consciousness and being was possible given the conditions and the readiness to commit one-self to work for it.

The first phase of Gurdjieff's search was concerned with the strange phenomena that he observed from his childhood and which no one could explain to him. The phenomena include all the effects familiar in spiritualistic seances as well as clairvoyance and tele-pathy. There are also cases of miraculous healing which he person-ally witnessed, and the appearance of rain in response to prayer. All these occurred while he was still a boy: probably between eight and eleven years of age, from 1885 to 1888. The stories told have a common element that is often overlooked by readers who take them as no more than examples of psychic phenomena in general. Gurdjieff draws attention to an action that is natural in its opera-tion, but not to be explained in terms of known laws of physics and biology. The inference is that there must be substances other than those of the physical world, and that these substances and their trans-formations must be governed by other laws. The common tendency to invent a name for something inexplicable and then treat it as having been explained is ridiculed in the 'hysteria' hypothesis offered by the chief physician Ivanov, to account for the Yezidi who cannot leave a circle drawn round him on the ground. In effect, Gurdjieff in this first stage of his search sets the scene and states the problem: "If there are phenomena, the reality of which we cannot deny but which cannot be fitted into our accepted conceptual framework, then something is wrong with that framework and we must look for another."

Gurdjieff says that "there was not a single book on neuro-pathology and psychology in the library of Kars Military Hospital that I had not read and read very attentively". It is hard to date this statement. He mentions the year 1888 as the date when the Yezidi incident occurred and in the same connection refers to his having started to drink. It seems that he was then eleven years old, but the claim to have read—in Russian which he had only recently started to learn—numerous medical treatises, cannot be taken too seriously. He says elsewhere that his education was completed by about 1891 by the saintly Bogachevsky, later to become Father Evlissi of the Essene Brotherhood, who taught him the doctrine of *conscience* that became one of the central elements on his own account of man's transformation. The contrast between morality, which is relative to time and place, and conscience, which is eternal and universal, was always in the forefront of Gurdjieff's teaching.

Gurdjieff spent some time in Jerusalem and the surrounding mountain country. He said that there was an Essene monastery close to the Mount of Temptation in which very ancient wisdom had been preserved. He connected some of the 'sacred dances' he taught later with this brotherhood. He asserts that he himself had "been among the Essenes, most of whom are Jews, and that by means of very ancient Hebrew music and songs, they had made plants grow in half an hour!"[a] A similar story is told in *Beelzebub's Tales* in the Bokharian Dervish chapter. More than one of the ritual dances that Gurdjieff said came from the Essenes was based on a cycle of seven. It seems fair to conclude that Gurdjieff intends to convey that this cycle was a link between ancient schools that included the Sarmān and the Essene Brotherhoods.

He also refers to a visit to Mount Athos, then dominated by Russian monks some of whom were *Staretz* or Masters. He makes no reference to the tradition that I have heard, not only in Greece, but in Asia also, that Mount Athos was the centre of a brotherhood that was open to all religions and knew the secret of the Second Coming of Jesus. If he had reached a positive conclusion regarding this tradition, he would have left some direct or indirect reference. We learn from other sources of his close connection with Russian Orthodox monks and teachers. We know that the Eastern churches have admirable spiritual exercises, some of which Gurdjieff taught his own pupils. He refers to a journey to Abyssinia with Professor Skridlov. He stayed for three months in Abyssinia where he followed up indications he had found in Egypt of the importance of the Coptic tradition. At the end of his life, I more than once heard him speak of Abyssinia, even referring to it as his 'second home', where he hoped to retire and finish his days. He also mentioned the special knowledge of Christian origins possessed by the Coptic Church that had been lost by the Orthodox and Catholic branches of Christianity.

He was still faced with the problem of finding people who could understand and explain to him all he had witnessed and show him how to live by objective conscience rather than by subjective morality. He claimed later that he had discovered the solution to these problems by his own unaided endeavours, making use of all that he had

[a] *Meetings with Remarkable Men*, p. 133.

learned about human physiology and psychology and special techniques such as hypnotism and suggestion. Gurdjieff was an experimental scientist in the Western tradition. He was not satisfied with isolated phenomena and insisted upon the need for an all-embracing hypothesis that would link many phenomena together. Nevertheless, he could not find for himself all that he needed and was prepared to devote himself for many years to the search for the 'lost knowledge'. He was able later to teach people how to attain for themselves the state of consciousness in which they could understand the hidden operations of the human psyche. This does not reduce the significance of Gurdjieff's own search, but rather provides an additional motive for understanding it. Which brings us to the second phase of Gurdjieff's search that we have to reconstruct from even less coherent material than his boyhood tales.

Gurdjieff did not make the task easy. Hints are scattered throughout his writings and in the conversations that he had with his pupils, both individually and in groups. It would be impossible to reconstruct either the routes or the chronology of his journeys, if he had not also mentioned historical events that can serve as landmarks. Let us consider one minor event that is, nevertheless, significant both for piecing together the sources of his teaching and for verifying his references to places he visited. In the Fourth Book of the *Third Series*, he refers to three occasions when he was nearly killed. He writes: "Even without considering the many other events unusual in human experience, which had taken place in the accidentally peculiar pattern of my past life, it would be enough to recall that strange and inexplicable destiny pursuing me, which consisted in that I was wounded three times in quite different circumstances, each time almost mortally and each time by a stray bullet. . . . The first of these three incomprehensible fateful events happened in 1896 on the Island of Crete, one year before the Graeco-Turkish War."

We know that in 1894 a secret society, the Ethniki Etairea, had been organized to foment trouble in Macedonia and that the Russian Government supplied it lavishly with money and encouraged Greeks living in the Caucasus to join it. This was in 1895, when the Cretan question was coming to the fore. There is little doubt that Gurdjieff joined the Ethniki Etairea as a means of getting where he wanted and that he did, in fact, go to Crete in 1896 after his stay in Egypt. The war between Greece and Turkey did break out as he said, one year later in 1897. Now, why should Gurdjieff want to go to Crete? In the chapter "My Father",[a] he refers to the legend of the 'Flood before the Flood', and to the Imastun Brotherhood whose centre was an island formerly called Haninn which was "approximately where Greece is now situated". The word Imastun is said to mean in ancient Armenian 'wise man' or Master of Wisdom and there is little doubt that Gurdjieff intended to convey the belief that there had been such a group that he describes as constituting 'a whole caste spread all over the earth'.

References to Atlantis abound in Gurdjieff's writings. Miss Crowdy asserted that Atlantis symbolizes 'conscience' that was submerged in the unconscious part of man and has no other meaning. This symbolical interpretation may be one of several meanings, but there is little doubt that Gurdjieff also intended the story of Atlantis to be taken literally. I accompanied him on his last expedition out of Paris to visit the caves of Lascaux in the Dordogne, in order to see the famous rock paintings. He told us that he did not agree with the Abbé Breuil's dating, 30,000 years before the present, because "the paintings were the work of a brotherhood that existed after the loss of Atlantis seven or eight thousand years ago". Gurdjieff associated Atlantis with 'pre-sand Egypt', the map of which he obtained by guile from an Armenian priest near Nakhichevan, not very far from the frontier of Iraq, on his first journey with Pogossian. He connects Cairo, Jerusalem and Crete in his various references to the brotherhood of the Masters of Wisdom. It is particularly interesting that he decided to go to Crete in 1896, just after Arthur Evans had made his first search for the palace of Minos, during which he found seals that connected Crete with the cities of Mesopotamia. It is very likely that Gurdjieff learned of these discoveries from archaeologists whom he met in Egypt, particularly Professor Skridlov, and that this determined him to join the Etairea and find out for himself. The stray bullet that led to his being brought "while still unconscious by some unknown Greeks to Jerusalem", is the link with the next phase. From Jerusalem, he made the overland journey through Anatolia back to the Caucasus that I mentioned in Chapter 1.

Putting all these clues together, we can see how important it is to take account of Gurdjieff's readiness to make use of political situations to further his own researches.

The series of journeys undertaken by Gurdjieff between 1890 and

[a] *Meetings with Remarkable Men*, Chapter II.

1898 were mainly directed to the verification of the conviction he had reached at the age of fourteen, "that there really was a 'certain something' which people formerly knew, but that now this knowledge was quite forgotten".[a] He refers to the intensive reading of ancient Armenian literature that he and Pogossian had undertaken and continues: "We had lost all hope of finding any guiding clue to this knowledge in contemporary exact science, in contemporary books or from people in general and so we directed our attention to ancient literature". Elsewhere he says that in 1892, he "arrived at the definite conclusion that it would be utterly impossible to find out what I was looking for among my contemporaries".[b] At that time, he would have been fifteen years old.

Gurdjieff describes his first expedition with Pogossian in sufficient detail to enable us to follow it on the map. His objective was to discover traces of the Sarmān Brotherhood. Yet, when they discovered the map of pre-sand Egypt, near the town of Z (probably Zakho), in a strangely irresponsible way the travellers abandoned their objective although they were only 150 miles from the 'Valley of Izrumin', which may be the valley in which the sanctuary of Sheikh Adi, the main centre of the Yezidis was and still is situated. Gurdjieff refers to the Yezedis as a small sect, "living in Transcaucasia, mainly in the regions near Mount Ararat",[c] whereas they are distributed widely in Iran, Iraq, Kurdistan and the Caucasus.

Gurdjieff mentions an Armenian Book *Merkhavat* which describes the Sarmān Brotherhood as 'a famous esoteric school which, according to tradition, was founded in Babylon as far back as 2500 BC'. If he was on the track of such an important key to the mystery he wanted to unveil, why did he abandon the search, unless he saw in his 'map of pre-sand Egypt' a clue to the same enigma? It seems likely that Gurdjieff did become convinced somewhere about 1896, that is, at the age of nineteen, that a society did exist which "possessed great knowledge containing the key to many secret mysteries".[d]

Mosul, three hundred miles to the north, is near the cities of Nineveh and Nimrud, which were the capitals of the Assyrian kings. The

[a] Ibid., p. 87.
[b] *The Herald of Coming Good*, p. 18.
[c] *Meetings with Remarkable Men*, p. 66.
[d] Ibid., p. 90.

Sarmān Society must have moved between them before going north. In this region, one has a strong sense of the continuity of tradition. Gurdjieff appears to have returned to the Caucasus by way of Mosul, crossing the mountains at the pass by which so many conquerors had entered Syria. I once asked him if he had seen the Armenian inscriptions referring to Hulagu, the grandson of Jenghis Khan, at Mar Behmen near Mosul; and, in reply, he spoke of the great importance of this area and the belief that it was the site of the original Garden of Eden with four rivers flowing from it. He added that Mosul had once been the centre of the Sarmān Brotherhood, who were the successors of a society that had existed since the loss of Atlantis.

The next area we have to examine is Gurdjieff's interest in Babylon. He went there twice, once with Skridlov on their return from Abyssinia and once with the Seekers of the Truth. The first visit was in 1894 and lasted three months. This was the time when he made telepathic contact with the Society of Adherents of Legominism referred to in Chapter 24 of *Beelzebub's Tales*. At that time, the Germans were conducting their great excavations and preparing to remove, with the connivance of the Turkish Government, the incomparable Ishtar Gate and many other monuments to the greatness of Babylon as it was in the seventh century before Christ. At that time, the modern practice of filling in archaeological excavations was not followed, and the houses and walls of Persian Babylon were left standing. Although the roofs and upper storeys had disappeared, the feeling of being in a living city was still powerful when I first visited Babylon in 1953. It must have been much stronger when Gurdjieff went there in 1894. The vivid accounts he gives in *Beelzebub's Tales* of the Club of the Adherents of Legominism must have been based on the impression of that visit.

The second visit was probably made in 1897 shortly after the Cretan adventure. It is described incidentally in chapter 8, 'Ekim Bey' of *Meetings with Remarkable Men*.

I think that the group of fourteen, headed by Prince Yuri, who spent a month in Baghdad, found little of interest except the tomb of Sheikh Abdul Kadir of Jilan, the founder of the Kadiri order of Sufis. They must have spent most of their time in Babylon recreating the life of the wise men who lived there 2,500 years before. Gurdjieff accepted as historical the legendary meeting of wise men, including Pythagoras and representatives of Buddha and Lao Tzu who were his contemporaries. This assembly took momentous decisions regarding the Master Idea that was to rule mankind for the succeeding epoch. Gurdjieff asserts that this Assembly was organized by a brotherhood established several thousand years earlier still, after the loss of Atlantis.

If we accept the account in *The Herald of Coming Good*, he went alone, at the age of twenty, to Central Asia, and through the introduction of a street barber, found his way into a Sufi monastery where he came to the conclusion that 'the answers for which I was looking . . . can only be found, if they are at all accessible to men, in the sphere of man's subconscience mentation". After this, he resumed his wanderings and seems to have decided to join forces with the group of Seekers of Truth headed by Prince Yuri.

The gradually dawning hope that there might be individuals and communities possessing real knowledge, led to the third phase of Gurdjieff's search. When we read the various accounts he himself gave in *Meetings with Remarkable Men, The Herald of Coming Good*, and *Life is Real Only Then, When "I Am"*,[a] there seems at first a hopeless contradiction as to what happened during these years. The first source suggests that the search was conducted mainly by The Seekers of the Truth, which is strengthened by the account in Ouspensky's *In Search of the Miraculous*, where Gurdjieff is reported as saying that 'after great difficulties, he found the sources of this knowledge in company with several other people who were, like him, also seeking the miraculous'.[b] The other two books give the impression that Gurdjieff discovered what he was looking for by his own efforts and especially by his own experiments with people. The latter version is supported by Ouspensky's account in which Gurdjieff says that "when quite young he made several long journeys in the East . . . in the course of which he came across many phenomena telling him of the existence of a certain knowledge of certain powers and possibilities exceeding the ordinary possibilities of man. Gradually, his absences from home and his travels began to follow one definite aim. He went in search of knowledge and the people who possessed this knowledge."

The contradiction is more apparent than real. *Meetings with*

---

[a] This title will commonly be called hereafter the *Third Series*.
[b] *In Search of The Miraculous*, p. 36.

D

Remarkable Men is, as its title implies, an account of the people Gurdjieff met and worked with; it is not concerned with his private researches. In *The Herald of Coming Good*, Gurdjieff wished to convey the enormous burden he had carried and the importance of his personal contribution in order, as he put it, to 'shear' those who could produce money for his undertakings. In *Third Series*, Gurdjieff was, more than anywhere else, autobiographical and therefore disclosed facts about his private life that do not appear elsewhere. Even so, there is much that he does not tell us. We can deduce much from *Beelzebub's Tales* which in many places are obviously and admittedly autobiographical. 'Beelzebub as Professional Hypnotist' was certainly Gurdjieff himself. A photograph of him taken at this time shows him dressed as a professional magician (plate 1). He set himself up as a wonder-worker in Tashkent and no doubt did cure drug addicts and drunkards, as I myself saw him do in Turkey in 1921. He probably had some connection with the Russian Secret Service, which was almost necessary in order to travel freely in that politically troubled time. He is most reticent as to his political activities and this is scarcely surprising. The only reference to a political mission is the account of his journey with Pogossian on behalf of the Armenian Nationalist Society, the Dashnakzutiun.

It is pretty certain that the facilities he enjoyed for travelling in Central Asia on his way to Afghanistan, Chitral, Kashgaria and Tibet were obtained in the capacity of agent for the Russian Government. His almost uniformly hostile references to England, and especially his attack on the Younghusband Expedition into Tibet in 1903, suggest that he was in conflict with the authorities of British India. I can personally confirm that he had an unfavourable dossier in New Delhi because, as an intelligence officer in Constantinople in 1920, I first heard of Gurdjieff in a dispatch from New Delhi warning us of a 'very dangerous Russian agent, George Gurdjieff, who was in Georgia and had applied for a permit to come to Constantinople'. By accident, very soon after I received this message, I was invited to dinner by my friend Prince Sabaheddin to meet an old friend of his whom he regarded as a most exceptional man in the field of occultism and spirituality. This was Gurdjieff and, as I have described in *Witness*,[a] I was very soon convinced that he was far more

[a] *Witness*, J. G. Bennett, Hodder & Stoughton, London 1962.

important as a source of real knowledge than as a former agent of the Tsarist regime. Anyone who knew the Caucasus at that time would suspect that a man who could get permits and move freely through the Bolshevik and Social Democrat areas must have a secret pull with the authorities. This conclusion was confirmed to me many years later by Sir Paul Dukes, whose knowledge of the Russian situation between 1917 and 1920 was far more intimate than mine.

It seems probable then that Gurdjieff was able to use the resources of the Russian Empire to further his own plans, and was even able to penetrate into Tibet from the direction of the Karakoram at a time when it would have been impossible for an Englishman to enter from India. It is more than probable that he also was able to travel as a healer and wonder-worker, and so reach people in Central Asia who would have avoided Russians both as infidels and as a threat to the independence of the Khanates of Turkestan. There is an enormous difference in Asia between being tolerated and being accepted. Acceptance itself has many gradations. Most Asiatics are genuinely spiritual people and, if they recognize in a person a sincere spiritual search, they disregard differences of race or creed and open doors that are not even perceived by the ordinary traveller. This I know from my own experience in many Asiatic countries, and Gurdjieff was far more qualified to evoke confidence and gain full acceptance. He was able to accomplish in ten years what most travellers would never begin to recognize as a possibility. This is only a small part of the story. I am sure that Gurdjieff was recognized as a man with a mission and was given special help that would not have been given to anyone else.

When we come to examine the full range of ideas, doctrines, methods and techniques that Gurdjieff brought to the West, we may well doubt if one man could have accomplished so much. He himself tells us that a group effort was responsible. The Seekers of the Truth consisted of fifteen to twenty men and one woman. It included specialists in several domains all driven by a common urge to find 'real knowledge'. They travelled on two or possibly three occasions as a group in their 'major expeditions'. They also travelled singly or in twos and threes. Sometimes one of them spent a long period of time at a particular centre where he sensed the opportunity of penetrating more deeply into the teaching available. At various times, they met and shared their experiences. It seems, however, that all did not go perfectly smoothly. I have heard that men who claimed to have been members of the society of Seekers of the Truth spoke of Gurdjieff as having taken an independent line and broken away from the others. Gurdjieff more than once said, in my hearing, that he had taken and used certain ideas for purposes that were not approved by the brotherhood in which they had originated. Ouspensky strongly suspected that at some time something went wrong with Gurdjieff's search. My own opinion is that he did gain access to centres that were not open to other members of the society and felt bound to take the opportunities that offered themselves.

It is probable that the first major expedition was through north Persia over the Amu Darya into Transoxiana and included Merv, Samarkand, Bokhara and Tashkent. Presumably they went right up the valleys to the high country where the railway ends for when the party broke up, Gurdjieff returned by way of Andijan and the Trans-Caspian Railway. This journey brought Gurdjieff right into the area where the Khwajagān had dominated the spiritual scene for centuries and were still active as Naq'shbandi and Kadiri Dervish communities. On such a journey, one would be certain to hear of solitary dervishes or sheikhs with small followings. I myself, when travelling alone in these regions, as late as the 1950's, again and again heard of Sufi Masters whom I was recommended to visit. From such visits and conversations, one always learns something—but to piece together the fragmentary insights is possible only if one puts into practice what one is learning. This explains Gurdjieff's periods of withdrawal before going further afield.

By 1899, when Gurdjieff was only twenty-two years old, he had spent one long period in a Sufi *tekke* in Afghanistan. A *tekke* is a general term for a centre recognized as being a source of teaching and guidance. It differs from a Christian monastery in several ways. Firstly, the *tekke* is presided over by a sheikh who has reached the stage of *murshid* or masterhood. This sometimes requires twenty, thirty or even more years of service and training. The sheikh is personally responsible for the spiritual progress of his *murids* who are those who place themselves under his direction and accept his decisions. There are no vows in the sense that a Christian monk makes his profession; but there is an act of mutual acceptance between the *murshid* and *murid*. The initiation consists in giving the *murid* a *zikr* or exercise which is selected according to his personal needs. This act is also the means whereby the *murid* is enabled to participate in the spiritual action or *baraka* transmitted by the sheikh. In a later chapter, we shall have to examine closely the place of *baraka* in Gurdjieff's teaching. The question at this point is whether or not Gurdjieff ever became a *murid*, in the strict sense of the word. It seems likely that he received several initiations without attaching himself to a particular *tarikat*. He would be accepted as a welcome guest, and recognized as having outstanding spiritual qualities and, therefore, entitled to be given access to some, if not all, of the secrets of the *tekke*. I myself have been accepted in this way at more than one *tekke* and given to understand that if I were prepared to make a prolonged stay, I might be initiated into the deeper secrets. I have also been told that, if I were to go to such and such a *tekke* several hundred miles away, I might find a sheikh on a higher level and participate in a more intensive *baraka*.

It is certain that Gurdjieff was in every way more qualified than I to penetrate into the secrets of Sufism. He also spent far more time and travelled during a more favourable period when there was freer movement between the countries of the Middle East and Central Asia than was possible after the World War and the Russian Revolution. He once told Ouspensky (*In Search of the Miraculous*, p. 37) that real knowledge was not hidden, but that, on the contrary, those who possessed it were deeply concerned to make it available to those who could receive it and use it wisely. Gurdjieff, to the end of his life, was totally receptive to new ideas and new impressions and in his youth must have been a joy to the Sufi communities and individuals whom he met in his travels. He must also have been a sore trial, for he makes no secret of his self-willed determination to do things his own way and of his disregard of all conventions. It may well be that some times he overstepped the mark and was sent away before he had received all that might have been given to him.

We must return to the year 1899 when, according to the account he gives in "The Material Question",[a] the members of the Community of Truth Seekers (as he calls it in this context) were preparing for their last 'big expedition through the Pamir region and India'. He describes as an interlude the wild story of the 'Great Universal Workshop' that he set up in Ashkabad on the TransCaspian Railway. Among other feats of roguery, he describes his success in buying and

---

[a] *Meetings with Remarkable Men*, p. 252.

converting women's corsets and selling them in the towns of Kras-
novodsk, Kizil Arvat, Ashkabad, Merv, Chardjui, Bokhara, Samarkand and Tashkent. This is a spread of 800 miles and Gurdjieff
claims to have made a profit of 50,000 roubles in three and a half
months. There may be much exaggeration and fantasy in the account,
but even Gurdjieff could not have invented some of the extraordinary stories. He must have been then twenty-two years old and
had already learned a great deal from his meetings with dervishes
and especially the *tekke* in Afghanistan; but had not yet found the
centre of the Sarmān Brotherhood which was the culmination of his
search.

An expedition, about which he says very little, was made from
Orenburg through Sverdlovsk into Siberia. In *Beelzebub's Tales*,[a] he
describes a legendary civilization, Maralpleicie, the Reindeer Culture, which may have lasted from the end of the Ice Age until the
onset of the warm period of the seventh millennium BC, when the
Siberian steppe was well watered and highly fertile. I think that his
reference to 'a certain purpose connected with the programme drawn
up by that same group of Seekers of Truth', confirmed by the
explicit mention of Professor Skridlov's archaeological researches
entitles us to infer that the group had already formed their own
theory of the origins of the real knowledge for which they were seeking. Very few people would at that time have regarded Siberia as a
fruitful ground for such a search. It is possible that this expedition
was made at an early stage, perhaps in 1895, before Gurdjieff had
been to Crete and had discovered traces of the catastrophe of 1500 BC,
but I think this very improbable.

Putting together the four expeditions, to Egypt, Crete and the Holy
Land, to the Sudan and Abyssinia, to Iran and Transoxiana and
finally through Siberia, I conclude that the Seekers of the Truth had,
by 1899, satisfied themselves that there had been schools of wisdom
in north-east Africa, the Levant, Central Asia and the northern valleys
of Siberia. This agrees with the evidence that I have pieced together
in Volume Four of *The Dramatic Universe*; that there were four
independent sources of human culture and language that came together to produce the modern world. When he came to write
Beelzebub's Tales, Gurdjieff chose to convey this information in the
form of allegories and myths that could be read in different ways. It

---

[a] *Beelzebub's Tales*, Chapter XIX, p. 185.

seems that he intended to convey a very definite and literal message in his description of the various centres of culture in Africa, the Levant, Central Asia and northern Siberia. If so, the expeditions to these regions acquire a clear significance, and they also give us one key to understanding the aims of the group of Truth Seekers, The other key is given by his emphasis on the archaeological character of their researches and the aim of finding traces of ancient wisdom.

The last great expedition started in 1900, and as described in the chapter "Peter Karpenko" of *Meetings with Remarkable Men*, was to pass through the Pamirs and India. In the course of this journey, they met the Afghan *ez-ezounavouran*, that is in the Turkoman dialect one who is working on himself for the salvation of his soul. This man is said to have given them a comprehensive account of 'the astral body of man, its needs and possibilities of manifestation according to law'. It seems improbable that this expedition did in fact reach India, as at that time a large party of Russians entering by way of the Kabul River would have been highly suspect to the Afghan frontier guards, and even more so to the government of British India.

As it is said that Peter Karpenko died in Russia two years after from a severe gunshot wound, it seems likely that the party returned to Russia by way of the Amu Darya and the Central Asian Railway. Gurdjieff may possibly have remained behind, because the next we hear of him was in Tibet. Gurdjieff must have been involved, and pretty deeply so, in the political struggle between Russia and British India for domination in Afghanistan, Chitral, Kashmir and Tibet. He says specifically that he was in Tibet one year before the outbreak of the 'Anglo-Tibetan War'.

We now come up against the difficult task of deciding whether Gurdjieff did indeed play any significant political role in these events. It has been suggested that Gurdjieff was known in Tibet as the Lama Dorjieff. Gurdjieff himself lent colour to this suggestion by telling—as I heard him in 1949—how he came to the Tibetan frontier and gave his name and papers made out in Russian. He said that there is no letter 'g' in Tibetan and so they pronounced his name Dorjieff and gave him a pass in Tibetan with this name on it. Gurdjieff told one of his characteristic stories, which might be literal fact or pure fantasy, about his Tibetan marriage. He said that his eldest son had become a lama and had made such spiritual pro-

gress that at a relatively early age he had been appointed the abbot of
an important lamasery. "Once," said Gurdjieff, "when I was in Paris,
he came to visit me with a retinue of monks. They were all astonished
when he knelt down and asked for my blessing. He remained for one
month and then returned to Tibet and even now is the head of a group
of monasteries."

These stories suggest that Gurdjieff had spent a considerable time
in Tibet and encourage us to identify him with the famous Lama
Dorjieff who went as emissary from the Dalai Lama to bring a con-
fidential message to Tsar Nicholas II. This sensational story is made
highly implausible by examining the published photographs of the
Lama Dorjieff who could not by any stretch of the imagination be
taken for Gurdjieff. Furthermore, the Lama Dorjieff is said to have
been the tutor of the Dalai Lama in his youth, a task that could not
conceivably have been allotted to any but a born Tibetan, probably a
Rin-Po-Chhe lama who had been associated with the Dalai Lama in a
previous incarnation. In any case, if it had been Gurdjieff, he would
need to have been in Tibet at the age of twelve and remained there
at least fifteen years: from 1888 to 1903. In short, the Dorjieff story
cannot be taken literally.

Another possible explanation is that Gurdjieff took advantage of
the similarity of name to travel freely in Tibet and visit lamaseries
that would otherwise have been closed to him. He certainly had a
deep respect for Lamaism. In *Beelzebub's Tales*, he asserts that a group
of seven lamas possessed both knowledge and spiritual powers un-
paralled elsewhere on earth, and that the accidental death of the chief
of the group had destroyed one of the hopes of mankind. A further
point is that in one of his most remarkable spiritual exercises
Gurdjieff placed 'Lama' on the same footing as Muhammad,
Buddha and Christ and asserted that there was a special concentration of spiritual power in a certain place between Tibet and
Afghanistan.

In his talks with Anna Durco, she asked him, as a child might,
why he had no hair. He replied, *'Tam gdie ya bil vsie bili'*. 'Where
I was, all were like that'. He added that they had red garments with a
bare shoulder exposed, a wooden staff—land barren in the background. She said that he seemed to be describing a vivid memory
of a time when he was dressed as a lama.

We can here consider a further clue given in the programmes of
his 'movements' demonstrations given in Paris and New York in

1924. He ascribes various dances and rituals to monasteries in Sari in Tibet, Maxari Sherif in Afghanistan, Kizilgan in the Keriya Oasis in Chinese Turkestan and Yangi Hissar in Kashgar. This indicates a very extensive stay in these regions.

This brings us to Gurdjieff's statement in the *Third Series*, Book IV, which reads: "Under such conditions of tension, years passed; then, for this unfortunate physical body of mine, came another year of destiny, 1902 when I was punctured by a second stray bullet. This occurred in the majestic mountains of Tibet, one year before the Anglo-Tibetan War. On this second occasion, my unfortunate physical body was able to elude destiny because near me there were five good physicians, three of European education, and two specialists of Tibetan medicine, all five sincerely devoted to me. After three or four months of unconscious life, for me had flown still other years of constant physical tenseness and unusual psychic contrivances." He writes much further on that his convalescence occurred in Sinkiang "at a place located on the south-western edge of the Gobi Desert". He adds that it was near to the city of Yangi Hissar.

It seems probable that Gurdjieff was, in fact, a Russian political agent, but not the famous Lama Dorjieff. He had access to Tibetan lamaseries and learned the techniques of energy control and other psychic, rather than spiritual, powers in which the Tibetan lamas are perhaps the world's greatest specialists. This interpretation is strengthened by Gurdjieff's association of this period with his full elucidation of the secrets of the 'Astral Body' of man. I think it is relevant that in *Beelzebub's Tales*, Gurdjieff uses the term *Kesdjan* body to designate what is usually called the astral body. *Kesdjan* is the combination of two Persian words that would be used in Afghanistan.

The Armenian plots, the Cretan rebellion against Turkey and the Anglo-Tibetan War were certainly not Gurdjieff's only contacts with war and revolution. He refers (*Third Series*, Book IV,) to: "my propensity during this period for always travelling and trying to place myself wherever in the process of the mutual existence of people, there proceeded sharp energetic events, such as civil wars, revolution, etc." and adds that this propensity had sprung from his sole aim of "understanding the exact significance and purpose of the life of man". He goes on to say: "During such events I had collected material for clearing up the problems of my principal aim in a more concentrated form and therefore more productivity. Secondly, as a result of the memory in my automatic mentation of the sight of all sorts of terrors flowing from the violent events I had witnessed, and finally from accumulated impressions arising from conversations with various revolutionists in the previous several years, first in Italy and then Switzerland and still more recently in Trans-Caucasia, there had crystallized in me, little by little, besides the previous unique aim, another also unconquerable aim. This other newly arisen aim of my inner world was summed up in this, that I must discover, at all costs, some manner or means for destroying in people the pre-dilection for suggestibility which causes them to fall easily under the influence of 'mass-hypnosis'.''

When did Gurdjieff first go to Europe? He mentions in his account of Mme Vitvitskaia (*Meetings with Remarkable Men*, pp. 126–7), that he was in Rome as a very young man and saw her one and a half years before one of the big expeditions of the Seekers of the Truth; and, by connecting this with Professor Skridlov, he suggests that it was the Siberian journey. In this case, Gurdjieff must have gone to Italy and Switzerland in 1896 shortly before his Cretan adventure, probably as a representative of the Ethniki Etairea, the Greek revolutionary society mentioned earlier.

The events in Trans-Caucasia, in the passage cited above, certainly refer to the abortive Russian Revolution of 1905. The Russo-Japanese War with its humiliating reverses had turned the Russian people against the government of the Tsar. The famous night attack of February 5th, 1904, in which half the Russian fleet had been destroyed in Port Arthur, failed to arouse a patriotic response. The Home Minister Plehve was blown up with his carriage in July. This and many other acts of violence were attributed to the Union for Liberation founded by Lenin in London. It is likely that, conforming to his plan of penetrating into the 'holy-of-holies' of every movement, Gurdjieff joined the Caucasus branch of the Union. Before open revolution broke out in 1905, Gurdjieff had been wounded and returned to Central Asia. Nevertheless, his contact with the revolutionary movement was probably more than transient. In later life he used to speak of the injustice of the Tsarist regime in a way that shocked Ouspensky and others who had belonged to the aristocratic party.

After Gurdjieff had recovered from the bullet wound he had collected in Tibet, he returned to the Caucasus to be with his family. He no doubt got involved in the revolutionary movement and it is possible that Djugashivili, the Georgian revolutionary, later to become world-famous as Joseph Stalin, was in the same group. It has recently been alleged that Stalin was a Tsarist agent which gives rise to many interesting speculations. I certainly myself heard Gurdjieff say that he had known Stalin and had been at the seminary with him. Whether this was fact or fantasy, Gurdjieff most positively asserts that he was wounded by a stray bullet "at the end of 1904 in the Trans-Caucasian Region in the neighbourhood of the Chiatur Tunnel". It may well be that he was both a revolutionary and an agent of the government. When I was in that line of business myself, I knew several who cheerfully played a double role without, as Gurdjieff would have put it, 'experiencing any remorse of conscience'.

Before continuing the story of this most critical period of Gurdjieff's life, I must recall his description of the years 1902–4 as "years of constant physical tenseness and unusual psychic contrivance". I think it can fairly be deduced that he completed during this time that transformation which consists in liberating the astral or *kesdjan* body from its dependence on the physical body. From 1904 onwards Gurdjieff seems to have changed radically both the aim and the method of his search.

Returning to the Chiatur Tunnel, which is between Tiflis and Batum, I must quote extensively from Gurdjieff's own account. He wrote: "Speaking about this third stray bullet, I cannot here deny myself the opportunity, for the pleasure of some and for the displeasure of others of my acquaintance of the present time" (i.e. 1935), "of now saying openly about this third bullet, that it was plunked into me, of course unconsciously, by some 'milashka' from among those two groups of people, fallen from one side under the influence of imperious superiors 'accidental upstarts', who together laid then, of course also unconsciously, the basic foundation stones of the ground-work of the, at least today, indeed 'Great Russia'. There then proceeded firing between the so-called Russian Army, chiefly Cossacks, and the so-called Gourians."

Gurdjieff goes on to say that he connects those events of 1904 with an experience that occurred to him on November 6th, 1927, and the completion of his self-appointed tasks.

He continues: "During the third time, near me there was only

one man and that a very weak one." A most interesting account follows of his experience in caves in the Caucasus and his gradual
recovery. As the Cossacks had by then gained the upper hand and
were 'poking about and arresting every 'suspicious' inhabitant who
was not a native', Gurdjieff decided to go into the Trans-Caspian
region and after various adventures, set out in the direction of
Central Asia. Taking the account in his own words (*Third Series*,
Book IV), "After overcoming every kind of great and small
obstacle, I came to the city of Yanghi Hissar in former Chinese
Turkestan where, from old friends of mine, I supply myself with
money and then find myself in that same place where I had lived
several years before, while recovering my health when it had been
shattered because of stray bullet number two.

"This place is located on the south-eastern edge of the Gobi
Desert and represents to my mind the most fertile of all the parts of
the surface of our earth. And concerning the air of this place and its
salutary influence on everyone inhabiting it, I will say that it is truly
purgatorial. If in reality there exist Paradise and Hell, and if from
them arise any radiation, then the air in the space between these two
sources would surely have to be similar to this. For on one side is
soil which almost literally grows from itself every kind of earthly
flora, fauna, and phoskalia, and right next to this fertile soil is
an area of many thousands of square kilometres representing
literally hell, where not only nothing crops up, but anything that happens to get in its midst, which originated elsewhere, is destroyed in
a very short time, leaving no trace. Namely, here on this small
singular piece of the hard surface of our Earth, the air of which, that
is, our second food, is transformed between the forces of Paradise
and Hell, in me there had proceeded also in an almost delirious
condition, just that self-reasoning concerning which in my consciousness . . . there flashed an idea which appeared to me entirely
absurd."

This passage is typical of Gurdjieff's uncanny power of conveying factual, psychological and universal notions in one utterance. The
universal principle here exemplified is that the Divine Reconciling
power is evoked by the conflict of joy and suffering, by the
simultaneous experience of Paradise and Hell. 'Purgatory' represents
the purifying action that results from submitting oneself to the
struggle of yes and no. In psychological terms, the reference is to the
transformation of our emotional nature through liberation from the

'pairs of opposites'. The astral or *kesdjan* body remains attached to the physical body until the liberation has been accomplished. It is clear that Gurdjieff wishes us to understand that he achieved this liberation at the age of thirty-two when he had passed through the two near-death experiences. The age of thirty-two is significant because, according to many traditions, this is the age at which a man destined for a high degree of human perfection attains the 'first liberation'.

Gurdjieff was then at the stage of 'crystallization' in which a man has the strength of a unified being but is still conditioned by his own essential characteristics. Gurdjieff admits that he was then in a very dangerous state. He was nicknamed 'the Tiger of Turkestan'; the powers he had gained before and during his stay in Tibet were psychic rather than spiritual. He knew well enough that this was not what he wanted and he knew that the next step would involve sacrificing much of what he had acquired.

In *Third Series*, he left an extraordinary account of his own searching into his own state and the decision he made.[a] Without this record, we should have very little to help us in understanding the transition. He describes his recovery from his second gunshot wound and links it with what happened after his escape from the Caucasus.

He had been left in Tibet by his companions to convalesce, and after six weeks was sufficiently recovered to plan to leave *en route* to see his relations in the Trans-Caucasus. On the night before leaving, in the silence of the mountains, he found himself reflecting on the significance and purpose of life 'with a critical faculty of unprecedented strength'. He recalled the blunders of his past search and saw how he should have acted. Succumbing to an attack of physical weakness he tried to invigorate himself by going to a nearby spring and pouring the icy water over his body. While he became still weaker from this treatment and was obliged to lie down, his mind became exceptionally active and the thoughts that ensued remained with him clearly for the rest of his life.

He was dismayed at the prospect of having to resume the state of frustration that he had experienced in the previous six months, "not only to experience feelings alternating, almost regularly, between remorse for the inner and outer manifestations of my ordinary waking state, and loneliness, disappointment, satiety, etc., but primarily to

[a] The passages quoted below are excerpts: the text should be read in full: *Life is Real Only Then, When "I Am"*.

be everywhere haunted by the terror of 'inner emptiness' ". Whereas
he had attained almost the extreme limit in the powers of the mind,
"I could not attain the state of 'remembering myself' even
sufficiently to hinder the associations flowing in me automatically,
from hereditary factors of my nature. As soon as the accumulation of
energy which enabled me to be in an active state was exhausted, at
once associations of both thoughts and feelings began to flow in the
direction of objects diametrically opposite to the ideas of my consciousness. . . . From one side it is clear, that it is necessary to
'remember myself' during the process of ordinary life also. And,
from the other side, that there is a necessity for the presence of
attentiveness which is able to merge, in case of contact, with others.
In my past life I had tried everything, even had worn relics of all
kinds on my person, nothing helped. Perhaps these did help a little
while I carried them on me, but if so, it was only at the beginning; as
soon as I stopped carrying them or got used to them, in a moment it
was as if before. There is no way out whatsoever. . . . However,
there is; there is one exit only—to have outside myself, so to say,
'A never-sleeping-factor, a reminding-factor.' Namely, a factor
which would remind me always, in my every common state, to
'remember myself. But what is this! ! ! Can it be really so? ? ! !
A new thought! ! ! . . . Why could I not, in this instance also, look
to a 'universal analogy'? And here also is God! ! ! . . .

"God represents absolute goodness; He is all-loving and all-for-
giving. He is the Just Pacifier of all that exists. At the same time, why
should He, being as He is, send away from Himself one of his nearest,
by Him animated, Beloved Sons, only for the 'way of pride' proper
to any young and still incompletely formed individual, and bestow
upon Him a force equal but opposite to His own? . . . I refer to the
'Devil'. This idea illuminated the condition of my inner world like
the sun, and rendered it obvious that in the great world for the possibility of harmonious construction there was inevitably required
some kind of continuous perpetuation of the reminding factor. For
this reason our Maker Himself, in the name of all that He had
created, was compelled to place one of His Beloved Sons in such an,
in the objective sense, invidious situation. Therefore I also have now
for my small inner world to create out of myself, from some factor
beloved by me an alike unending source. . . . .

"I came to the conclusion, that if I should intentionally stop
utilizing the exceptional power in my possession which had been de-

veloped by me consciously in my common life with people, then there must be forced out of me such a reminding source. Namely, the power based upon strength in the field of *Hanbledzoin* or as it would be called by others, power of telepathy and hypnotism. . . . And so, if consciously I would deprive myself of this grace of my inherence, then undoubtedly always and in everything its absence would be felt. Never as long as I live shall I forget what state of mind resulted then. . . .

"As soon as I realized the sense of this idea, I was as if re-incarnated; I got up and began to run around the spring, without realizing what I was doing, like a young calf. It all ended thus, that I decided, at the first opportunity to take an oath before my own essence, in a state of mind known to me, never again to make use of this property of mine."

The second sojourn in the same place was again the occasion of a revision of Gurdjieff's life aim. We have already seen the profound effect made on him by witnessing the terrible consequences of 'mass-hypnosis' and he now set himself the task of finding how to free people from their propensity to suggestibility. This represents a dramatic departure from the earlier objective of gaining access to the knowledge and powers possessed by the schools of wisdom. The change was, in part, due to his decision to put aside the exercise of his psychic powers for his own personal benefit and, in part, the consequence of the compassion aroused in him by his growing awareness of the dilemma of modern man. He saw man's power to dominate and destroy nature increasing side by side with a pro-gressive decline in self-discipline and loss of inner freedom.

After 1905, we hear no more of expeditions of the Community of Truth Seekers. Gurdjieff entered upon the fourth phase of his search, which was now directed to understanding the secrets of the human psyche. He says that he went to 'a certain Dervish Monastery situated in Central Asia' where he spent two years in study of the laws of hypnotism and suggestion, and other features of the human un-conscious. I would hazard a guess that this was a Yesevi *tekke* where Gurdjieff was able to learn a great deal about the use of music and rhythm in which the Yesevis were specially qualified. It is likely also that they introduced him to the 'stop exercise' described in pp. 351–6 of *In Search of the Miraculous*. (The *ariks* or irriga-tion canals referred to are a feature of all that region.) Although

Gurdjieff in some places gives the impression that he was working on his own, other passages show that he entered fully into the life of this *tekke* and learned many of the techniques that he used later in his own Institute. I should mention here that, although Ahmed Yesevi was one of the successors of Yusuf Hamadani, he is by no means universally accepted as one of the Masters of Wisdom. The modern Yesevis have such close connections with Tibet and China that they are regarded with suspicion by the more orthodox Sufi brotherhoods. This may account for the attitude of Naq'shbandi sheikhs whose opinion of Gurdjieff I have tried to ascertain. The Masters of Wisdom, as we saw from Gudjduvani, were not favourable to sacred dance and music.

Gurdjieff found little to attract him in orthodox Islam. He claims that he made the pilgrimage to Mecca and Medina in company with Sart Dervishes, but had found nothing significant for his search. He adds that he had made it clear to himself that if there was anything in the Muslim religion, it must not be sought in the 'Holy Places' as "everyone says and believes, but in Bokhara, where from the beginning the secret knowledge of Islam had been concentrated, this place having become its very centre and source". This statement would be astonishing and difficult to take seriously if we had not seen the immense importance of the Khwajagān and their successors, the Naq'shbandi Sufis, whose centre up to the end of the nineteenth century was in Bokhara. Generally speaking, the Naq'shbandi Sufis do not have *tekkes* in the sense of fixed places where a group of dervishes live and work under the direction of a sheikh. Their principle is expressed in Abdulhalik Gudjduvani's formula *'halvat dar anjumen*: in the world but not of it. They used their outward life as the means of developing their inner life and do so to this day. This is one reason why I infer that Gurdjieff went to a Yesevi *tekke*, especially as the Yesevis were stronger in Tashkent than in Bokhara.

Direct confirmation of Gurdjieff's connection with the Yesevis has been given from his talks with Anna Durco. When speaking of folk-dances, he said that in Tashkent (which he pronounced Djash-kent), there were special dances, but that further away there were very very special dances. Before one could see these one had to have a *palalikanina* which both in Sanskrit and Romany means a sponsor. There they taught the Yesevi (pronounced by Gurdjieff Yiesef) dances and he had found a teacher who could teach by dancing what others taught by books. He said that only very very few people had the capacity to read the language of symbols. He then made a most significant statement—extraordinary for anyone, but strange indeed made to a child who fortunately remembered it word for word. "In one place symbol, in another technique and in another dance". This corresponds so exactly to the distribution of the Naq'shbandi, Djellali and Yesevi dervishes and shows their common affiliation to the Khwajagān by tying together threads whose connection would otherwise have been a matter of conjecture. He added that Yesevi "teach dancing same as put seed in the ground, but seed very hard, this green plant grow slow because need much time to grow, need very long time to give fruit, even much water will not help grow. Sometime this hard seed stay in ground for a long time—when begin to grow, change everything, all landscape can change. When symbol and technique grow together then give another plant, then grow quick and for other purpose. Special dance—sacred—very few can do. When symbol, technique, dance come in one place—then dance sacred for very special purpose."

It seems that Gurdjieff wished to leave this clue to his search in such a way that it could not be followed up prematurely. I always felt that the Yesevis had a special significance for Gurdjieff, but had no direct evidence until I read Anna Durco's story.

The period from 1905 to 1907 was not likely to have been without its abscences from the *tekke*. In Central Asia, dervishes are always on the move and when it is seen that they need some special training, they are sent to a sheikh who is a recognized Master. Gurdjieff asserts that he collected the ritual dances, rhythmic exercises and music that formed such a significant part of his method in Tashkent, Chitral, the Pamirs, Kashgaria and Kafiristan. All these places would have been within travelling distance of the Yesevi *tekke*, which may itself have been in or near Kashgar.

Gurdjieff, in the programme for his demonstration of temple dances in Paris in 1923, refers to an order founded at the end of the nineteenth century with its chief monastery in the city of Tangri-Hissar, in Kashgaria. Tangri-Hissar means God's Castle in any Turkish dialect of Central Asia. Gurdjieff says that the members of this order took the slogan 'We who tolerate freedom' as their watchword. They were known to people of the surrounding country as 'They who renounced'. The dervishes who formed this order were drawn from the Kubravi, the Kaljandar, the Naq'shbandi, the Djellali and Kadiri orders. This combination is very remarkable, as the orders in question do not normally make use of the *Sama* or sacred music and dance.

Gurdjieff refers also to the religious exercises of the Matchna monks who live in the eastern part of the Gobi Desert. These latter belong to a quite different tradition from the Kashgarian order, are affiiliated to the Yesevis and have a very close connection with Tibet and Tantric Buddhism. Many of the temple dances are assigned an origin in Tibet.

The 'Great Prayer', attributed to this order, is one of the most remarkable examples of symbolic language and, at the same time, an expression of the different *Hal* or states through which a dervish passes in the process of freeing himself from the illusion of existence.

In 1907, Gurdjieff said: "I began to give myself out to be a 'healer' of all kinds of vices and to apply the results of my theoretical studies to them affording them at the same time, of course real relief.[a] This continued to be my exclusive preoccupation for four or five years in accordance with the essential oath imposed by my task, which consisted in rendering conscientious aid to sufferers, in never using my knowledge and practical power in that domain of science except for the sake of my investigations, and never for personal or egotistical ends. I not only arrived at unprecedented practical results without equal in our day, but also elucidated almost everything necessary for me."

At some time during this period, it would seem that Gurdjieff finally made his way into one of the sanctuaries of the Sarmān Brotherhood. He describes this in a way that makes it impossible to date it accurately. He specifically says that it was the "chief monastery of the Sarmoung brotherhood" and that it was his last meeting with Prince Yuri, whom he had known for thirty-five years. This latter statement is patently absurd as Gurdjieff, at that time, was himself only thirty-five years old. *Meetings with Remarkable Men* is written not as a narrative but as a series of pictures of people and isolated events. It does not follow that it is all fantasy or that the events described do not fit into a coherent account of Gurdjieff's search. His stay of three months at the Sarmān sanctuary must have come at a late stage, because he himself makes it clear that he regarded it as a very great achievement and a sign that he had progressed beyond the level of teaching to be found in a Dervish *tekke*.

The importance for our enquiry is due in part to the need to ac-

[a] *The Herald of Coming Good*, p. 20.

count for the extraordinary cosmological or theological notions that Gurdjieff embodied in his 'system'. We saw no evidence that, with all their wisdom and their powers, the Khwajagān were concerned in such matters. The advanced astronomical and mathematical achievements of the learned men of Bokhara and Samarkand stood apart from the psychological and human services of the Khwajagān. The study of what Gurdjieff always called the "laws of world creation and world maintenance" must have been confined to centres no longer accessible to ordinary dervishes. Gurdjieff's friend Bogga Eddin (the Russian for Bahauddin) stands for the ordinary Sufi of the Naq'shbandi or Kadiri tradition. He is left behind when Gurdjieff is invited to the Sarmān sanctuary. The role of Soloviev is from start to finish fantastical. The account of his death—with his neck gnawed by a wild camel in the Gobi Desert—upsets any possible chronology. He may probably be inserted here because Gurdjieff wanted to include the elaborate play-acting of the Gobi Desert adventure at this particular point. The entire group of Seekers of the Truth, including "the experienced astronomer Dashtamirov", who does not appear elsewhere, abandoned the undertaking "although they had already done much towards the discovery of the legendary city which they had expected to find on their journey". It seems to me that the whole story is an allegory of the search that looks for 'real knowledge' somewhere 'out there' as if it were hidden away in a legendary city in the midst of the Gobi Desert. In contrast with this, the Sarmān sanctuary is 'within' and it reveals its secrets to those who can die consciously as Prince Yuri did.

While these allegorical interpretations were probably intended by Gurdjieff, he gave such precise details about the sacred dances of the priestesses and the way they were trained that he must refer to a real event. When we came to learn the sacred dances, we discovered that some of the most significant were based on combinations of the laws of three and seven and, in particular, on the enneagram symbol. I believe that Gurdjieff was, in fact, given access to cosmological and theological ideas that deserve the epithet 'supernatural' used by Professor Saurat.

We have still to fill in the story of the years from 1907 onwards. Gurdjieff told me once that he spent a long time in and near Tashkent which was a convenient centre for meetings of people from the different Khanates of Turkestan, and also for visitors from the East and West. In the little prospectus he issued in Constantinople in

1920, he says that he first founded his Institute in Tashkent. Let us take it, then, that Gurdjieff's period as professional hypnotist and wonder-worker was from 1908 to 1909 or 1910. He says that he decided "to make use of my exceptional, for the modern man, knowledge of the so-called 'supernatural sciences', as well as of my skill in producing different 'tricks' in the domains of these so-called sciences, and to give myself out to be, in these pseudo-scientific domains, a so-called 'professor-instructor' ". He gives as his reason for this decision the growing craze for 'occultism', 'theosophism', 'spiritualism', etc. He set himself to come into contact with people belonging to what he called "these vast organizations, where people forgather to reach certain special results by studying one of the aforementioned sciences".

The purpose of this undertaking was to give him the opportunity of studying people in both their conscious and their unconscious manifestations, to further his aim of helping people to attain 'inner freedom'. This is in accordance with the change of plan made in 1905, from the search for people with real knowledge to the experimental verification of the conclusions previously reached.

I must record a remark he made at my last talk with him. He spoke about the work he had started in Turkestan and said: "Remember what I now say. Begin in Russia, finish in Russia." At the time, I did not notice the significance of his reference to Tashkent. Only when I was preparing the material of this book, did the reference to 'finish in Russia' make sense to me. It seems clear today that the completion of Gurdjieff's work requires that all that he found in Central Asia should be made available in the West.

We have now reached the end of the stage that can properly be called Gurdjieff's search. He is conscious of a mission and sets himself to fulfil it. The mission is to awaken mankind to the 'Terror of the Situation' and for this he needs helpers who can join with him in spreading the message. The next phase begins with Tashkent and ends in Fontainebleau at the Château du Prieuré.

5

Gurdjieff's Mission

IN 1909, Gurdjieff was thirty-two years old and had built up an extraordinary repertoire of ideas, techniques and powers that he referred to sometimes as his 'system' and sometimes simply as his 'ideas'. He had started to experiment with people and was creating for himself a reputation as a wonder-worker. In order to move fast, he set himself to gain the confidence and support of the occult and theosophical societies that had many followers among the Russians and other Western people who lived in the important growth centres such as Tashkent. Industries were beginning to attract capital, trade was flourishing and the Russian Government was doing everything possible to stabilize its authority in the Khanates of Turkestan and to extend its influence.

Gurdjieff writes: "The ensuing circumstances of my life were so favourable to me that, within six months, I succeeded not only in coming in contact with a great number of these people, but even in being accepted as a well-known expert and guide in evoking so-called phenomena of the beyond in a very large circle."[a] He gave public demonstrations and also accepted pupils for training. His procedure was then, as it was later, to attract large numbers of people and select from them those with whom he wished to work. He sweepingly described all the occult and spiritual societies as "workshops for the perfection of psychopathism" and said that he was able, by observing "various manifestations in the waking state of the psyche of these trained and freely moving guinea pigs allotted to me by destiny for my experiments", to resolve many of the practical problems that would arise in carrying out his aim to "help people to attain inward freedom".

[a] *The Herald of Coming Good*, p. 22.

We are now at one of the decisive moments of Gurdjieff's life. He was about to commit himself to the creation of a school of his own. He resolved to introduce mankind to a new way of thinking and to renewed understanding of the cosmic purpose. What had in past ages been hidden as mysteries except to small esoteric groups, could at last be communicated widely, thanks to the spread of education and new media of communication. Equipped with the knowledge discovered during his search, he now proceeded to interpret it to the world of today and apply it in forms suited to contemporary conditions. And he added his own original solutions to cosmic problems that had so far escaped attention in both Western and Eastern cultures. He set himself at the same time to teach how latent human powers could be realised. Man had ceased to function as an integrated whole and had lost his sense of direction, as a result largely of unbalanced development and lack of co-ordination. In particular, while the reasoning faculty had made such striking progress in the last three millennia, the other faculties had failed to keep pace in development, and in some respects had indeed become weaker. And the psyche and nervous system had lost their powers of harmonious co-ordination, without which there could be no truly directed and fully effective action. He was impelled by a sense of urgency; far in advance of his generation he recognised that humanity would play the key part, for better or for worse, in determining the future balance of the biosphere.

This book does not purport to give any comprehensive account of Gurdjieff's ideas: this has been undertaken elsewhere. But a brief explanation of some of the key conceptions is given for the benefit of the general reader to illustrate the development of his thought; and as he deliberately adopted an obscure style and terminology a note on this is added as an appendix. Again, as this book is not a manual of instruction, the descriptions of Gurdjieff's methods do not go beyond what is needed to trace his story. He harnessed a variety of techniques, but these are united by the principle that the different sides of man's nature have to be developed together in harmony, that the instinctive and motor functions have to be co-ordinated with the emotional and mental, and the whole brought within the discipline of the will. Since such co-ordinated training cannot be accomplished by conventional methods of education, he introduced and adopted methods proved in the distant past.

According to his customary procedure, before entering upon a new phase of his activity, Gurdjieff made experiments to test the feasibility of what he had in mind. When he came to the moment of decision, he appears to have consulted a brotherhood in the very heart of Asia with which he had close relations. He recorded that he decided to confide his intentions to this brotherhood. The very heart of Asia probably refers to the region of Kashgaria rather than Bokhara or Taskent. He often spoke of the Keriya Oasis as a place where for centuries an esoteric community had preserved high knowledge. He visited this centre a number of times between 1902 and 1912. Either this or some similar community was his point of contact with the Masters of Wisdom. His intention was to secure their future co-operation. As a result of long discussions about all sorts of mutual obligations, referring on his side chiefly to his future religious and moral actions and on their side to accepting the responsibility for guiding the inner world of individuals that he would entrust to them, they came to a certain definite agreement. This account is slender evidence indeed that Gurdjieff recognized any authority other than his own conscience. Apart from this passage we have no other evidence that Gurdjieff set up his Institute with the authority or at least the approval of a higher school, but he spoke both in Russia and at the Prieuré of schools in Central Asia with which he was in communication and to whom he sent specially prepared pupils. I told him in 1923 of my ambition to go to Turkestan and of my meetings with Yesevi dervishes from Tashkent. He said that, if I remained with him for two years, he might send me. That is all I ever heard of it; but I was left with the conviction that Gurdjieff had contact with high-level sources with whom he could consult.

Piecing together the fragments of information, it seems that he was established in 1910 and 1911 as a professional teacher of the occult with his headquarers in Tashkent. By the autumn of 1911, he had acquired a solid reputation among the members of three large-scale independent 'workshops' but decided to give them up and to undertake the organization of his own 'circle' on quite new principles, with a staff of people specially chosen by him. This he regarded as the prototype of his Institute for the Harmonious Development of Man. Tashkent was a meeting ground for a variety of cultures, Shamanism was still a force among the nomad tribes of the north. Buddhism was the religion of the local Tadjiks. There were Nestorian Christians and Russian Orthodox. The great majority of the settled population were Muslims, having been converted as far back as the eighth century. Gurdjieff was at home with them all. In selecting Tashkent as his first centre of activity, Gurdjieff showed the strength of the bond that held him to Central Asia. Those who are born and bred in the European tradition, whether they live in Europe or one of the newer countries, can only with difficulty enter into the feelings of the people of Central Asia whose culture was ancient when Europe was still in the Stone Age. In 1910, Central Asia was still remote, even for the Russians who had set themselves to conquer and colonize it; but for those who were born there it was the centre of the world and everlasting. Belief in magic and the spirit world was taken for granted; but, since the decline of Shamanism, genuine magicians were rare, and a man possessing Gurdjieff's extraordinary powers would exercise a powerful influence on natives and Russian colonists alike.

Here we must take account of Gurdjieff's assertion that on the 13th of September 1911 he took a special oath binding himself "in his conscience to lead in some ways an artificial life, modelled upon a programme which had been previously planned in accordance with certain definite principles". He also said that he had set himself the task of leading this artificial life for twenty-one years, up to the year 1923. Most of the people who met Gurdjieff during those years felt that he was in some way hiding himself and that it was impossible to know who he really was. Sophie Grigorievna Ouspensky, his most devoted pupil, wrote him a letter in 1925, which she used later to have read to those who were close to her, in which she told Gurdjieff that for her he was the great enigma, unknown and unknowable. Ouspensky wrote: "Many people got the impression that he was a gourmand, a man fond of good living in general, and it seemed to us that he often *wanted* to create this impression, although all of us already saw that this was 'acting'. Our feelings of this 'acting' in G. was exceptionally strong. Among ourselves we often said we never saw him and never would. In any other man so much 'acting' would have produced an impression of falsity. In him 'acting' produced an impression of strength, although, as I already mentioned, not always, sometimes there was too much of it." Ouspensky does not attempt to explain this feature of Gurdjieff's 'artificial life' though he gives many instances of it.

We must, therefore, go back to Gurdjieff's own account. He

writes: [a] "This protracted and, for me, absolutely unnatural life, absolutely irreconcilable, too, in every way with the traits that had entrenched themselves in my individuality by the time of my maturity, was the direct consequence of my decision founded upon the results of my previous study of a whole series of historic precedents with a view, first of all, to preventing, by outward manifestations of myself to a certain degree unnatural, the formation, in relation to me of that, already noted from ancient times, 'something', termed by the Great Solomon, King of Judah, *tzvarnoharno*[b] which, as set out by our ancestors, forms itself by a natural process in the communal life of people as an outcome of a conjunction of the evil actions of so-called 'common people' and leads to the destruction both of him that tries to achieve something for general human welfare and of all that he has already accomplished to this end." He adds, as a second reason for his vow to live an unnatural life, that it would counteract "the manifestation in people with whom I came in contact of that inherent trait which, embedded as it is in the psyche of people and acting as an impediment to the realization of my aims, evoked from them, when confronted with other more or less prominent people, the functioning of the feeling of enslavement, paralysing once and for all their capacity for displaying the personal initiative of which I then stood in particular need". Elsewhere Gurdjieff wrote that "a mark of the perfected man is his ability to play to perfection any desired role in his external life while inwardly remaining free and not allowing himself to 'blend' with anything proceeding outside of him".

We have to take Gurdjieff's 'acting' or role-playing into account when we try to interpret the many diverse impressions recorded in books by people connected with him for a shorter or longer time. The entire period during which Gurdjieff attempted over and over again to set up an organization of his own, corresponds to the twenty-one years of his 'unnatural life'. It was not until 1935 that

---

[a] *The Herald of Coming Good*, p. 12.

[b] The term *tzvarnoharno* is almost certainly derived from the Zend and Pahlawi word *hvareno*, meaning majesty, or the impression produced on ordinary people by those who have the royal afflatus. The *hvareno* principle is part of the Avestan tradition developed by Zoroaster, and while Gurdjieff never refers directly to Zoroaster and the importance of this tradition as at least one of the sources of the Sarmān system, he drops hints here and there that he had a profound grasp of the principle.

he finally abandoned this plan and set himself to achieve his aim by preparing people to carry on his work after his death.

He embarked on the task of setting up his own organization because of the discovery that only a very limited range of types of people become interested in occult and theosophical circles. "Meeting then a great number of people usually composing such circles, I had elucidated and established the fact that in such societies I found generally people of three or four definite 'types', whereas it was necessary for me—in order to observe the manifestations of man's psyche in his waking state—to have at my disposal representatives of all the 28 'categories of types' existing on Earth as they were established in ancient times."[a]

He organized three small groups of people of as varied types as he could muster in the course of three years. He probably refers here to the three years from 1909 to 1912 which included his time as 'professional hypnotist'. In 1912, while still based upon Tashkent, he came to the conclusion that the arrangements were too loose and that he would have to work with people more intensively than was possible in the monthly meetings of the theosophical circles.

At that time, Gurdjieff was engaged in various money-making enterprises and probably could not devote much time to his 'groups'. "I engaged in the most varied enterprises, sometimes big ones. For instance, I carried out private and government contracts for the supply and construction of railways and roads; I opened a number of stores, restaurants, and cinemas and sold them when I got them going well; I organized various rural enterprises and the driving of cattle into Russia from several countries, chiefly from Kashgar; I participated in oil-wells and fisheries; and sometimes I carried on several of these simultaneously. But the business I preferred above all others, which never required my specially devoting to it any definite time or needed any fixed place of residence, and which moreover was very profitable, was the trade in carpets and antiques of all kinds."[b]

While he conducted these enterprises he directed his groups, "on the one hand, observing and studying the material already available, and on the other, satisfying as conscientiously as possible those in whose psyche the passion of curiosity was deeply rooted, and impartially destroying in those others, in whom the predisposition

---

[a] *The Herald of Coming Good*, p. 23.
[b] *Meetings with Remarkable Men*, p. 270.

proper to all men for acquiring a real 'Being' was not yet atrophied, all their previous illusions and erroneous ideas".[a] Here Gurdjieff describes the practice he followed all his life of 'giving people what they are able to receive'. He counted on finding in this way men and women capable of making the commitments and sacrifices necessary for 'work on oneself' who could become assistants in his future work. Group meetings had not produced the required conditions, either for his observations of people or for their own development, and he concluded that "in a broadly planned public organization embracing almost all the interests of contemporary life", he would be able to bring together for his observation types of people previously lacking.

Gurdjieff felt it necessary to justify his action in bringing people under scrutiny, ostensibly to enable them to learn about the 'beyond', but in reality to serve as guinea-pigs for his experimental researches. He writes: "I consider it necessary to speak of the mental and emotive associations which gave rise to this decision which was in complete harmony with my conscience. Towards the end of all my reflections at that time, as a result of which I had at last firmly decided to organize such a public Institute, there arose in my entirety then, as has always happened in similar cases, that strange impulse which is proper to my peculiar individuality and which automatically compels me to consider always each new task in life also from the point of view of 'objective justice'. My reasoning with myself was as follows: To make use of people, who display a special interest in an Institute founded by me, for purely personal ends, would surely strike those around me as a manifestation of egotism. But, at the same time, of the people who had anything to do with such an Institute, those in whom the predisposition for acquiring data for the impulse of 'objective-conscience' and for the formation of 'essential-prudence' had not been entirely atrophied, could in this way alone profit by the results of knowledge, amassed by me due to exceptional circumstances of my life, and use them for their own benefit."[b] A year later (1934) he wrote: "On this occasion, I will say only that, after some years," (i.e. after 1909) "I found it necessary to originate somewhere an institution for the preparation of 'helper-instructors' in order to be able to put into the lives of people what I have already learned. When this need arose then, after all kinds of

[a] *The Herald of Coming Good*, p. 23.
[b] *The Herald of Coming Good*, pp. 24, 25.

'comparative-mentation', I selected Russia as most appropriate for this purpose. With this aim, I found myself in 1912 in the heart of Russia, the city of Moscow, where I at once started to organize such an institution under the name of 'The Institution for the Harmonious Development of Man'." There is no indication in these passages that Gurdjieff was undertaking a mission on behalf of the Sarmān Brotherhood or any other group of Masters. He does not even mention his former colleagues, in the group of Truth Seekers.

The basic principle on which the Institute was to be founded was to create *conditions in which man would be continually reminded of the sense and aim of his existence by an unavoidable friction between his conscience and the automatic manifestations of his nature.*[a] I have put this passage in italics because it must be thoroughly assimilated by anyone who wishes to grasp how Gurdjieff worked and why he did so many things apparently unaccountable and hard to accept.

Gurdjieff wrote in 1932 that, when he set up his Institute, he chose Russia 'which at that time was peaceful, rich and quiet'. Nothing could be farther from the truth. A bitter struggle between Tsar Nicholas II and the Fourth Duma was in progress. The court was in a state of frenzy over the precarious health of the Tsar's only son, Alexis, who suffered from hereditary haemophilia. Rasputin had already gained his sinister ascendency over the Tsarina and through her was driving the prince and his father to the brink of madness. The moderate party lost its leader Stolypin by assassination and nothing remained except the bitter struggle between the extreme reactionaries, incited by the court, and the revolutionaries inspired by Lenin and Trotsky.

It would seem that Gurdjieff ranged himself with the nobility. It is quite likely that he was presented to the Tsar as a possible saviour of the Crown Prince or at least as a man of extraordinary powers. I infer this from the chapter in *Beelzebub's Tales* which describes his meeting with the Tsar: it is hard to believe that Gurdjieff could have invented this story except from first-hand knowledge. He always spoke warmly of Nicholas II and once described him as a good man and very compassionate, but little more than a Warwick in his inability to influence events.

Gurdjieff asserts that he arrived in Moscow with a fortune of a

[a] *Meetings with Remarkable Men*, p. 270.

million roubles and "two invaluable collections, one of old rare carpets and the other of porcelain and what is called Chinese cloisonné".[a]

In Moscow, and a little later in St. Petersburg, he arranged a series of lectures which attracted a number of intellectuals and men of science, and the circle of people interested in his ideas soon began to grow. He began to prepare everything required for launching the Institute. He purchased an estate near Moscow, ordered equipment from various European countries and was even arranging for the publication of his own newspaper. The outbreak of war and the invasion of Russia by the Germans seems to have come as a complete surprise to him. With hindsight this seems to have shown a singular inability on his part to read the situation, but the whole of Russia was in a bemused state. Gurdjieff did not in the least understand the European political situation and remained a stranger to it all his life. He had lived in Central Asia, where Russian influence was growing steadily. The Russo-Japanese War and the abortive revolution of 1904–5 had been forgotten and the Russian Empire was an overwhelming fact that no one imagined could soon disappear.

Gurdjieff seems to have been associated with the moderate party surrounding the Tsar and, at one time, even to have been canvassed as a counter to the hated Rasputin. But the Tsarina, Alexandra Feodorovna, was immovable. She was hypnotized by Rasputin's prophecy that his death would toll the knell of the Russian monarchy. Nevertheless, the general atmosphere of the court and the attitude of many of the aristocracy and intelligentsia were strangely susceptible to any kind of promised miracle. There were various circles devoted to spiritual and occult leaders. Gurdjieff's included people who were fully aware of the urgent need for accommodation with the liberal party, the 'Octobrists' who, since 1905, had represented the chief hope of constitutional progress. His position with the aristocracy must have been well established, for he was able to meet and marry a lady-in-waiting to the Tsarina, the beautiful and talented Countess Ostrowska, who was with him to the end of her life.

The disastrous mishandling of both strategy and loyalties on the front was aggravated by the total incompetence of Nicholas II and his chosen ministers. The Tsar assumed the post of Commander-in-Chief and spent much time on the German Front where he prevented effective decisions from being taken. Communications with Russia's

[a] *Meetings with Remarkable Men*, p. 270

Western Allies became ludicrously unrealistic: no one was willing to face the fact that the entire system was breaking down and would never be repaired. The administrative machinery of Russia was based on a highly centralised control that could not adapt itself to war. Food distribution began to break down and the government would not see that this made revolution inevitable, even in the absence of revolutionary leaders and revolutionary plans. Strikes in key industries increased in scale and duration simply because the workers needed food and had no other means of showing it. Signs of demoralization were visible everywhere, yet no one was willing to recognize them.

In spite of the conditions, Gurdjieff went on with the organization of his groups and found his most valued pupil and helper, Peter Damian Ouspensky, in April 1915. Ouspensky was giving lectures in Moscow and St. Petersburg with titles such as "In Search of the Miraculous" and "The Problems of Death". He was brought to see Gurdjieff by a chance acquaintance and was at once impressed by his mastery of subjects which Ouspensky asked him to explain.

He did not speak to Ouspensky about his Institute but gave him to understand that he had active groups working in Moscow and at a *dacha* an hour's journey away. Ouspensky soon undertook to organize groups in St. Petersburg and eventually became very closely associated with Gurdjieff's work. He has left a detailed account of both the content and the method of Gurdjieff's teaching in the years 1915–17, up to the time of the October Revolution. Gurdjieff stopped going to St. Petersburg, but Ouspensky and his wife went regularly to Moscow to get instructions and glean new ideas to work on.

The entire period of this group lasted little over a year, from July 1915 to September 1916. During this time, Gurdjieff had been pouring out ideas of astonishing force and originality and had demonstrated techniques including his own exceptional powers, as he put it, 'in the field of Hanbledzoin'. It was during this period that Gurdjieff appears to have spoken of an 'Inner Circle of Humanity', of 'schools' and 'ways' and particularly in a way that suggested that he fully accepted a fairly strong version of the 'Inner Circle'. He apparently did not tell Ouspensky and the others of the work he had been doing in Turkestan before he came to Moscow.

Gurdjieff was now forty years old. Ouspensky describes him as a man of oriental type, no longer young, with a black moustache and piercing eyes, who made the impression of a man poorly disguised, and the sight of whom embarrasses you because you see he is not what he pretends to be and yet you have to speak and behave as though you do not see it.[a] This sense of remoteness remains throughout Ouspensky's account of his time with Gurdjieff and finally led to his making a separation between Gurdjieff and his ideas. The consequences of this separation were far reaching, and led ultimately to a complete breakdown in the relationship between these two extraordinary men. Fortunately, Ouspensky recorded and subsequently published the greater part of what Gurdjieff taught during the four years that they were in contact. So far as I am concerned, this material, which Ouspensky used for his own teaching in the years from 1922 to 1940 when he had his groups in London, constitutes the most valuable corpus of ideas and methods that I have come across in fifty years of searching. Nevertheless, something essential was missing. Not only did Gurdjieff say nothing—or at least nothing was reported by Ouspensky—about his work in Central Asia and the aims that he had set himself in coming to Russia; but he gave the impression that the work depended exclusively on personal effort that each man had to make for himself. The idea, which is so important in Christian doctrine, of *enabling Grace*, without which work on oneself is impossible, was never mentioned. Nor was the Sufi notion of *baraka*, which refers to the same supernatural action that must be transmitted from person to person. I have no doubt that Gurdjieff was fully aware of the importance of this action because he spoke to me personally about it only five years later at Fontainbleau.

How did it come about that Gurdjieff gave out such an incredible wealth of ideas and teachings on almost every subject of interest on the transformation of man, and did not refer to the key to making it all work, the transmission of higher energy or *baraka*? I believe that the explanation is to be found in what Gurdjieff wrote about in his original plan to set up his Institute in Tashkent. His aim was not to initiate an action, but to study people of many types in order to find a way to help them to liberate themselves from the universal disease of suggestibility, which makes them 'believe any old tale'. If people came to him and were ready to work with him on his own terms, but without losing sight of their own aim, they could profit from the contact. If they could not do so, he was not responsible. He had put aside for the time his plans for the Institute; they could not

[a] *In Search of The Miraculous*, p. 7.

be realized in such conditions of complete fluidity when no one could count on remaining in one place for a month ahead.

In June 1917, Gurdjieff made an experiment which no one else at that time recognized as such. He collected twelve or fourteen people together at Essentuki on the northern slopes of the Caucasus Mountains to work with them day and night for six weeks with unparalleled intensity. Ouspensky writes that, during this period, Gurdjieff unfolded to them the plan of the whole work. They "saw the beginnings of all the methods, the beginnings of the ideas, their link, their connection and direction. Many things remained obscure for us; many things we did not rightly understand, quite the contrary, but in any case, we were given some general propositions by which I thought we could be guided later on."

From Ouspensky's account of the six weeks at Essentuki in the summer of 1917, it is evident that this was for Gurdjieff a most important experiment to test the methods he intended to use in his Institute. When the experiment was ended, he abruptly dismissed the group, to the dismay of those who could not understand what he had been doing.

The following year, Gurdjieff made a second experiment—this time near Tuapse, close to the shore of the Black Sea. Ouspensky arrived from St. Petersburg, which he had left on the eve of the Bolshevik coup of October 21st, 1917. Gurdjieff had collected a group of ten, which included Dr. and Mrs. Stjernwal, Thomas de Hartmann and his wife, Olga. Ouspensky "noticed that there was something wrong. There was not a trace", he writes, "of the Essentuki atmosphere." There was no kind of 'work' in the sense of what had been at Essentuki. Soon they moved to Tuapse, where they lived for two months. Gurdjieff sent messages to those of the groups who had remained in Moscow or St. Petersburg, and finally some forty people assembled. The new phase of the work began in March 1918, with a different system involving external activities of the most varied kind. Strict rules were imposed. Gurdjieff for the first time introduced the group to the rhythms and dances which he told them were mainly of dervish origin.

Ouspensky does not appear to have understood that in all these activities Gurdjieff was experimenting and testing the various techniques he intended to introduce in his Institute. Ouspensky summarizes the programme in one sentence: "In addition to exercises, dances, gymnastics, talks, lectures, and house work, special work was

Plate 1 Gurdjieff as Professional Hypnotist

Plate 2
Gurdjieff's Mother

Plate 3
Gurdjieff's Wife,
Mme Ostrowska

organized for those without means." This describes the life of a Yesevi community in which families live together in strict obedience to the sheikh, learning the required range of exercises and disciplines and, at the same time, engaging in one or more enterprises to provide for their material needs.

For the first time, Gurdjieff proposed that the group should be given an external form. He also organized public lectures to attract interested people. With all this, Ouspensky was deeply disturbed by the direction the work was taking. He had assumed that the groups in Moscow and St. Petersburg and the community at Essentuki, which was a natural sequel, represented the work as Gurdjieff intended to develop it in the future. He felt at home and, in spite of some misgivings about Gurdjieff's treatment of individuals—such as Mr. Zakharof who was dismissed to St. Petersburg and returned a dying man—he was prepared to support Gurdjieff in all his undertakings. He even said the 'work' alone made it possible to live through the horrors and absurdities of the collapse of Tsarist Russia. Gurdjieff had an uncanny capacity for diverting people's attention from his private purpose and intention, so as to leave himself freedom of decision. None of Gurdjieff's pupils were able to follow his line of thought, even when he made no secret of it.

So it came about that Ouspensky did not participate in a further experiment in reproducing under conditions of great external stress, an expedition similar to those undertaken by the group of Seekers of the Truth, twenty years earlier. Gurdjieff describes this experiment in detail in *Meetings with Remarkable Men*, (pp. 271–6). His main practical concern was to save twenty young men of military age who had joined him in the Caucasus, and also to extricate himself and his most devoted followers from the perilous situation that had developed as a result of the clash between the Cossacks and the Bolsheviks. He refers to his interest in dolmens and his wish to verify certain alignments of stones, reported to exist in almost inaccessible regions of the Caucasus Mountains. He therefore began to spread the rumour that he knew of enormously rich deposits of gold and platinum. He proposed to organize a prospecting expedition which would bring in great wealth to the Provincial Government. In all this, he was also demonstrating to his pupils the power of suggestion and the ease with which people could be made to 'believe any old tale'. The outcome was that he was given unlimited facilities, including the use of two railway wagons, to take him and his party to Maikop at a time when, owing to the constant movement of troops, it was almost unthinkable for one man without baggage to travel by rail.

The rest of the journey over the mountains to Tiflis is described both by Gurdjieff and by Thomas de Hartmann. Gurdjieff says of the journey: "In my opinion, we got out safely because in the common presence of these people—although in the grip of a psychic state in which the last grain of reasonableness vanishes—the instinct inherent in all human beings for distinguishing good from evil, in the objective sense, was not completely lacking. And, therefore, instinctively sensing in my activities the living germ of that sacred impulse which alone is capable of bringing genuine happiness to humanity, they furthered in whatever way they could the process of accomplishment of that which I had undertaken long before this war".[a]

Neither Ouspensky nor de Hartmann, who held very different personal viewpoints about Gurdjieff, appeared to have grasped that he was seeing events on a very different time scale to themselves. He had set himself the task of introducing into the modern world ideas and techniques that were supremely necessary if mankind was to survive the crisis of which the Russian Revolution was only an early symptom. Whether or not he was confident that events would make this possible, he was at least bound to act as it they would. He was not concerned with immediate survival: his past life amply demonstrated his indifference to personal hardship and even the imminence of death. He acted consistently in all his various experiments with people in his plan to set up a system of training and personal development that would produce 'free' men and women. He was not concerned with the problems of individuals who, in any case, had to solve their own problems if they were to progress at all.

The journey from Maikop to Tiflis is perhaps over-dramatized in Hartmann's account. Gurdjieff also somewhat exaggerated the difficulties he encountered when he reached Tiflis. By that time, the Armistice between Turkey and the Allies had been signed at Mudros on 30th October 1918, twelve days before the surrender of the German army in France. An Allied army of occupation was in control of Constantinople. A British infantry brigade was sent to Georgia early in 1919, both to cut off any threat from the Turkish side and to strengthen the morale of the Social Democrat governments of

[a] *Meetings with Remarkable Men*, pp. 274–5.

Georgia and Azerbaijan. The Western Allies were very dependent at that time upon supplies from the oil field of Baku and it was considered vital to keep the pipeline from Baku to Batum flowing. For the first time since the collapse of Russia, there was an area of relative calm in the southern Caucasus. Trade with the West was opened through the Dardanelles. Pilgrims from Central Asia were making their way to Mecca to take advantage of the first opportunity for five years of going to the Holy Places. There was a very active movement of Armenians, Greeks, and Jews all seeking to restore trade on which their life depended.

Gurdjieff was quick to size up the situation. He arrived in Tiflis and found members of his family who had escaped from the twofold devastation of the retreating Russian army and the equally disordered advancing Turks. His father had been killed near Alexandropol. Others had died of typhoid. He sent messages everywhere to tell his family and pupils to join him and, according to his own account, found himself responsible for housing and feeding two hundred people, including nephews, nieces and other children. He very quickly organized a regular carpet business in which he was helped by the first Englishman to come in contact with him, Major Pinder, the British intelligence officer responsible for the security of the Baku–Batum pipeline and a colleague of mine in the General Staff Intelligence of the Army of the Black Sea, commanded by General Sir George Milne.

Within three weeks the carpet business was bringing in such an income that there was not only sufficient money for all to live on, but a great deal left over. At that time, British, French, Italian and American officers in Constantinople were recklessly buying oriental rugs of all kinds, and the merchants in the bazaar and the shops in Pera were offering unheard-of prices for carpets from Russia and Turkestan. There was also a wholesale trade direct to all the ports of Europe and America. Gurdjieff soon acquired the reputation of being a big-business man and gained the confidence of the Georgian Government. He decided to establish his Institute there. The flood of refugees from the north had created a serious housing shortage; but, as Gurdjieff puts it: "The Georgian Government met me halfway and directed the mayor of Tiflis to assist me in every way to find a building worthy of such an important establishment of general public significance." Several members of the Tiflis Municipal Council had become interested in Gurdjieff's work and did all they could, but nothing suitable could be found and the Institute was established in temporary quarters.

At that time, there was a very strange and unusual climate of thought and feeling in Tiflis. There was a lull, which everyone knew was precarious, in the revolutionary break-down of society. There was plenty of money about, but little chance of travel, for the Allies imposed severe restrictions on travellers attempting to go through the Bosphorus towards the freedom of Europe. The British Navy was in complete control of the Black Sea, including the Russian ports of Odessa and Novorossisk. The Georgians are not a race that take much thought for the morrow, but there was in Tiflis, as in every city, a proportion of serious people who were looking for some way of understanding 'life', that was proving so completely different from what anyone could have foreseen. These attitudes, incomprehensible then to Europeans, who still believed that the world would 'return to normal', are no longer strange to us who have lived through a Second World War, through great economic crises, the sudden collapse of empires and the atom bomb. We now see before us the threat of total collapse of the human society on earth: there is nowhere to take refuge. In 1918, the threatened collapse was total but local, and many turned to the idea of escape. Others saw that change of place would alter little and began to look for a new way of life.

Gurdjieff saw that he could attract those who were able to see and think clearly. He invited all his former pupils to help him. Ouspensky, at the time, was in a state of great doubt as to his future in connection with Gurdjieff. He was even rather taken aback to see his name among the 'specialist teachers' of the Institute. He quotes from the prospectus a passage which reads: "With the permission of the Minister for National Education, the Institute for the Harmonious Development of Man, based on George Ivanovitch Gurdjieff's system, is being opened in Tiflis. The Institute accepts children and adults of both sexes. Study will take place morning and evening. The subjects of study are: gymnastics of all kinds, rhythmical, medical and others: Exercises for the development of will, memory, attention, hearing, thinking, emotion, instinct and so on." After describing the various activities that would be carried on, the prospectus went on to inform readers that Gurdjieff's system "was already in operation in a whole series of large cities such as Bombay, Alexandria, Kabul, New York, Chicago,

Christiana, Stockholm, Moscow, Essentuki and in all departments and houses of the true international and labouring fraternities".

The absurdity of these claims was in keeping with Gurdjieff's self-imposed task of acting at all times in such a way as to make it hard for people to accept him without reservation. No doubt, neither Ouspensky, nor the other pupils who at this time began to draw away from Gurdjieff, suspected that his strange behaviour was dictated by the decision to prevent people from becoming too dependent on him. It was not until much later that he explained why he had acted as he did. Ouspensky had seen that he was constantly 'acting', but had taken this in a positive way until the 'acting' began to be directed towards himself. In order to achieve his object, Gurdjieff had been obliged to show them something of the range of his ideas and powers and they had formed exaggerated expectations of what he might be able to do for them. Now that the situation had changed and Gurdjieff needed to organize his work on the lines of the Institute that he had set himself to establish, he could no longer play the same role as before.

Ouspensky did not take the Institute project too seriously. He regarded it as no more than an external form needed to regularize Gurdjieff's activities. He even said "that this outward form was somewhat in the nature of a caricature".[a] Ouspensky and most of the others who had belonged to his own group in Moscow had serious doubts about Gurdjieff. Most of them were prepared to accept Ouspensky's formula which distinguished the system as something wonderful and significant from Gurdjieff, the man, with his balance of good and bad qualities.

About this time, through Thomas de Hartmann and his wife, two important recruits joined Gurdjieff. They were Alexander de Salzmann and his young wife, Jeanne. They very soon became invaluable helpers in organizing the dances and rhythmic movements, the demonstrations given to the public, having been in Tiflis since the revolution, they had got to know many influential people.

Gurdjieff kept his Institute in Tiflis going for several months; but, when the British War Office decided to withdraw the brigade and all its officers, the collapse of the Social Democratic Government became inevitable. At that time, I was at the head of the political intelligence branch of the British General Staff in Turkey, and among the tasks

[a] *In Search of the Miraculous*, p. 381.

assigned to me was the care of a mission for the Second Socialist
International, which in desperation the Allies were sending to Tiflis
to strengthen the morale of the Georgian Government. I for my part
was confident that, if we had maintained a military presence in the
Caucasus, the Bolsheviks would have stopped north of the mountains and independent governments could have maintained a
neutral zone that would for many years have contained the Bolshevik
threat to the Caucasus. The mission headed by Ramsay MacDonald
and Camille Huysmans returned from Tiflis with an urgent plea for
continued support of the Menshevik Government. Unfortunately,
rigid strategic principles prevailed, and as neither the French nor the
Italians would support us, the British brigade was withdrawn, and
soon afterwards the Caucasus collapsed.

Gurdjieff was faced with a momentous choice. He could go west
into Europe, or east into Turkestan where he was known and knew
his way about. He could count on finding a safe haven there for himself and those of his followers who wished to go with him. He proposed an expedition into Persia to several of them, but eventually
went only with one companion. I surmise that this journey was not
so much to examine the situation—which he knew far better than
that in Russia—as to see and consult people in whose judgment he
had confidence. I think this is the right interpretation of something
he said about his coming to Europe being with the approval of his
'teacher'. So the great decision was taken, the 'work' was to go to the
West and Gurdjieff was to sever his connection with Russia. Some of
his pupils elected to stay. Some went back to Moscow and St. Petersburg, soon to become Leningrad, others remained in the Caucasus.
He himself liquidated his affairs, turning his effects partly into cash
and partly into a selection of particularly valuable carpets. He applied
for visas for Turkey for himself and some of his family, though
most of the latter could not travel with him at that time. He provided
those of his followers, who wished to go, with money, but wisely
left them to make their own travelling arrangements. He arrived in
June, 1920 at a rather critical moment, as the Greek Army was then
advancing into Eastern Thrace and threatening to occupy Bursa and
Ushak. No one knew what the Turks would do in front of this pro-
vocation.

The British Navy and the Army of the Black Sea were responsible
for the security of this area. The French had taken Syria and the
Italians western Anatolia and the islands. This meant that I, as head

of the political branch of military intelligence, had to keep myself informed of all 'suspicious' arrivals. Apparently, as I mentioned in the
last chapter, Gurdjieff had a formidable dossier against him in New
Delhi and we received a dispatch warning us that he might now be a
Bolshevik agent. At that time, we had the famous 'Dunster Force'
in northern Iraq keeping watch on the critical area between Kars,
Tabriz and the Caspian Sea. It seems that Gurdjieff's movements had
become known to General Dunsterville. It is possible that Gurdjieff
had some connection with the so-called 'Christian Army of Revenge'
under the bloodthirsty Armenian General Antranik, who succeeded
in setting up an independent Armenian republic. Whatever the reason,
Gurdjieff was regarded as suspect and found it impossible to get permission to leave Turkey. He was, however, perfectly free to organize
his own work in Constantinople and particularly in the districts of
Galata, Pera and Tatavla, which were almost entirely inhabited by
Armenians and Greeks. He certainly had friends among Turks as well
as Christians, as my own first meeting with him in the Palace of Prince
Sabaheddin on the Bosphorus witnessed, and he was able to rent a
house near to the Galata Tower in Yemenedji Sokak No. 13. This
was not easy at that time as Constantinople was crowded with Allied
troops, and inundated with Russian refugees arriving in increasing
numbers from Odessa and other Black Sea ports, as well as with
demobilized Turkish army officers and men.

Once again, Gurdjieff decided to set up a branch of his Institute. I
have a copy of the prospectus he gave me at the time:

*A group of people, who have long been interested in questions
of the development and perfection of the 'self' reached the conclusion that in every centre of culture there should be an appropriate
organization for such questions.*

*Having learned that Mr. G. I. Gurdjieff is, by chance, in
Constantinople, these people applied to him with the request that he
should help them to organize a branch of the Institute for the
Harmonious Development of Man in Constantinople. Mr. Gurdjieff
has given his consent.*

*As the organization of a branch of the Institute with the integral
programme which experience shows to be necessary is not possible
under present conditions, it has been decided initially to open a
branch with a restricted programme with the intention of extending
the programme at the earliest opportunity.*

In the meantime, the following classes have been opened:
1. *Harmonic and Plastic Rhythm.*
2. *Ancient oriental dances*
3. *Medical Gymnastics*
4. *Mime*

For the present, the Institute will acept only pupils of the second and third categories.

The Instructors are people who have previous experience in the establishments of the Institute:

Mme Jeanne Matignon—harmonic rhythm
Mme J. Ostrowskaia—plastic and ancient oriental dances
Professor Th. de Hartmann—music
Dr. Stiernval—medical gymnastics

Mr. G. Gurdjieff, as director general, has taken responsibility for the organization, pending the arrival of the person specially charged with the direction of the Constantinople branch of the Institute.

Provisionally and until a permanent place is organized, the work will be conducted at Pera, Tunnel, Rue Yemenidji No. 13.

Mr. Gurdjieff will give lectures twice a week [on Thursdays and Sundays] at the centre. He will alone conduct public discussion on questions of religions, philosophy, science and art from the esoteric viewpoint. Special attention will be directed to systems for the study of man and to theories of 'superman' in the eastern sciences. He will also review contemporary integral sciences in the light of the ancient sciences, medicine, chemistry, psychology, etc.

The aim of the lectures is to make known to the public of Constantinople the scientific and philosophical material collected over a long period of years in the course of researches in different countries, especially Asia. All the material is unpublished.

The themes of the lectures will include the following:
1. *Selected extracts from accounts of journeys in Turkestan, Pamir, Tibet, Chitral, Kafaristan, Afghanistan and Baluchistan.*
2. *Is India really the country of miracles?*
3. *Excavations in Delhi and the valleys of the Hindu Kush, in Armenia, Babylon and Egypt.*
4. *Is the soul eternal? Is the will free?*
5. *The law of the octave.*

6. *What is the essential defect of contemporary science?*
7. *What does contemporary man represent?*
8. *What is hypnosis?*
9. *'Magnetism', 'emotionalism', 'mysticism'.*
10. *'Fakirism', 'monachism', 'dervishism' and 'yogism'.*
11. *The science of numbers, of symbols and diagrams.*
12. *Ancient sacred art.*
13. *The science of poisons.*
14. *Magic.*
15. *Proof of the unity of origin of all religions.*
16. *Explanations and demonstrations of the various feats and sleights of hand performed by fakirs, spiritualists, diviners and fortune tellers.*

The lectures will be delivered in Russian, Greek, Turkish or Armenian, according to the audience. All receipts will be used to help impoverished students of the Institute.

The cover of the prospectus shows the 'emblem' of the Institute with the Enneagram symbol, many symbolic objects and a picture of Gurdjieff as a young man.

The prospectus is not dated, but I fancy it was printed in September 1920 and was probably not seen till later by Ouspensky, who had come to Constantinople in January and had started to give public lectures in the Russky Mayak (lighthouse) in Pera. In August, he started to have group meetings in the flat I shared with Mrs. Beaumont close to the German Embassy. Gurdjieff and Ouspensky again made friends and Ouspensky was helping him actively with the organization of the Institute. Thomas de Hartmann and his wife were organizing concerts for a newly formed and remarkable Russian orchestra drawn from the principal orchestras of Moscow, Kief, Kharkow and Odessa. By chance, I became involved in this enterprise and so met Ouspensky the Hartmanns and Gurdjieff himself independently, without realizing at first that they were connected.

I went only once to the Institute headquarters in Yemenidji Sokak. Yemenidji Sokak is a steep narrow street with tall narrow buildings. No. 13 is three doors from the Grand Rabbinate where Gurdjieff obtained the use of a large room in which I saw for the first time a 'demonstration' of Gurdjieff's rhythmic exercises and ritual dances. I remember most vividly the 'Initiation of a Priestess' in which

Gurdjieff's wife, Mme Ostrowska, was the central figure. Gurdjieff told us that his system developed all sides of a man's nature, and that the exercises we had seen were not only to acquire control of the body and its movements and postures. The exercises had complicated patterns that called for a powerful effort of mental attention. In combination with the mime—which was indeed extraordinary and unlike anything I had seen before—they acted upon the emotional nature. I asked if this was the entire training, and he explained that he had brought together a comprehensive system of ideas and methods that he intended to bring to the West as soon as the political situation would allow. I saw Ouspensky at the same demonstration and, for the first time realized that he and Gurdjieff were connected.

As Gurdjieff had at that time a group trained in the exercises, he decided to make this the central feature of his Institute in Turkey. In particular, he intended to complete the ballet called the "Struggle of the Magicians". A very severe training of body, mind and feelings is required to enable the ritual movements to be carried out correctly. It is quite different from ballet training, in which the basic elements are automatized, leaving the dancer to interpret the theme through his mind and feelings. In Gurdjieff's exercises, the body must be itself in a high state of consciousness which unites the three functions of thought, feeling and bodily sensations into a single integral act of expression. I had seen a variety of Sufi demonstrations including the Rufai or 'howling' dervishes and the Mevlevi or 'whirling' dervishes. The closest to a Yesevi ritual were the Helveti dervishes whose elaborate ritual included some quite complicated movements of body, head and arms. Gurdjieff's movements seemed to combine these and have something besides. I witnessed for the first time the 'stop' exercise in which the pupils rushed towards the audience and were caught by a command from Gurdjieff and piled up on the floor in strange attitudes which they held as if frozen. For some reason, this reminded me strongly of a night I spent in a Rufai *tekke* on the Asiatic side of the Bosphorus.

The work of the Institute in Pera continued until the summer of 1921. Meanwhile, I had gone to England to act as interpreter at the so-called 'Conference for the Pacification of the Near East', which was held in St. James's Palace in January and February. By March, I was back in Turkey, having resigned my commission to take up the interests of the Ottoman Imperial Princes, amongst whom I had several personal friends. I was also then able to help Gurdjieff in

one of his amazing business deals. He had cured a Greek youth of
drunkenness and drug addiction, in return for which he received a
half-interest in a ship that had been requisitioned by the British
Navy. As the Navy no longer required it owing to the changed
situation in Anatolia, I was able to get it released, and Gurdjieff sold
his share for a large sum of money that he used to get his group away
to Germany, for which he had no difficulty in getting visas. This time
he left behind him a fairly large group of interested people, who
continued to study his ideas theoretically. In the exchange of
populations that occurred some years later, the Greek members of
this group moved to Salonika, from where they kept in contact with
Gurdjieff to the end of his life. I believe he visited them in the 1930's.

Gurdjieff remained in Constantinople from June 1920 to
September 1921. Meanwhile Ouspensky's *Tertium Organum* had appeared in Nicholas Bessarabov's translation and attracted the
attention of Lady Rothermere. She tracked Ouspensky down to
Constantinople and arranged for him to come and lecture in England. He left in August 1921 and I met him soon after in London,
and was able to hear him lecture in English for the first time.

Gurdjieff took his group through Roumania and Hungary to
Berlin. He rented a hall in Schmargendorf, a suburb of Berlin which
was then in the throes of the terrifying inflation that totally destroyed the value of the German mark. Anyone arriving in Berlin with a
supply of foreign money was rich and Gurdjieff was able to travel
freely in Germany in search of a suitable centre. Alexander de Salzmann had known Germany well before the war, and his wife, Jeanne,
had been a pupil of Jacques Dalcroze, the founder of Eurythmics.
Owing to inflation, the Dalcroze Institute, at Hellerau near Dresden,
had been unable to continue, and Gurdjieff saw the possibility of
using it as the headquarters of his own work, at least until Dalcroze
was in a position to start again. He could have bought the place outright and might have done so, if he had not been told that a group
of wealthy English people, attracted by Ouspensky's lectures, were
prepared to establish him in England and guarantee his expenses.

The German situation was then very unpleasant: it is almost incredible that a revolution did not break out. Only the amazing
discipline of the German people prevented it. It was probably this
situation more than anything else which decided Gurdjieff to try his
luck in England. Unfortunately, with all the influence that could be
brought to bear by Lady Rothermere and Ouspensky's rich and

distinguished friends, the Home Office would not give Gurdjieff and his group visas for more than a month. Although a large house in Hampstead had been found and all was prepared for launching the British branch of the Institute, it had to be abandoned, and Gurdjieff went back to Berlin, where his main group was going through a very intensive training.

Surveying the ten years from 1911 to 1921, we can see that Gurdjieff was pursuing a clear and consistent plan. To others, his actions may have appeared eccentric and inconsequent, but he was evidently driven by the conviction that his mission was important for mankind, and that the Higher Powers would provide the means to fulfil it. I believe that at that time he was in communication with dervish communities in Asia. He gave me the impression of a man who had a well-defined programme. He said that he was able to call on help from people who knew the importance of his task. It is impossible to convey the sense of complete assurance with which he threaded his way through the complications of countries devastated by war and revolution. Ouspensky, who had many friends in Europe, was much more uncertain and anxious for assurance that he would be able to settle in England. Gurdjieff gave the impression that he could and would establish his Institute where it was best for his mission: when he decided to give up the plan for a London headquarters, it was because he liked Paris rather than because London did not like him.

6

The Institute at Fontainebleau

GURDJIEFF'S decision to abandon London was a great disappointment to the English group, who had been electrified by his extraordinary talks that gave us a foretaste of what could happen if the Institute were set up in Hampstead, as we had hoped. I have notes of a lecture he gave on the 15th of March, 1922. I include parts of it here to convey an impression of the way Gurdjieff's ideas were first presented to us. It must be remembered that nothing had yet been published. Ouspensky had told us startling things, but had kept to what we could observe and verify for ourselves. Gurdjieff had with him two translators, one English and one Russian. He spoke in reply to a question by Orage about the means of achieving the radical change of being that Ouspensky had told us was both necessary and possible. Gurdjieff introduced the idea of essence and personality in characteristic terms, speaking, as Ouspensky never had, of the possibility of using hypnotism in order to change personality. He explained that the deeper changes we hoped for could not be brought about by the action of a third person, but must be the results of one's own suffering and sacrifices. "Personality", he said, "is not our own, we are not born with it. It is acquired from our contact with sleeping people, so that it must be asleep. It does not want to waken, it wants to be hypnotized. Essence is asleep, but it is not hypnotized. It is all we are born with, and what comes out of that by natural development. Personality is what we acquire in life. It is on the surface, so it changes very easily. Change of essence is difficult, sometimes perhaps impossible.

"You have to understand that there are two kinds of change in personality. There is unconscious change. This is temporary. One set of experiences drives out another. Then the situation returns, and personality becomes as it was before. Conscious change in personality can be permanent. If we observe personality, we can find out what has to be changed, in such a way that it will not return as it was before.

"When you learn to observe yourself, you will learn to distinguish between what belongs to essence and what belongs to personality. Then you will be able to classify everything in yourself, and come to know essence. Personality cannot control essence. It can only prepare the way so that essence can wake up. Real control can only be in essence. All control in personality is imagination.

"People are related to one another by personality and by essence. It is chemical. In two people perhaps personalities love each other, but essences hate each other. Their essences will always quarrel, but personalities will forgive.

"First you must understand the situation as it exists now. What you call 'will' in yourself is only from personality. It has no connection with real will. Something touches personality, and it says 'I want' or 'I do not want', 'I like' or 'I do not like', and thinks it is will. It is nothing. It is passive. Will can be only in essence. Such as you are now, your essence has no will, only automatic impulses. The desires of essence are your own desires, but they are not conscious, they are not will. They arise automatically in you because you are like that.

"Essence and personality are even in different parts of the brain. Nearly everything that belongs to personality is in the formatory apparatus. Essence cannot use all this material, so it has no critical mind. It is trustful, but because it does not know, it is apprehensive. You cannot influence essence by logical argument or convince it. Until essence begins to experience for itself, it remains as it always was. Sometimes situations arise where personality cannot react, and essence has to react. Then it is seen how much there is in essence. Perhaps it is only a child, and does not know how to behave. It is no use telling it to behave differently, because it will not understand your language. Personality can easily be influenced, especially in modern man. Personality gives itself up to every suggestion, however absurd. Maybe sometimes the mind knows better, but then essence is timid. The mind may know that it ought to love all, but essence cannot, so it remains only words.

"With most people, essence continues to receive impressions only until it is five or six years old. As long as it receives impressions it grows, but afterwards all impressions are taken by personality and essence stops growing. Sometimes if education is not too unfavourable, the essence may continue to grow, and a more or less normal human being can result. But normal human beings are the exception. Nearly everyone has only the essence of a child. It is not natural that in a grown-up man the essence should be a child. Because of this, he remains timid underneath and full of apprehensions. This is because he knows that he is not what he pretends to be, but he cannot understand why.

"You cannot tell how essence can be changed and take a normal part in your life until you have more knowledge. For this, you need a new 'language'. At present, I could not tell you even if I wanted to. By self-observation, you will come to know what has to be changed and why; but, even if you know what has to be changed, you cannot find out how to work for yourself. Because essence is unique, each one needs an individual programme. But to establish an individual programme a long study is needed, not only by oneself, but also by others. This is how it is arranged for people in the Institute. When they come, they begin to study themselves, and others study them also. After a long time, it is possible to arrange for each one his own corresponding programme of work."

I quote from this and other lectures to illustrate the connection with the teaching of the Khwajagān. A man cannot enter the way so long as personality dominates. The surrender of personality is the *fana-i-ahkam* which is not true *fana*, but nevertheless indispensable if the seeker is to come under higher influences. The first surrender of essence is *fana i ef'al* and the final surrender of being is *fanai sifat*—the words *ef'al* and *sifat* stand for the outer and inner aspects of the essence. In all Gurdjieff's lectures at that time, the Sufi origin of his teaching was unmistakable for anyone who had studied both.

Gurdjieff's visits to London continued over a period of about two months during which he was also searching in France. I did not, at that time, renew my personal contact with him partly because I was travelling in connection with my work for the Turkish Imperial family, but chiefly because I was unable to help with what was then most urgently needed; to provide money to enable the Institute to be established. By July 1922, Gurdjieff had given up the idea of settling in London. After several months of search and negotiation, he succeeded in arranging a strange deal with the widow of Maître Labori, famous for his defence of Dreyfus, who had left her the Château du Prieuré in Avon near Fontainebleau, formerly the home of Mme de Maintenon. Most of his pupils had remained in Berlin until he was ready to house them. He brought them rather prematurely to Paris in July—

a move that cost him more money than he could afford. It was not until October that he could occupy the Prieuré. He describes the predicament in which he found himself as "one of the maddest periods of my life".

"When I walked through the gates of the Château du Prieuré, it was as though, right behind the old porter, I was greeted by Mrs. Serious Problem. My one hundred thousand francs, down to the last sous, had already been scattered to the winds, partly in paying the rent of the property and partly in the expense of living for three months in Paris with so many people. My situation was further complicated by the fact that, when I arrived in Paris, I spoke no Western European language."

He began to look for the possibility of obtaining a loan. Ouspensky had some wealthy friends in London, particularly Ralph Philipson, a Northumberland coal owner, who was reputed to be a multimillionaire and whose Russian wife had become an enthusiastic supporter of Ouspensky in all that he did.

This was the first time he departed from the principle he had imposed upon himself fifteen years before—to take on himself sole responsibility for the accomplishment of his work, without accepting material help from the outside. He divided his time between Paris and the Prieuré where he was constructing the famous Study House from a surplus aircraft hangar that he acquired free from the French Air Force for the work of removing it. He spent much of his time in Paris seeking ways of making money. He undertook the cure of drunkards and drug addicts. He was able to start various business ventures, including a project connected with the Azerbaijan oilfields, which were still under the nominal control of private owners. This project, about which I heard much at the time, because of my own connection with the Turkish Imperial family's claims to the concessions for the Mosul oilfield, brought Gurdjieff both cash and useful connections in America. He also had a remarkable flair for setting up restaurants. He helped two groups of Russian émigrés to start restaurants in Montmartre which later became famous, and sold his own interest at a good profit.

As soon as the Prieuré was occupied, people from the London groups began to go there, either on visits or to 'stay forever'. Dr. Maurice Nicoll and Dr. Alsop, two very successful doctors and leading exponents of Jungian psychology, sold their practices and went with their wives and children. A. R. Orage sold the *New Age*, to the consternation of literary London. Several of our lady members, including Dr. Bell, also a psychoanalyst, Miss Crowdy, Miss Gordon and Miss Merston, went with the same determination to go and see it through to the end. In the spring of 1922, we were all given copies of the prospectus of the Institute which had been translated into English, German and French.

As this document links the new phase with the previous attempts to found the Institute in Turkestan and Russia, I shall quote from it extensively (*The Herald of the Coming Good*, p. 28) The prospectus starts with a preamble, declaring that modern civilization has deprived man of the possibility of progressive and balanced development towards a new type of human being, a development which is due to occur if only in the course of time and according to the law of general human progress. It goes on to say that "the general psyche of the modern man is split into three, so to say, completely independent 'entities', which bear no relation to each other and which are separate both in their functions and in their manifestations, whereas, according to historical data, these three sources formed, in the majority of people, even in the time of the Babylonian civilization, one indivisible whole, which appeared to be at once a common repository of all their perceptions and the radiating Centre of their manifestations". The reference to Babylon is not to the late Babylonian period, but to the earlier time of Sargon and Hammurabi. This is shown by Gurdjieff's saying that the split in man's psyche occurred 4,500 years ago. He criticizes here as elsewhere, the modern system of education which perpetuates the divisions in man's psyche and says :

"Because of this one-sided education of the modern man, upon the attainment of his majority these three entirely independent sources or centres of his life; that is, firstly, the source of his intellectual life, secondly, the source of his 'emotional' life, and thirdly, his instinct or his 'motor' centre, instead of fusing inwardly in the normal way to produce common outer manifestations, have become, especially of late, quite independent outward functions, and not only the methods of education of those functions, but also the quality of their manifestations have become dependent on special outer subjective conditions.

"According to the deductions based on detailed experiments made by Mr. Gurdjieff himself, as well as those by many other people who have seriously thought about this question, every really conscious perception and manifestation of man can result only from the simultaneous and co-ordinate working of the three aforesaid sources, which make up his general individuality, and each of which must fulfil its role, that is, furnish its own share of associations and experiences.

"The complete achievement of the requisite and normal manifestation in each distinct case is possible only upon the co-ordination of the activity of all these three sources.

"In the modern man, partly owing to his abnormal education during his preparatory age, and partly owing to influences due to certain causes of the generally established abnormal conditions of modern life, the working of his psychic centres during his responsible age is almost entirely disconnected, therefore his intellectual, emotional and instinctive motor functions do not serve as a natural complement and corrective for one another, but, on the contrary, travel along different roads, which rarely meet and for this reason permit very little leisure for obtaining that which should in reality be understood by the word 'consciousness', wrongly used by modern people today.

"As a result of the lack of co-ordinated activity on the part of these three separately formed and independently educated parts of man's general psyche, it has come about that a modern man represents three different men in a single individual; the first of whom thinks in complete isolation from the other parts, the second merely feels, and the third acts only automatically, according to established or accidental reflexes of his organic functions. These three men in one should, in accordance with the foresight of Great Nature, represent, taken together in responsible age, one man as he ought to be: the man-without-inverted-commas, that is, the real man.

"These three, who were deliberately shaped by Great Nature to compose one complete whole, as a consequence of not assuming at the right time the habit of mutual understanding and aid, through the fault of men themselves and of their false education, produce this result that, in the period of responsible manifestations of the modern man, they not only never help one another, but are, on the contrary, automatically compelled to frustrate the plans and intentions of each other; moreover, each of them, by dominating the others in moments of intensive action, appears to be the master of the situation, in this way falsely assuming the responsibilities of the real 'I'.

"This realization of disconnected and conflicting activity of the centres of origin, which ought to represent the psyche of man, and, at the same time, of the complete absence of even a theoretical conception of the indispensability of an education corresponding to these separate, relatively independent parts, must inevitably lead to the conclusion that man is not master even of himself.

"He cannot be master of himself, for not only does he not control these centres, which ought to function in complete sub-ordination to his consciousness, but he does not even know which of his centres governs them all.

"The system applied in the Institute for Man's Harmonious Development for observing human psychic activities clearly demonstrates that the modern man never acts of his own accord, but only manifests actions stimulated by external irritations.

"The modern man does not think, but something thinks for him; he does not act, but something acts through him; he does not create, but something is created through him; he does not achieve, but something is achieved through him. In order to avoid undesirable results and unexpected consequences in working upon one's self, it is necessary to submit to the discipline of special and strictly individual methods, aimed at the development of new and particular 'inertias', by means of which, under the direction of an experienced guide, the old ones may be regulated and altered, in other words, it is necessary to develop new faculties, which are unattainable in ordinary life, and which man can neither develop unaided nor by the help of any general method.

"The programme of the Institute for Man's Harmonious Development includes the practical application of a special 'line-of-work', from which a careful choice of some definite type of work is made for every person, according to his abnormally constructed psyche, the automatic activity of which has to be developed or diminished."

As I myself did not go to the Prieuré until 1923, I have to draw from notes that were kindly given to me by Miss Gladys Alexander, one of Ouspensky's pupils with whom I had been working. She wrote:

"Pending the opening of the Prieuré, a few went straightway to Paris to join the pupils who had journeyed with Mr. Gurdjieff from Russia and Turkey. In London, meanwhile, all kinds of alarming rumours concerning the hard life of the Prieuré ran riot. Fear perhaps of painful shocks to personalities, and of exhausting trials of physical endurance led to much exaggeration and confused understanding.

"Whether by intention or not, a newcomer to the Prieuré usually passed unnoticed, and for days I was at a loss to know how to introduce myself to Mr. Gurdjieff. Then I realized that I had to make an effort to approach him. His response was immediate—"Not be afraid", he said, "not fear".

"Life was spurred to a highly accelerated pace. It ranged from the heavy toil of an old-fashioned kitchen and scullery, from the work of the house and the laundry, the flower and kitchen gardens, to the care of horses, donkey cart, sheep and goats, cows and calves, hens, pigs, and dogs. It was lived in a seething atmosphere of speed and tension, of zeal and high hopes, punctured by bouts of inertia and criticisms, of lively friction and wordy contests. It was, indeed a melting pot designed to reduce to their intrinsic value the ingredients that boiled and simmered within.

"In the salon after supper we practised the movements and also the Dervish dances. Though superficially I had essayed the technique of Dalcrose, of the ballet and Isadora Duncan, I had found in them no medium for the plastic expression of a threefold form; but in the movements taught by Mr. Gurdjieff I recognized at once that indefinable something for which I had been searching.

"Later the parts of the Zeppelin hanger arrived to be erected into a Study House. From a low stage of hardened mud, a wide, open space overlaid with rugs and carpets reached to the far end, on one side of which a small enclosure, draped with hangings and furnished with rugs and cushions, served for the use of Mr. Gurdjieff. A little wooden railing surrounded the space, and separated it from an outer passage. Behind the passage ranged a bank of raised seats or divans, also spread with rugs and cushions for sitting or reclining. Within the space, goat skins covered the railings, serving as a back to a stretch of mud-hardened floor, also covered with similar skins to seat the pupils. The men were allocated to one side and the women to the other, meeting only on a central pathway, marked by the outline of the rugs, and upon the stage. The back wall of the stage was hung with Eastern instruments of music a grand piano stood nearby. The figure of the Enneagram was suspended above the stage, and later in script form the sayings of Mr. Gurdjieff were painted on white material attached to the roof. The seats outside the railings were reserved for onlookers, visitors and those not taking part in the studies. Long low windows painted in the colours and symbolic patterns of Persian rugs backed the raised divans. Two fountains, at first filled with gold and silver fish, were placed on either side near the doorway, and a single fountain below the middle of the stage at the head of the central path. The central fountain was set to play a sequence of changing colours.

"Here, after the day's work, the practice of movements continued, often till the small hours of the morning, when, as the warmth from the stoves died down, the winter cold drove us back to the slightly lesser chill of the Prieuré."

All this work on Gurdjieff's part demanded not only time and effort, but the expenditure of psychic energy in the form he described as *Hanbledzoin* (see Chapter 3). He taught that to produce this substance in quantities above the normal requirements of the physical body, either special exercises must be carried out, or intentional suffering of a particular kind must be self-imposed. The vow he had taken in 1911 deliberately to increase the difficulties of his life was the secret of his prodigious output not only of external work but also of ideas and of actions upon people that made those who met him ask themselves if he was an ordinary man or a supernatural being. The 'unnatural life' to which he had condemned himself was the only mode of existence by which his task could be accomplished.

Gurdjieff's uncanny power was once again brought to play in his dealing with Ouspensky. Ouspensky was a brilliant and dedicated exponent of Gurdjieff's ideas, and also a man who inspired confidence by his obvious integrity and sincerity. No one else in Gurdjieff's entourage could have gained the confidence of so many wealthy and influential English people. Gurdjieff's French-speaking pupils proved incapable of arranging for support either in France or Germany. Nearly all the money that launched the Institute came from England. Gurdjieff regained Ouspensky's confidence and affection to such a degree that throughout 1923 Ouspensky spoke about the Prieuré as an unique opportunity for those who could go to it.

I went first to the Prieuré in January 1923, shortly before the death of Katherine Mansfield. At that time, the work was very largely connected with the practical running of the place, but Gurdjieff spoke personally with the pupils that appeared to him to be promising, and from time to time he gave lectures. The following lecture, of which I was given a copy, was delivered on the 8th February 1923. It is important because it shows Gurdjieff's attitude towards Christianity and affirms that the aim of his work was to enable people to be Christians, in the true sense. He never spoke well of the Christian churches. One of the favourite sayings of his father was: "If you want to lose your faith, make friends with the priest." The following is a résumé, put together from several sets of notes :

"So long as man does not separate himself from himself, he can achieve nothing and no one can help him. To govern oneself is a very difficult thing—it is a problem of the future; it needs much power and demands much work.

"But this first thing, to separate oneself from oneself, does not require much strength, it only needs serious wish, the wish of a responsible man. If a man cannot do it, this shows that he lacks this wish. Consequently it proves that there is nothing for him here. What we do here can be suitable only for serious people.

"Our feelings and our thinking have nothing in common with 'us', that is, with our real selves. Usually our thinking is the result of our feelings. Our mind should live by itself, and our feelings should live by themselves. When we say 'to separate oneself from oneself', it means first of all that our mind should stand apart from our feelings.

"Our weak feelings can change at any moment, for they are dependent on many influences : on food, on our surroundings, and on chance circumstances that affect our desire to be important. But the mind depends on very few influences, and so, with a little effort, it can be kept in the desired direction.

"Even a weak man can give the desired direction to his mind. But he has little control over his feelings; great power is required to give direction to feelings, and to control them. Man's feelings do not depend on him : they can be good-tempered or bad-tempered, irritable, cheerful or sad, excitable or placid. All these reactions happen independently of him. A man may be cross because someone pushed him or scolded him. Or he may be cross because he has eaten something that has produced this effect.

"If he has no special attainments, nothing can be demanded of him. Therefore, one cannot expect from him more than he has. From a purely practical point of view, a man is certainly not responsible in this respect; it is not his fault that he is what he is. So I do not take this into consideration, for I know that you cannot expect from a weak man something that requires strength. One can make demands of a man only in accordance with the strength he has to fulfil them. Naturally, the majority of people present are here at the Institute because they lack this strength and have come here to acquire it. This proves that they want to be strong, and so strength is not demanded from them.

"But I am speaking now of the other part of us—the mind. Speaking of the mind, I know that each of you has enough strength, each of you can have the power and capacity to act not as he now does.

"The mind is capable of functioning independently but unfortunately it also has the capacity of becoming identified with the moods and feelings, of becoming a mere reflection of the feelings. In the majority of those present, their mind does not even try to be independent, but is always merely a slave of their moods.

"Every man can achieve this independent mind; everyone who has a serious wish can do it. But no one tries, and so, in spite of the fact that they have been here so long, in spite even of the desire they had for so long before coming here—they still stand on a level below that of an ordinary man; that is, the level of a man who never intended to do anything.

"I repeat again—at present we are not capable of controlling our states, and so it cannot be demanded fom us. But when we acquire this capacity, corresponding demands will be made.

"And so I say that a serious man, a simple, ordinary man, a man without any extraordinary powers, whatever he decides, whatever purpose he has set himself, that purpose will always remain in his memory. Even if he cannot achieve it in practice, theoretically he will always keep it in his mind. Even if he is influenced by other dictates, his mind will not forget his aim. He has a duty to perform and, if he is honest, he will strive to perform this duty, because he is a man.

"No one can help in this remembering, in this separation of oneself from oneself. A man must do it for himself. Only from the moment that a man has the ability to achieve this separation can another man help him.

"It is true that to have a constant wish to separate one's thoughts from one's feelings is not easy, but the mind must always remember this wish. It must remember that you came here realizing the necessity of struggling only with yourself, and be thankful to anyone who gives you the opportunity to engage in this struggle.

"The programme of the Institute, the power of the Institute and the aim of the Institute can be expressed in one sentence: *The Institute can help a man to be able to be a Christian.*—Simple! That is all! But it can do so only if a man has this wish, and a man will have this wish only if he has a place where a constant wish can be present. But before *being able* one must *wish* to be able.

"Thus there are three periods : *to wish, to be able, and finally to be*. The Institute is the means. Outside the Institute, before one comes, it is necessary to *wish*. But here one can learn *to be able* and *to be*.

"The majority of those present here call themselves Christians, but practically all are 'Christians in quotation marks'. Let us examine this question :

"Dr. Y., are you a Christian? What do you think, should one love one's neighbour or hate him? (Answer: One should love). Who can love like a Christian? It follows that to be a Christian is almost impossible. Christianity includes many things; we have taken only one of them, to serve as an example. Can you love or hate someone to order?

"Yet Christianity says precisely this—to love all men, to bless those that hate you. But this is impossible. At the same time it is quite true that it is necessary to love. Unfortunately, with time, modern Christians have adopted only the second half of the teaching and lost the first—which should have preceded it. First one must *be able to love*, then only can one love. But how can one be able? It is the knowledge of this that is lost.

'It would be unjust for God to demand from man what he cannot give. So He gave this knowledge not once but many times. Only man is a fool and throws this precious knowledge away.

"Half of the world is Christian, the other half has other religions. For me, a sensible man, this makes no difference. Originally they all had the same ideals as Christianity. Therefore it is possible to say that the whole world is Christian—the difference is only in name. And it has been Christian not one year but thousands of years. There were Christians even before the coming of Christ. So common sense says to me 'For so many years men have been Christians, and God Himself in the person of Jesus Christ lived among them—how can He be so unreasonable as to demand the impossible?'

"But it is not like that. Things have not always been as they are now. People have only recently forgotten the first half of their religion and through this have lost the capacity for *being able* to follow the teachings of Christ. And so it became indeed impossible.

"Let everyone ask himself, simply and openly, whether he can love all men? If he has had a cup of coffee, he loves; if not, he does not love. How can that be called Christianity?

"In the past, not all men were called Christians. Some men of one and the same family were called Christians, others only half-Christians, yet others were non-Christians. So in one and the same family there could be the first, the second and the third. But now all are called Christians. It is despicable, unwise, naive and dishonest to bear a name without justification. The Bible says:

" 'A Christian is a man who is able to follow the commandments.'

"A man who is able to do all that is demanded of a Christian, both with his mind and in his feelings, is called a Christian without quotation marks. A man who, in his mind, wants to do all that is demanded of a Christian, but who can do so only with his mind and not with his feelings, is called a half-Christian. And a man who can do nothing even with his mind, is called a non-Christian.

"Try to understand the significance of what I wished to convey by this lecture."

Gurdjieff's lectures were given at irregular intervals and usually with no advance warning. He was frequently absent from the Prieuré and, when there, drove himself mercilessly in physical work, in directing movements and in seeing important people. Those who had been to Ouspensky's meetings in London were fortunate in having a theoretical background. Perhaps this explains why there were practically no Americans or Europeans at the Prieuré in 1923.

In the spring of 1923, Gurdjieff began to broaden the basis of his work. I quote again from Miss Alexander's notes:

"One evening Mr. Gurdjieff announced that, in general, work so far had been like that of oxen, and as such inadequate. He then widened the scope of its directions with exercises in memory and attention, which we were to combine with our daily activities. And many other exercises of the kind, in great variety, were tried and practised. To me they were very difficult, often confusing (perhaps intentionally so) and even unnerving. When discouraged by the failure of repeated efforts, I told him that I was quite unable to do them, he just said, 'I know you can't'. I had not then realized that the machine is what it is and cannot be anything else, nor how the proneness of human nature to compare results and failures to those of others only increases the difficulties by distracting attention.

"Apart from these studies, the scheduled programme of the subjects to be taught at the Institute lay dormant, nor had those in quest of health found the cures they hoped for, or perhaps believed in. The driving force of the first shock had weakened, much of Mr. Gurdjieff's method of training was difficult to understand. Only the nettles could be grasped, and how many had the tenacity to do so?

"One day, however, Mr. Gurdjieff offered us a choice of instruction from a wide selection of trades and handicrafts. In assent to each announcement we were told to hold up our hands. We replied with vigorous armraising, sometime without a dissent. So far as I remember we could learn to cobble shoes, to tailor, to make stays, to create hats, to weave rugs and carpets, to massage, to paint, to sculpture, and even to become electricians. But despite our ready response little if any instruction materialized, though it was remarkable how the mere prospect of it revived our flagging energies. We lived on anticipation.

"Later, however, we received a stimulus of another kind, the least expected, namely, the fast. Mr. Gurdjieff explained that it must only be undertaken voluntarily and without fear. It was desired to effect a change of metabolism, and to be of any benefit the first preliminary was an enema. For most it was permissible to drink water only. In one case the fast began with prostokvasha, the Russian sour milk, in another with oranges in plenty. Its duration also varied. For some it lasted a day, or two or three days, for others a week, even a fortnight. The doctors took daily note of weights, temperatures and pulses. The usual work continued. To break the fast, strong bouillon was given the first day, and beef-steak the second. The fast was loyally carried out.

"It was a brilliant summer. Mr. Gurdjieff decided to have a section of the forest cleared for the building. It was said to be for a permanent central hall for the Institute. As the great trees fell, the burning sun beat down upon the bare earth, and the massive roots and stumps of the trees had to be hacked and dug to the accompaniment of exercises in memory and attention. It was a gruelling task. But there was the cold water of the fountain basin in which to bathe, the larger bowl of sour milk and the rare appearance of red wine to gladden the heart, and the weekly beatitude of our fundamental cleanser, the Russian bath. Yet, once again, not a stone of the new building was ever laid. In its stead, from its unfertile soil, sprouted sweet corn and beans.

"At the weekends, the Prieuré received many visitors from Paris and elsewhere, and on Saturday evenings some of the local inhabitants of Fontainebleau and Avon were invited to watch demonstrations of the movements and exercises. These occasions were staged, as it were, in full dress. The Russian bath and supper over, the day's labours set aside, we donned our white costumes, keyed to the tension of a public performance. Those summer evenings, fading into nights spiced with the aroma of the forest, are unforgettable. I can still hear the clanging of the entrance bell as the people streamed in, passing by the long flower beds to the study house, with the garden fountain playing a coloured rhythm of changing lights to the fitful dancing of the glow worms."

To give an idea of the way the work went, I will repeat just one of many stories about the furious work to get the Study House completed in time for the Christmas celebrations. Tchekhovitch, who was continuously engaged on the job, was fixing the trusses about 25 feet above the ground. He was so exhausted that he fell asleep precariously balanced on a narrow beam. None of the others noticed; but Gurdjieff entered, took in the position at a glance, motioned to them all to remain perfectly still and climbed like a cat on to the truss and along it until he could hold Tchekhovitch steady. Then he went for him like a fish-wife and sent him off to sleep for forty-eight hours after which all went on as before. Again and again, the inexperienced builders were confronted with lifting and fixing problems they could not solve and always Gurdjieff appeared at the critical moment to show them just how the job could be done.

I went for a longer visit in July and August 1923. Mrs. Beaumont, with whom I had entered Ouspensky's group and who was also completely committed to the work, could not come with me because she had to go with her mother to Dax to take the waters. I have the letters which I wrote to her at the time. Reading them they remind me how naive was my attitude towards Gurdjieff and his work and the lack of understanding of myself also. When Mrs. Beaumont later came to the Prieuré, she had a very strong but mixed impression of Gurdjieff. She went back to Ouspensky and said to him:

"I can see that Mr. Gurdjieff is an extraordinary man, but I cannot tell if he is good or bad. He seems to be both together." Ouspensky categorically assured her that Gurdjieff was a good man and that she should be confident that I would receive benefit from being with him, providing I remembered that Gurdjieff had said that we must believe nothing that we had not verified for ourselves.

When I was at the Prieuré, I was taken to see the 'laboratory' but, as none of the large-scale apparatus had yet been installed, I could not tell if it was intended to be taken seriously. At that time, Gurdjieff could not speak either English or French and I was fortunate in being able to talk to him freely in Turkish, which he spoke perfectly, though with an accent that was more that of Central Asia than the Ottoman Turkish I knew. This may be the reason why I was lucky enough to have several private talks with him that were the envy of the other people from England, who were mostly older and more important than I was. One day, he took me in his big car for a drive in the forest of Fontainebleau, ending up in a clearing from which we could look down on the Prieuré. He sat on a fallen tree and he told me how he intended the Institute to develop, how it would become a centre of training and research not only into the powers of man himself, but into the secrets of the solar system. He said he had invented a special means for increasing the visibility of the planets and the sun and also for releasing energies that would influence the whole world situation. Looking back, I can see how, in my naivete and inexperience, I accepted all these claims and was ready to devote myself to helping Gurdjieff to realize them. Soon after this, Gurdjieff did indeed show me how to release energies such as I had never before experienced and to know things I could not possibly have known otherwise. I believe that, with all the exaggerations and absurdities, Gurdjieff was seriously planning a great undertaking and moreover intended to do this on his own initiative and responsibility.

One of Gurdjieff's lectures made a great impression on me: I have frequently reread it and it has always deepened my understanding. He spoke about Freedom and Pride. I kept only a summary which I reproduce in full:

"Freedom leads to Freedom. Those are the first words of Truth. You do not know what is truth because you do not know what freedom is. All the truth that you know today is only 'truth' in quotation marks. There is another truth, but it is not theoretical: it cannot be expressed in words. Only those who have realized it in themselves can understand that truth.

"Now I will give you a detailed explanation of those words I have spoken. It rests on the following basis. The freedom I speak about is the freedom that is the goal of all schools, of all religions, of all times. And, in truth, I tell you that this freedom can be a very great one. Everyone wishes for that freedom and ever strives for it: but it can never be attained without the first kind of freedom that I will call the

Lesser Freedom. The Greater Freedom is the liberation of ourselves from all influences acting outside ourselves. The Lesser Freedom is the liberation of ourselves from all influences acting within ourselves. For a start—for you who are beginners—the Lesser Freedom is a very big one indeed, as it is not subject to your dependence upon outside influences.

"You have to understand that so long as you are the slave of inside influences you cannot come under the action of outside influences. This is perhaps even a good thing, so long as you have no inner freedom. You must understand that the man who is freed from inside influences begins to fall under the play of outside influences.

"Inner influences, that produce in you inner slavery, come from many independent sources. That is to say, there is a great heap of independent factors that cause a man to be inwardly a slave. These influences are different for different people. In one case one influence is strongest, and in another case another. But in every one without exception there are so many factors of slavery that, if you had to struggle with each one separately, and free yourselves from them one by one, you would need such a long time that half a lifetime would not be enough.

"Therefore we must find such a means or method of working as will enable us to destroy simultaneously as many as possible of the enemies within us from which flow these influences that produce slavery.

"As I have said, there are very many independent enemies: but two of the chiefest are Vanity and Self-Love. In one doctrine, these are even called the chief ambassadors of the Devil. It may be added, by the way, that for some reason they are called Madame Vanity and Monsieur Self-Love. I have quoted merely two of these inner enemies as characteristic, because it would lead too far to mention them all now.

"We have also many slaves within us—each of these slaves wishes to be free, but it is difficult for each slave to work directly and straightforwardly. It is especially difficult for our slaves to contend with these enemies, because none of our slaves has enough time. At one moment one slave is present: at another moment it is another slave, and to contend with these enemies requires a great deal of time. In the upshot, it has to be done indirectly in order that we can get rid of several of the enemies simultaneously.

"For this we have to understand how these enemies work and from where they get their power. You must know that these representatives of the devil stand all the time on our threshold and deny entry to all outside influences—both good and bad. Accordingly they have both good and bad sides. If anyone wishes to limit the entry of outside influences, it is well for him that these sentinels exist. But if, for some reason or other, anyone wishes that every kind of influence should enter him, then he must free himself from these two sentinels. Only it is necessary to understand once and for all that it is impossible to select the influence one wishes. For example, it is impossible to select only good influences. The sentinels are only undesirable for those whose real aim is freedom. Those who have this aim must strive by every means in their power to liberate themselves first of all from these two enemies—vanity and self-love.

"To do this there are a heap of methods and many different means. But I, Gurdjieff, would personally advise you to get rid of them, without subtilizing, by merely reasoning simply and actively with oneself.

"This is possible by active mentation: and I must warn you that, if you fail or find it impossible by this means, then some other means must be found, because there is no hope of going further until some of these enemies have been eradicated.

"For instance, self-love or false pride takes up half of our time and half of our life. If anyone or anything outside us should hurt our pride, we are injured, not only for the time being, but for a long time afterwards. And that wounded feeling, acting by inertia, closes the portal and so shuts out all life.

"*I live!* Life is outside. I am life so long as I am connected with the outside. If life only exists inside me, this is no life at all. When I 'behold myself' I find that I am linked up with the outside world. Everything lives after this wise and cannot exist without this linkage.

"One experience fades away and hardly has time to do so when another takes its place. Our machine is so built that it has not various places in it in which different experiences can subsist at one and the same time. In us, there is one place where experiences can be, and if that place is occupied by experiences of one kind that are undesirable, there can be no question of its being occupied by experiences of another kind that may be desirable. You have to grasp and realize as a fact that your experiences cannot lead to any kind of achievement or liberation unless you have lived through them. You must have experiences—even more perhaps than you can possibly imagine, both pleasant and unpleasant—but you must not let them make slaves of you. On the contrary you must use them in order to prepare a place in which you can be free.

"We do not own ourselves and do not possess real pride of self. Pride of self is a big thing. As much as we must blame pride as it is ordinarily understood, so much do we need that real Pride which unhappily does not exist in us.

"Pride of Self is the sign of being in possession of oneself. If a man has Self-Pride it proves that he is. But, as I said in the beginning, Self-Pride is also the Devil's representative. Self-Pride is the chief enemy, the chief obstacle to all our aims and achievements. Pride is the main tool of the representative of hell. Pride is also one attribute of the soul. By pride it is possible to discern the spirit. Pride of Self is the indicator and proof that such a one is part of Heaven. Pride of self is 'I'. 'I' is God. Consequently it is needful to have pride. Pride is hell. Pride is heaven. These two, both bearing the same name, externally both of the same substance, are wholly different and opposite. No one by merely superficial examination—even if he continues through a whole lifetime—will ever succeed to discern one from the other.

"There is a saying: 'Those who have Pride are already half-free.' And if we take those who are sitting round here, each one has so much pride that he has more than enough and to spare. This is the paradox. We are full to the brim with pride and yet we have not the slightest freedom for ourselves. The aim must be to have Pride. If we attain to have pride we shall thereby be made free from many of the foes who are installed within us. We may even free ourselves from the main ones—Madame Vanity and Monsieur Self-Love.

"If you wish for Freedom—even the Lesser Freedom—you must be ready to pay a big price.

"Sometimes people complain to me that they cannot do the tasks I give them. What do they expect? It is enough if you see the possibility of doing them—the rest depends upon the strength of your own wish to be free. At present you cannot do, because you are not free.

"You must understand that you cannot begin with freedom—freedom is the goal, the aim. People say that God created man free. That is a great misunderstanding. Freedom cannot be given to anyone—even by our all-loving Creator Himself. God has given to man the biggest thing he can—that is the possibility to become free. The desire for freedom exists in every man worthy of the name—but people are stupid and they think they can have outward freedom without inner freedom. All our evil comes from this stupidity. Unless we desire, first of all, to be free from our own inner enemies, we shall only go from bad to worse.

"Therefore everyone must examine himself and try to find in himself a sincere wish to be free from the forces of vanity and self love acting in him. That inner slavery is the worst degradation for man, it is the Hell in which man allows himself to exist. The sincere wish to be free from that degradation is the beginning of real pride."

Gurdjieff's lectures which were always given at unexpected moments were for most of us the high spots of life at the Prieuré. One in which Gurdjieff explained the working of 'higher emotional energy' made a great impact upon me, because it followed a day of the most intense experiencing, when I for the first time discovered that it is possible to make contact with a source of energy that is beyond consciousness. This coincided with a time when I was seriously ill, indeed all my experiences were coloured by my health. I had a return of dysentery contracted in Izmir in 1919 and I recklessly overworked myself. The work in the gardens reminded me of Dervish communities in Turkey. The hot summer of 1922, the constant need for water, the Turkish bath and feasts on Saturday evenings were all reminiscent of the East. But, most of all, the Study House reminded me of the Sema Hanes of the Dervish communities outside the walls of Constantinople. In such an atmosphere, it was strange to see English men and women at home, though it must be confessed not one of them gave the same impression as the Dervishes I had seen only three or four years earlier.

In place of the inscriptions from the Qur'an and sayings of the Prophet, that one would see in a Sema Hane, Gurdjieff had placed round the ceiling a series of his own sayings. These were written in a strange script slightly resembling Arabic but reading vertically. We were expected to learn this script and I preserved all the aphorisms— one of which is reproduced in plate 12. There were about a dozen when I was there, but they were constantly added to and the final series was so interesting that I reproduce it in its entirety:

1. *If you have not a critical mind by nature it is useless your staying here.*
2. *Only he who can look after another's can possess his own.*

Plate 4
Gurdjieff departing
for Washington

Plate 5
Dr. Stjernwal and
Thomas de Hartmann
at the Prieuré

Plate 6   Gurdjieff's 'Kosshah' in the Study House

Plate 7   The Russian Bath at the Prieuré

3. *The more difficult the conditions of life, the greater the possibility for work, provided you work consciously.*

4. *Only he can be just who can enter into the position of others.*

5. *We can only strive to be able to be Christians.*

6. *I love him who loves work.*

7. *Judge others by yourself and you will rarely be mistaken.*

8. *Here one can only create and direct conditions, but not help.*

9. *Know that this house can be useful only to those who have already recognized their nothingness, and believe it possible to change.*

10. *The best means of obtaining felicity in life is the ability to consider externally always, internally never.*

11. *Man is born with the capacity for a definite number of experiences. Economising them he prolongs his life.*

12. *Consider only what others think of you—not what they say.*

13. *Love not art with your feelings.*

14. *Take the understanding of the East and the knowledge of the West, and then seek.*

15. *He who has got rid of the disease of "Tomorrow" has a chance of achieving what he is here for.*

16. *The highest achievement of man is to be able TO DO.*

17. *Here there are neither English nor Russians, Jews nor Christians, but only those following one aim—to be able to do.*

18. *Help only him who strives not to be an idler.*

19. *Judge not by tales.*

20. *It is a sign of a good man that he loves his father and mother.*

21. *Respect all religions.*

22. *If you know what is bad and continue to do it, you commit a sin that is difficult to forgive.*

23. *Only conscious suffering is of use.*

24. *Better be temporarily selfish than never to be just.*

25. *Like what it does not like*

26. *Remember that work here is not for work's sake but a means.*

27. *Energy used by an act of inner work is immediately converted for fresh use; that used by passive work is lost forever.*

28. *Practice conscious love on animals first; they are more responsive and sensitive.*

F

29. *One of the strongest motives for wishing to work on your-self is the realization that you may die at any moment.*
30. *Always remember that you are here having realized the necessity for contending with yourself; therefore thank everyone who affords an opportunity.*

I suppose that no one could evaluate the strains to which Gurdjieff had been subjected. He had no experience of European life. He did not understand and had never liked the British people and he was in desperate straits for money. He compelled himself to behave in an unnatural way in order to produce the energy he needed and yet he had to gain and hold the confidence of the people on whose material help he depended. This was a dilemma to which he had vowed he would never find himself exposed and yet there was no avoiding it.

In spite of the obstacles, Gurdjieff during the period from November 1922 to December 1923 had accomplished something that had never been seen in Europe before. He created conditions for work that enabled scores of people to discover and verify for themselves the potential for transformation that is latent in every human being. The basic method was simple: it consisted in offering pupils the opportunity and the means of stretching to the limit the capacity of their physical body for work, for attention, for the acquisition of skills, and for the production of psychic energy. The daily routine was exacting in the extreme. We woke up at five or six in the morning and worked for two hours before breakfast. Afterwards there was more work: building, felling trees, sawing timber, caring for the animals of almost every domestic species, cooking, cleaning, and every kind of domestic duty. After a quick light lunch and a period of rest, one or two hours were devoted to 'exercises' and 'rhythms' accompanied by music usually played by Thomas de Hartmann on the piano. Sometimes, there would be fasts lasting one, two, three or even up to seven days during which all the work continued as usual. In the evening, there would be classes in rhythms and ritual dances which might go on for three, four or five hours until everyone was totally exhausted.

One lecture made a very significant reference to 'the Sufis':
"In certain of the ancient doctrines it is said that 'When God created man, the same day he also created two spirits for each man,

the spirit of God and the spirit of Evil, or Angel and Devil, side by side. The angel he set on the right shoulder and the devil on the left shoulder of man.'

"There are other ancient doctrines in which it is said: 'When God sent the spirits on to the planets to work, the spirits asked God "What are we to do there?" God divided up the spirits into their separate natures and said: "You on the right hand will try to lead the living into Paradise, and you on the left hand, you shall try to lead the living into Hell."

" 'And here one of the head ones asked: "What means do you allow us to adopt with the different people?" To this, God answered; "You may have recourse to any method you like, but let the following fundamental difference exist between those methods and means: Let the plan of the spirit on the right hand be to work through man's activities and let the spirit on the left hand work through what, so to say, 'does itself' in man; for the spirit of the right hand, through man's active nature and consciousness, and for the spirit of the left hand, through man's passive nature and unconsciousness."' "

"These two doctrines I refer to are ancient ones. At the same time, *pari passu* with these ancient doctrines, there exists another doctrine right down to the present day, and one that other religions do not recognize.

"The majority of religions breathe, act and live according to holy writ, commandments and precepts.

"At the same time a teaching existed of wise men who tried to realize for themselves every religion, and all legends and all doctrines dispassionately. They did not blindly submit. Before accepting anything, they beforehand realized it for themselves. Whatever they could realize for themselves, they accepted. What they could not, they rejected.

"In this way a new religion was formed, although the material of which it was formed was adopted by other religions. The doctrine I am speaking of is the teaching of the Sufi; this same doctrine respecting the angel and the devil is to the following effect:

"Every action of man, every thought, each of his movements, either proceeds from the angel or the devil. What is derived from all intensive activity takes the form of a second, but much finer organism in the shape of a certain shell or casing, made of real matter, which can be sensed or recognized as being of one sort or the other. Each shell has the faculty of submitting to certain laws and to certain effects." Gurdjieff went on to speak about breathing exercises, but did not wish these to be referred to in public.

No description of the external life at the Prieuré can give any adequate idea of what was happening inside people. They could see for themselves that miracles were possible and were occurring before their eyes. They could see people as they really were behind the habitual masks and patterns of outward behaviour. They could experience in themselves the states of consciousness that Ouspensky had described, but which the work in London had never enabled them to attain.

But in spite of these results there was something not right. It was too frenzied, we were all in too much of a hurry to 'enter Paradise at all costs by next week', as Gurdjieff put it. Ouspensky concluded that many of his people had been far too precipitate in giving up their life and occupations in England, in order to devote themselves entirely to work with Gurdjieff. Among these were outstanding men like Orage and Nicol, and women of great strength of character like Ethel Merston and Dr. Bell. Few, at that time, were ready to accept that the process of transformation takes time and that each stage must be completed if the next is to go forward properly. We all wanted to run before we could walk.

Looking back, it seems that Gurdjieff was still experimenting. He wanted to see what European people were capable of. He discovered that they were prepared to make efforts that few Asiatics will accept —for the simple reason that on the whole Asiatic people are not in a hurry. This difference is deceptive and it may be that Gurdjieff misjudged the capacity for effort, and took it for ability to accept the need for inward change. As I see it now, we did not really grasp the profound change of attitude towards oneself that is needed before the process of the 'Work' can act freely in us. We were perhaps misled by Gurdjieff's insistence on effort and yet more effort. This insistence was probably needed with Asiatics and even Russians who as Gurdjieff put it are turkeys, half-way between peacocks and crows. The British people in 1922, still had that puritanical streak that makes us believe that what is good for us must necessarily be hard and even unpleasant. So one could see men and women accepting with alacrity the most absurd demands and outrageous behaviour on

Gurdjieff's part, whereas the French had one look at what was going on and quickly turned away.

This brings me back to the life of the Prieuré in 1923. While the whole week was devoted to intensive work, Saturday was a feast day. Nearly every Saturday evening there was a special meal with wines and spirits to drink. Guests were invited both by Gurdjieff himself and his privileged pupils. The master bedrooms of the château were reserved for special guests. They were called 'the Ritz' and were well furnished and carefully kept, whereas the rest of us slept in the servant's quarters and were lucky if we shared a room with congenial companions. The Prieuré became quite well known from press articles in England and France. Gurdjieff and his followers were called 'the Forest Philosophers' and it was customary for visitors from Paris to come out late on Saturday evenings to watch demonstrations of rhythms and sacred dances as well as pseudo-magical phenomena brilliantly stage-managed by Gurdjieff, de Hartmann and Alexander de Salzmann. I saw several of these demonstrations and could not guess how they were done until they were explained to me.

In Central Asia ritual feasts are part of the Dervish way of life. The *Chamodar*, or Master of the Feast, is a very ancient institution, and Gurdjieff himself said that he had adopted customs that had favourably impressed him during his long sojourn in Turkestan. One of these customs was the ritual that Gurdjieff called the 'Science of Idiotism'. He explained that in a Sufi community, which he used to visit, a method of teaching had been handed down from antiquity which consisted in tracing the path of man's evolution from a state of nature to the realization of his spiritual potential. I have put together the contents of many talks in the following account:

"There are twenty-one gradations of reason from that of the ordinary man to that of Our Endlessness, that is, God. No one can reach the Absolute Reason of God, and only the sons of God like Jesus Christ can have the two gradations of reason that are nineteenth and twentieth. Therefore the aim of every being who aspires to perfection must be to reach the eighteenth gradation. You must understand that the people you know do not have any reason at all. They live in their dreams and have no connection with reality. Whoever has any contact with reality is called an Idiot. The word idiot has two meaning: the true meaning that was given to it by the

ancient sages was *to be oneself*. A man who is himself looks and be-
haves like a madman to those who live in the world of illusions: so
when they call a man an idiot they mean that he does not share their
illusions.

"Everyone who decides to work on himself is an idiot in both
meanings. The wise know that he is seeking for reality. The foolish
think he has taken leave of his senses. We here are supposed to be
seeking for reality, so we should all be idiots: but no one can make
you an idiot. You must choose it for yourself. That is why everyone
who visits us here and wishes to remain in contact with us, is allowed
to choose his own idiotism. Then all the rest of us will wish from
our hearts that he will truly become that idiot. For this alcohol was
used by the ancient sages; not to get drunk, but to strengthen the
power to wish."

Gurdjieff had a fixed ritual in proposing the toast of the idiots.
The Director started with ordinary idiots, going on to the super
idiot, then the arch idiot. The fourth, the hopeless idiot, was again
and again chosen by Gurdjieff for an explanation of what he meant
by dying an honourable death. The false hopeless idiot is satisfied
with himself and does not see that he is a 'candidate for perishing
like a dog!' The true hopeless idiot sees his own complete nothingness and does not realize that this death of self is the guarantee of his
resurrection. From this stage he becomes a compassionate idiot, whose
reason has opened to enter into the sufferings of others. The sixth is
the squirming idiot who is not yet ready for help. There are then
three 'geometric' idiots—square, round and zigzag—who represent
stages in the establishment of true reason, at first only momentarily,
then comes the discovery of one's own identity and third the
desperate struggle to break free. Gurdjieff said of him that he 'has
five Fridays in the week'—an example of a meaningless saying that
communicates better than much good sense.

At the Saturday evening meals, the toasts seldom went beyond the
zigzag idiot, unless he wished to associate someone present with
the characteristics of one of the next series. These are the enlightened,
the doubting and swaggering idiots. Beyond these again are idiots
whose characteristics are deep in their essential nature. At each stage
there is a death and resurrection before a new gradation of reason is
attained.

Gurdjieff gave a most significant twist to the Science of Idiotism when he explained that no one could go beyond the enlightened idiot unless he had first 'consciencely descended' to the first gradation of the ordinary idiot. His explanations made it clear that he was referring to the same secret as Jesus when he said : "Except ye become as little children, ye shall in no wise enter the kingdom of heaven." Having heard scores of times Gurdjieff's explanations of the idiot toasts, I can only marvel at the insights into human nature that he was able to express in such simple terms. His talks about the tragic situation of the enlightened idiot whom 'even God could not help' invariably sent a shudder of horror down my spine. Nothing has done so much to convince me that we must totally shed any pretension to be 'special people' if we hope to attain true freedom.

When I was at the Prieuré, it was already known that Gurdjieff intended to take a group to America to demonstrate the sacred dances and exercises. When I spoke to him about my plans, he even suggested that I might go with him and help with the translation of his talks. One day Gurdjieff asked me how long I could stay at the Prieuré because he wanted to prepare my programme of work. I explained that I had little money, but hoped within six months to settle the affairs I was engaged in and then could help him. He said he did not need my money, but my work, and offered to provide me with money. I little dreamed of the dire straits in which he was at the time; but even believing that he had limitless resources, I could not bring myself to accept his help. I realized later how much my pride and self-love were involved, but at the time I thought I would soon be able to return. As things turned out I left the Prieuré in August 1923 and did not set eyes on Gurdjieff again for twenty-five years.

Work at the Prieuré at the close of the first year was focussed on the demonstration of Central Asian dance and ritual given at the Champs-Élysée Théâtre in December 1923. It made a notable impact. Miss Alexander decribed their departure for America :

"A few weeks later they were in New York, where groups had previously been organized. It was at these meetings that Mr. Gurdjieff, with a minimum of English words, spoke of the principles and methods of his teaching.

"They had little direct contact with the Americans and little opportunity to explore their city. They lived in furnished rooms, and, as at the Prieuré, practised the movements and exercises. Performances in the little Knickerbocker Theater were followed by visits to Boston and Philadelphia. At Boston they drew an audience from the professors and students of Harvard University."

The visit was a success financially and enabled the debts of the Prieuré to be paid off. There was much publicity but little understanding of what Gurdjieff wished to convey. He returned to France in April and gave himself six months to prepare for a return visit.

All plans were abruptly changed and many hopes were shattered on July 6th, 1924, when Gurdjieff, as he himself put it, "crashed with a car going at ninety kilometres an hour into a great tree alongside the road in Fontainebleau forest". Almost any other man would have died from the injuries he received. He was brought first to the hospital at Avon and soon afterwards to the Prieuré while still unconscious.

Many stories are told of the events of the succeeding days. There is little consistency in the accounts, which is not surprising as all were in a state of near hysteria from shock and grief. The English tried to carry on as best they could. For them Gurdjieff had not yet become a legend. It was otherwise with the Russians. Helpless refugees in a foreign land, few of them knowing the language and most of them believing Gurdjieff to be a superhuman being, they were indeed sorely stricken. The English were distressed to see them sitting silent and crushed, huddled together on the floor outside his bedroom.

Thus ended the second phase of Gurdjieff's life story. The great plan to set up a world organization to promulgate his ideas had to be abandoned; but his true life's work had scarcely begun and his chief legacy to prosperity was to come in the next phase. No one could have guessed what form it was to take.

7

Gurdjieff as Author

THE eleven years from 1924 to 1935 were dominated by Gurdjieff's decision taken when he was recovering from his accident to transmit his ideas in written form. When the accident occurred, he was forty-seven years old, and his writing phase ended when he was in his fifty-eighth year. This decision originated from the wish to "share with the other creatures of our Common Father similar to himself almost all the previously unknown mysteries of the inner world of man which he had accidentally learned". He had long recognized that his discoveries would have to be published in order to reach all the people who could benefit from them. He paid special attention to men like Ouspensky and Orage who had an established reputation as writers. Ouspensky said that Gurdjieff's power lay in the use of the spoken word. He called him the finest lecturer he had ever heard, able to convey to an audience, large or small, a sense of the reality and immediacy of the theme that he was exposing, in a way that even the most talented professional lecturer could not emulate. On the other hand, Ouspensky had a poor opinion of Gurdjieff's writing and said that, when it came to the written word, he could express Gurdjieff's ideas very much better than he could himself. Ouspensky describes how at his very first meeting, in 1915, he had been invited to hear a reading of a fragment called *Glimpses of Truth*, which had been written by one of Gurdjieff's pupils. He was asked his opinion as to its suitability for publication and had been obliged to say that it would not do. It was written in an amateurish way and failed to convey what it was really about. Shortly afterwards, Ouspensky had spoken about his intention to write, and Gurdjieff had agreed that he should do so, but only after verifying the essentials, and when he felt himself competent to give a satisfying exposition.

During the period from 1909 to 1924, nothing had, in fact, appeared except the prospectuses of the Institute published in Tiflis, Constantinople and Paris. The Institute was the core of Gurdjieff's work and he counted upon it to accomplish his aim. When he came to the moment of decision and found that he had to abandon the Institute, he once again felt his way by making experiments. To understand the extraordinary situation that had arisen, we must try to reconstruct the events that immediately followed his accident.

He was, in fact, so close to death that the doctors warned his family that there was little or no chance of his surviving. Only his immediate family were allowed to nurse him, his mother, his wife, Mme Ostrowska, and his sister, Sophie Ivanovna, to whom he was deeply attached. They were there throughout the first agonizing weeks, his mother having arrived with Sophie Ivanovna and her son Valentin in 1923. Encouraged by the success of the American trip, he had sent for his brother, Dimitri, who arrived with his wife and three daughters about the time of the accident. These circumstances reveal a significant pattern in Gurdjieff's life, for he noted the closing in of the family at critical moments.

The period was one of extreme tension. The Russian pupils were bewildered and hardly knew what was to become of them. Few of the English visitors to the Prieuré remained. Ouspensky had cut off all relations with Gurdjieff, but his wife, Sophie Grigorevna, remained at the Prieuré and, with Mme de Hartmann, kept the establishment going. Miss Alexander and others were so distressed by the strange atmosphere that they left the Prieuré.

Those of us who were in London at that time were exposed to the same sense of foreboding when Ouspensky spoke about Gurdjieff and the events in France. At a small meeting to which, though much the youngest, I was invited, he gave his own opinion, emphasising that it was no more than this. He said that, when a man was destined for a very high spiritual development, he must necessarily pass through a critical stage when the upper and lower natures of his self were divided: a great inner war then begins, which affects all around him, exposing them to risks which they may not be strong enough to meet. For this reason, he had advised Mrs. Philipson to withdraw the two orphan Polish boys whom she had adopted and sent to live with Mr. Gurdjieff in the Prieuré. She had hoped that, by being brought up with him, they would be able in the future to serve the 'Work' in a very special way. Our distress was accentuated when he later hinted to us that, in his opinion, Gurdjieff had gone out of his mind. In fact, those who had access to no other source of information continued to believe that Gurdjieff had simply gone mad; some even thought he was dead. This indicates the degree of isolation that Ouspensky imposed on his own followers.

At that time, Jane Heap, who had come to the Prieuré with her two adopted sons, decided to leave them at the Prieuré where they remained all through this period. One of them has written about his experiences, evidently unaware of the intensity of the events that were taking place around him. The sense of disaster which Miss Alexander felt in the Russian followers of Gurdjieff was perhaps due to an awareness of the situation greater than that of the English students.

Gurdjieff did not recover until it was too late to save the Institute. He wrote about this: "As a final chord, this battered physical body of mine crashed with an automobile going at a speed of ninety kilometres an hour into a very thick tree one week after my return to Europe from America. From such a 'promenade', it was discovered that I was not destroyed and several months later, to my misfortune, into my totally mutilated body there returned in full force, with all its former attributes, my consciousness." There is here a discrepancy of dates, for the accident occurred on the 6th of July 1924, several weeks after his return. He had, in fact, been very active during that time, having considerably improved his finances during the American tour and hoping to go again in the autumn. The accident changed everything.

Two unmistakable facts very soon became clear. First, due to his forced retirement from the Institute, all that he had prepared in the preceding three years in order to fulfil his inner aim was wasted. This aim had been formulated in 1909 as being "to discover some means for destroying in people the predilection for suggestibility which causes them to fall easily under the influence of mass-hypnosis". Also, if the damage to his physical body from the motor accident could be repaired, it would take time. As Gurdjieff came to himself and took stock of the situation, he saw that everything had gone to pieces. He was bitterly disappointed by the failure of Ouspensky and the English group to rally to his support after the accident. Nearly all his help came from America through Orage, who had thrown himself wholeheartedly into Gurdjieff's work, undaunted by the accident which ended guidance upon which he had counted when he undertook to organize groups in America. Perhaps, as Phillip Mairet has said in his *Life of Orage*, it was necessary that Orage should be thrown upon himself. He was far too much of an individualist to be able to play the role of second-in-command. So it came about that Orage was able to use his brilliant capacity for presentation, to put Gurdjieff's ideas to groups of interested people in New York, and later in Chicago and Boston. Although Gurdjieff recognized with gratitude that the money which Orage sent him regularly did enable the Prieuré to keep going, he could not accept that Orage's undertaking was the natural development of what he himself had launched a few months earlier. In fact, he regarded the work of the Institute as having been brought to a premature close and changed his plans accordingly.

It is not easy to say exactly what Gurdjieff expected from his pupils. He wrote: "One night, while still in bed and suffering from the insomnia which was habitual to me at that time, stirred by association, and remembering a thought concerning a plan which, during the last two or three months, had always perturbed me and even finally obsessed me—and which should have been realized at the time when I drew up the general scheme of means of attaining the aforesaid fundamental aim of all my life, which included the intention to spread the essence of my ideas by means of literature also, and which failed on account of the untrustworthiness and vicious idleness of those people whom I had specially prepared during many years for that specific purpose—it suddenly occurred to me that there was no reason why I should not take advantage of the present situation and should not begin to dictate myself the material for the realization of this aim."

This condemnation was not quite fair, inasmuch as he himself had stipulated that no notes should be taken of his lectures, and that nothing should be written until he was ready for it. We do not know what passed between Gurdjieff and Ouspensky that led to their break in January 1924, when Gurdjieff was leaving for America, but it is very probable that it had something to do with money, about which Ouspensky himself was very sensitive and Gurdjieff very wild.

However this may be, Gurdjieff tells us that, by the autumn of 1924, he could already move about the house and even, with the help of someone to support him, go into Paris by car. This was, for Gurdjieff, a period of great anguish in which his life's work seemed doomed to perish. His sufferings were aggravated by the realization that his wife and mother were both in the terminal stages of mortal sickness. His mother was suffering from a chronic liver complaint and Mme Ostrowska from cancer. He describes in several places the prodigious effort he had made to cure his wife's cancer by a technique learned in Central Asia which made use of astral power but which called for daily sessions which he alone could conduct. Hints he dropped later corroborate the view that the decision to close the work of the Institute was not due solely to his weak state of health. He spoke of his motor accident as the manifestation of a power hostile to his aim, a power with which he could not contend. He decided that he must change all his plans. In his own words: "Since I had not, when in full strength and health, succeeded in introducing in practice into the life of people the beneficial truths elucidated for them by me, then I must at least, at any cost, succeed in doing this in theory, before my death." This was written in 1934,[a] at the very end of his writing period, and one must presume that it represents his own considered opinion.

We must now return to the beginning of this writing phase. Just as he had made experiments when he started organizing groups, so now he experimented with writing. He says that it was not until the end of 1924, several months after the accident, that he was able to do this, initially dictating to a secretary. He tried to convey different aspects of his teaching in the form of short scenarios for the theatre or cinema, of which we know of four:

> The Cocainists
> The Chiromancy of the Stock Exchange
> The Unconscious Murder
> The Three Brothers

In the last of these, he represented the three-fold nature of man, physical, emotional and mental, by three brothers. In dialogues of the three characters, he "introduced certain ideas which have come down from ancient times, when the science of medicine was very highly developed, ideas of what is useful or harmful, satisfactory or unsatisfactory for one or other of the characters of the scenario in the process of transforming of this or that substance."[b]

[a] *Life is Real Only Then, When "I Am"*, Book IV.
[b] *The Herald of the Coming Good*, p. 44.

One scenario was based upon a legend which he had heard in childhood about the appearance of the first human beings on Earth. This seems to be the only reference that Gurdjieff makes to his source for Beelzebub as the character to represent the growing compassion with which an impartial being would survey the history of mankind upon the Earth. The reference to a legend directs our attention to Babylon, where Beelzebub was a minor member of the Chaldaean Pantheon and entered into various myths, rather than to the New Testament, where he is a synonym for Satan. Some of the main themes are examined in the next chapter. While in 1925 he wrote in outline the different fragments intended for publication, Gurdjieff had already decided to write three books. He intended with the contents of the first to achieve the destruction in the consciousness and feelings of people of deeply rooted convictions which in his opinion are false and quite contradictory to reality; with the second to prove that there exist other ways of perceiving reality and to indicate their direction; and with the third to share the possibilities which he had discovered of touching reality and, if so desired, even merging with it.

When he began to write he again encouraged visitors, now mainly from America, to come to the Prieuré. They came no longer to an organized 'Work' but rather to see him personally and to follow up the teaching that they had received from Orage. Orage himself used to come over at least once every year.

It is interesting here to look at this situation in the accounts given by the pupils who were there. According to Miss Ethel Merston, she co-operated with the Armenian-speaking students in making the translations. It is commonly said that these translations were made by Orage; but, in fact, Orage only visited the Prieuré at rare intervals and the work of translation was done continuously. Orage made various brilliant suggestions, and I believe at a later stage helped with the extraordinary idiom which was finally evolved. The work of translation was a strange process. At the start, Gurdjieff dictated in Russian to Mme de Hartmann, but as soon as he could write himself, he did so in Armenian, his mother tongue. This was translated into the poor Russian of the Armenians, improved by Mme de Hartmann and finally, it was translated into English by the English-speaking students. There was no one available who could translate into French, but a German secretary, who came to join Gurdjieff at the Prieuré shortly after his accident and who later became Mrs. Louise

March, undertook the German translation.

For a picture of the Prieuré as it appeared to the students, I quote again from Miss Alexander, who returned to the Prieuré after a long stay in Switzerland and Italy. She writes: "Life at the Prieuré had completely changed. The Institute as formerly organized was closed, 'never again,' Gurdjieff had said, 'to be re-opened'. Nor was he himself accessible as formerly he had been. Of direct teaching there was none, neither of movements nor of exercises. People could come and go, and, for themselves, perhaps discover there new values. In the salon, we listened to his music, and heard the first rough drafts of *Beelzebub* read aloud. For the rest we were free more or less to work each according to his conscience."

Almost as soon as he started writing, he also turned his attention to music. Between 1925 and 1927, he composed more than a hundred short pieces on Eastern and religious themes. Gurdjieff said that certain ideas could be grasped only if the emotions are tuned into them. He composed music to be played before the reading of particular chapters, and demonstrated the difference in understanding that this made possible. Other pieces were evocative of the life of Central Asia and based on recollections of the sacred music and dancing of various dervish orders. There was also a remarkable group of religious pieces, predominantly on the theme of death and resurrection.

Miss Alexander describes this period in her journal:

"From 1926, the Prieuré again came to life. Gurdjieff was, for the most part, inaccessible; but, when he did join in the activities, particularly on Saturday evenings, the feeling of security returned to the house. His writing came first and no one dared to interrupt him on any pretext. In 1926 and until the summer of 1927, all seemed to be going well. Gurdjieff was immersed in his writing but many Americans came and went. Some spent their vacation at the Prieuré, others were allowed to stay longer. Pupils received more personal attention, though there was no organized work such as there had been in 1923.

"He did not seek the solitude of his room, but did much of his writing away from the Prieuré. The Grand Café in Paris was named his 'Paris Office'. He also travelled, mostly by car, to the Alps and south of France and wrote in cafés, wayside inns or in the car. Often he would invite some of the American pupils to go with him on his motor trips. These were usually prepared in much excitement and, when he **was** ready to go, everyone gathered round to see him start. His departures were always disconcerting. Very often he would fix a time for going and would be ready half an hour earlier when those invited to go with him had to drop their preparations and rush to join him in the car. At other times, he would suddenly decide to work on *Beelzebub* and would sit at the wheel of the car for half an hour or an hour while everyone waited to know whether he would leave. Sometimes, ten minutes after leaving, the car would return, having failed to take the steep hill leading out of the Prieuré up into the forests of Fontainebleau. Often a mechanical failure would mean a return within a few hours. The journeys were terrifying for the people who could bring themselves to trust Gurdjieff's driving. Indeed there was certain justification, in view of his notorious propensity to accidents, and some people avoided going in his car and preferred to follow behind, which he only rarely permitted."

All had the impression that Gurdjieff was interested in their personal work and the amount of attention which he gave, especially to visitors from America, was astonishing.

It must be understood that the individual pupils, especially those who had been with him for years, were themselves going through very critical phases. Everyone was faced with the dilemma of dependence on Gurdjieff and identification with him. He had an unlimited power of instilling hope and confidence by his mere presence. However strangely or harshly he might treat his pupils, they could never doubt his infinite goodwill. Those who were able to make real progress knew that they must ultimately find the resources within themselves.

Gurdjieff had intended to publish the First Series of his work, *Beelzebub's Tales* in 1928. However, in order to judge the effect on different people, he held frequent public readings of *Beelzebub*. The inability of listeners to grasp his intention forced him to undertake a total revision of all that he had written. This brought him near to despair so acute that he even contemplated suicide.

In 1934 he described the situation in 1927 as he then saw it: "I think any reader can easily represent to himself what a dilemma then arose for me when, after working for almost three years with unimaginable difficulties, and being ready to die happily, I clearly understood that, of these writings of mine, people who did not know me personally would understand absolutely nothing."[a] He says that he finally came to a decision on the 6th November 1927. At that time, his health was bad and early one morning in one of the night cafés at Montmartre in Paris, tired to exhaustion from his 'black thoughts', he decided to go home and try to sleep a little. His miserable state that morning was further aggravated by the fact that during the preceding weeks he had not slept more than one or two hours in twenty-four and this last night he had not been able to sleep at all. He saw that it was necessary for him to re-write everything that he had written in order that it might be accessible to everyone. But he was confronted with the precarious state of his health. He writes:

"If all this which was written during three or four years of almost unceasing day and night work, were to be rewritten from the beginning . . . at least the same length of time would be required . . . But time is needed for the exposition of the second and third series; and time will be also necessary for inducting into practical life the essence of these writings of mine . . . But where can so much time be obtained? . . ." He says that his health was such that all the doctors who knew him and he himself, as an experienced diagnostician, would say that his expectation of life was not more than two or three years and that it would be impossible for him in this time to fulfil all his objectives. He says that he then decided to "Mobilize all capacities and possibilities in my common presence, both those personally achieved and those inherited, and until the moment of the arrival of the next New Year, which moment is that of my appearance on God's earth, to discover some possible means of satisfactorily emerging from such a situation; if unable to discover this means, then on the evening of the last day of the Old Year to begin to destroy all my writings, calculating the time so that at midnight with the last page to destroy myself also."

He says that after this, while trying outwardly to live and work just as before, lest his unusual state be noticed by those around him, he thought only of how to emerge from his desperate situation. Time went on, the Christmas holidays were approaching. One day, physically exhausted from a perilous drive over a pass in the Pyrenees, while sitting in a provincial café, he put the following question to himself: "What now, exactly, will it be necessary for me to do so that first of all I myself may be completely satisfied with my

[a] *Life Is Real Only Then, When "I Am"*, Book IV, Chapter I.

writing and, secondly, that completely corresponding conditions may be created for its spreading?" The answer that was formed was that both these wishes could be fulfilled only if three definite aims were to be realized. First, he should rewrite all his manuscripts, but in a form he now understood. Second, he should clarify for himself certain obscure and deep questions concerning the common psyche of man, and use this in his writings. Finally, he should seek physical and spiritual renewal so that he could direct the publication of his books with the energy and persistence that were peculiar to him in his youth. He calculated that these aims would require about seven years to complete.

For weeks he pondered over the problem. One might have expected a man with his immense energy and self-command to have confidence that he could see the task through. This is a mistake that such men often make: but Gurdjieff had a profound understanding of energy transformation and knew that he needed more energy than could come from his body. He had already expounded, in the early version of *Beelzebub's Tales*, the principle of conscious labour and intentional suffering: but here it could not be applied directly, for his physical body was about to collapse.

On his return to the Prieuré, instead of going into the house, he went to sit upon the bench where his wife and mother used to come and sit with him when he was resting from his writing. It then suddenly struck him that his output, or, as he put it—his 'labour-ability'—had been proportional to the intensity of suffering that he had experienced on account of the illness and approaching death of these two women, particularly that of his wife. He asked himself how it could come about that involuntary suffering of this kind could have such a positive effect upon his creative work. As a result of this, he began to see a principle connected with suffering which he had not previously understood, and which held the solution of his problem. This came to him while he watched the children around the Christmas tree on Christmas Day in 1927. By the following April he had completely worked out his plan. Thus he was able to complete the rewriting of *Beelzebub* and to go to America in order to raise the money for its publication and for renewing the life of the Prieuré.

We can begin to see that his extraordinary behaviour in 1928 and 1929 towards those who were closest to him was necessary for the creation of conditions for more active work. It is interesting to note

an observation perhaps familiar to those who have been seriously ill
and have been visited by friends. He says :

"Once during my reflections about the construction and functioning of the nervous system of man, I, by the way, remembered, and,
thinking further, very definitely established the following:

"During the second period of my, so to say 'Great Illness' after
the automobile accident, that is, when my consciousness returned,
while my body was still helpless, and when I was visited by different
friends, then, no matter whether they talked to me, or just remained
silent, for several hours after their departure, I felt very badly. Their
sincere sympathy in reality gave birth in me every time to thoughts,
which may be expressed as follows : 'came-sucked-me-out-like-vam-
pires-and-went-away'."

Before putting his plan into practice, Gurdjieff took what he calls
an oath before his own essence, an irrevocable decision, on the night
of the 6th May 1928. He decided, "under the pretext of different
worthy reasons, to remove from my eyesight all those who by this or
that make my life too comfortable." This sentence, which is really the
key to all that Gurdjieff wrote in this Fourth Book of *Life is Real
Only Then, When "I Am"*, recalls his early decisions regarding the
suffering that was required in order to fulfil his aims. Because of his
consummate ability as an actor, none of those with whom he was
living at that time could understand what it was that he had in mind.
They saw it, as an action that was for their own good, to place them
in front of opportunities of suffering for their benefit. They did not
realize that it was a necessity for Gurdjieff, to enable him to complete
his mission.

The visible outcome was the very difficult decision of sending away from Prieuré many of his closest friends and pupils.
He did so in such a way as to create opportunities for them
and they read this as important moments in their own development and their relationship with him. Among those who went
in this way were Dr. Stjernwal, his wife and children, who had been
with him for a very long time. I think he was probably the oldest
surviving pupil. He had also sent away Mr. and Mme de Hartmann.
The manner of their leaving was characteristic. Mme de Hartmann
had been the mainstay of life at the Prieuré and Mr. de Hartmann
himself the invaluable collaborator in the creation not only of the
music but also the sacred dances and movements. Mme de Hartmann
had immense organizing ability and was deeply devoted to Gurdjieff;

she had a practical understanding of the difficulty of relating the Eastern to the Western attitudes to life. Gurdjieff was aware that neither Thomas de Hartmann nor Olga were liberating themselves from their identification with him and with one another, an identification which hardly anyone who remained a long time in contact with Gurdjieff was able to avoid. Gurdjieff himself describes the incident which he created that was to make it impossible for the Hartmanns to remain. He told this story more than once over the dinner table in Paris many years later. He said that he had become aware that it was undesirable for his work and also for their personal development that people should make him too comfortable. The culminating incident occurred at the time of his Name Day Feast of St. George on the 23rd April 1928. He had spoken of his fondness for English kipper and said how pleased he would be if he could eat it for his birthday. It appears that Mme de Hartmann had immediately telephoned London to arrange for a case of kippers to be sent over, picked up in Paris and brought straight out to the Prieuré where they were prepared for the supper that evening. Gurdjieff made this a pretext for sending them away. The de Hartmanns went to live in Paris in 1929, on Gurdjieff's very strong insistence, but Mme de Hartmann visited the Prieuré from time to time. It was also about this time, I believe, that Alexander de Salzmann, who had joined him in Tiflis in 1918 and had been with him for ten years, helping him in the most decisive way in all aspects of his work, was obliged to leave and go off to Switzerland, where he became seriously ill and finally died.

We know that at this time he was also making things very difficult for Orage. The year before, two of his younger pupils, Ferapontoff and Ivanoff, had left for Australia; afterwards they joined me in Athens, and from them I heard many stories of the Prieuré. But neither they nor anyone who had been sent away diminished their loyalty and devotion to Gurdjieff. All that they could say was that they were not able to understand what it was that he required of them. It is significant that the flow of musical composition ceased in 1927. He never again composed music. It seems that those around him could not read the signs.

It was not until much later that he revealed his own personal reasons for these traumatic actions. They were necessary to enable him to gain the bodily and mental energy for completing his task. It is a very remarkable fact that no one who has written about Gurdjieff

—even from the most intimate acquaintance like the Hartmanns—seems to have understood what he himself had to suffer at that time. They saw him always as their teacher, concerned with the spiritual progress of his pupils, whereas, he was concerned with the fulfilment of his mission, which he saw upon a very much larger scale than those around him. He was not concerned with the immediate present but with the impact which his work and his ideas could have on the world over a long period of years. This is why he so frequently refers to the realization of his aims after his death.

Gurdjieff gave some hints that at this time he was not taking decisions entirely on his own initiative, but was consulting with the school with which he had previously been connected. He describes the period of Christmas 1927 to May 1928 as one in which he worked at his manuscripts only a few hours in the morning and the evening, the rest of the day being devoted to "writing letters of enquiry to some of his friends whom he respected or to thinking and working out in his mind the details of the general programme". Now these "friends whom he respected" would almost certainly not be his pupils in Europe or America. None of these could advise or help him, and indeed, he carefully hid his real problems from them.

Persons who were with him at that time, notably Miss Merston, were confident that he remained in touch with the schools in Turkestan. He spoke to them more than once of having arranged for certain people to go there for further training, and they saw letters arriving with postmarks from these countries. In fact, he continued to be in correspondence with friends in Asia right up till the end of his life. Many of us who went to visit him in Paris in 1948 and 1949 believed that he made more than one visit to Asia under the pretext of going to Germany. But this was always carefully concealed and, so far as those around him could tell, he was working entirely on his own and was in no need of personal help beyond care for his body.

The arrangements that he made for the carrying on of his work were so successful that he was able to complete the rewriting of *Beelzebub* within eighteen months. It seems that there were certain crucial sections that were dubious. We shall see later that he completely rewrote certain chapters, such as "Purgatory", even after working entirely on his own and was in no need of personal help ing:

"Firstly, 'puffed' three small booklets into ten substantial volumes.

Secondly, undersood from all sides not only different deep-rooted *minutiae* of the common psyche of man, suspected by me and intriguing me all my life, but constated unexpectedly many such 'delicacies', which, had they been known to Mr. Beelzebub, would, I dare say, grow the horns mentioned by me in the next to the last chapter of the first series of my writings, even on his hooves. Thirdly, my health is now in such condition at the present time, that not only, as you may see, I live and write such an already ultra-fantastic book, but intend to outlive all my past, present and future conscious enemies."

The steps Gurdjieff took to remedy his situation in October 1927 are vividly described in Chapter 1 Book IV of the *Third Series*. The distinction between involuntary and voluntary suffering is made clear in this passage. Chapter 2 of the same book, he compares voluntary and intentional suffering. All three kinds of suffering can bring great benefits. The voluntary can help us to achieve external aims while the intentional can transform our inner nature. The successful use of suffering led to the completion of *Beelzebub's Tales*.

With the work again going well, 1928 and 1929 were cheerful years, especially for visitors from abroad. Many Americans came in the summer of 1928 and again in 1929, and in 1930 he went again to the United States. He reports that he succeeded in fulfilling the greater part of the task set for him "in spite of all kinds of obstructive factors, those which arise according to law, as well as those engendered by various types amidst us who, unfortunately, bear also the name of 'man' ".

Gurdjieff regarded the writing of his second work as a means of refreshing himself from the very tense and difficult work of completing *Beelzebub*. Certainly *Meetings with Remarkable Men* is written with a much easier style, but it is a very profound work, the meaning of which escapes the casual reader. He continued to work, as before, travelling, principally in France, and writing almost solely in public places, such as restaurants, cafés, "dance-halls" and other—he calls them—"kindred 'temples' of contemporary morality". He recounts that, freed somewhat from his writing, he began to observe more carefully those who had some interest in his ideas. He was particularly concerned with those who had already begun to put into practice experiments which were supposed to correspond to his own ideas. He then says that he found something wrong—"so definitely 'all-wrong', that it was noticeable, of course with a certain knowledge of observation, even to every average person". At subsequent meetings, he began to observe them particularly, to understand how this came to be.

Among the followers of his ideas in New York, he observed the same phenomenon. This produced such a deep impression on him that he saw that it was necessary to take some drastic action. Arriving on the 13th November 1930, he attended a general meeting in the Carnegie Hall. While Orage was absent in London, a great number of people had come, many of whom had visited the Château du Prieuré.

There followed the incident of Gurdjieff's public repudiation of Orage, of Orage's arrival in New York and his volunteering to sign the undertaking of his group members not to have any further association with Mr. Orage. Gurdjieff described with great gusto the way in which the groups of Americans reacted to this shock. There is no indication that Orage or anyone else could see what were the reasons for his extraordinary behaviour. Orage took the breaking up of his groups simply as a lesson for himself and a means of insuring that they would make a fresh start. For Gurdjieff this was all part of the conditions which he created in order to make the fulfilment of his mission possible.

In presenting the situation to the American groups, Gurdjieff made use of the last chapter of *Beelzebub's Tales*, entitled "From The Author". This chapter contains the kind of presentation which Gurdjieff made during the First World War years to the groups in Russia. It brings back what he said in his lectures at the Prieuré and when he first went to America in 1924, but links it all with the introduction of new methods of work, of which most of his groups had previously no idea. Indeed, the new exercises that were being introduced in 1930 and the early part of 1931 seem to have been different from the exercises which he had shown people individually at the Prieuré between 1924 and 1929.

When Gurdjieff returned to Europe in 1930 after the break-up of the old Orage groups, there was a very small sum left in the treasury to be used for any purposes connected with his work. Paul Anderson, who was then treasurer, worked out a proposal for producing a mimeographed edition of *Beelzebub* from the chapters Gurdjieff had left with them. The funds available were just enough to pay for editing, proof-reading and printing of 102 copies, but not for binding. Two were reserved for Paul and Naomi Anderson who had done all the work, and the remainder were sold at prices varying from $10 to $100 according to what pupils could afford. One of the sets, beautifully bound, was given to me by Wym Nyland when I went to New York in 1952 to help in launching the Gurdjieff Foundation.

No authorized text was left either by Orage or by Gurdjieff himself. In some cases passages were missing and had to be reconstructed from memory. This was possible because the New York group had heard the chapters read many times from the time when Gurdjieff first brought them to New York in 1929. No one believed that a complete version could be produced, but it was done within three or four months. Copies were sent to Gurdjieff who smiled happily and seemed to be pleased. Copies were also sent to Orage for himself and Ouspensky.

The version of *Beelzebub's Tales* that was published at that time is of great interest. It is in some ways easier to understand than the final version, published in 1950, and the French translation, published a few years later. The greatest changes were made in the chapter "Purgatory". He also changed some of the 'key words', particularly the words describing the two fundamental cosmic laws. In the early version, the Law of Threefoldness is called *Triamonia*, whereas in the published version it is called the Law *Triamazikamno*, which in colloquial Greek means: I put three together. In the same way, the Law of Sevenfoldness in the old version is called the Law *Eftalogodiksis*, whereas in the later version it is called the Law *Heptaparapashinokh*, combining Greek and Armenian derivations. Why did Gurdjieff make these changes in the description of the Cosmic Laws? He invented all these words in order to give the reader the feeling of being in the presence of a Being of a different nature to ourselves, a Being who did not originate on this planet, and he achieves this effect in a masterly way. But, of course, there is very much more to this revision than the new words. In particular, the old version is much more explicit of the stages in man's development, which become disguised in the later version and are much harder for the reader to understand. Why should Gurdjieff have made a chapter that was already difficult even harder, if indeed the intention was that *Beelzebub's Tales* should be a means of bringing the ideas to the notice of the general public? Only someone familiar with his ideas, and prepared to devote a lot of time and hard study to the chapter could make anything of it. Gurdjieff has shown in his *Meetings with Remarkable Men* that he could tell stories in simple language, without confronting the reader with any linguistic problems. We also know that he spent no fewer than seven years in the writing of *Beelzebub*—as he himself says, sparing himself neither day nor night, constantly writing and rewriting. Therefore, we must assume that the writing of *Beelzebub* was in the form which he intended, and that the alterations were deliberate, in spite of making the ideas less accessible to the unprepared reader.

These changes in *Beelzebub* are striking enough, but there is an even greater contrast with the presentation of the ideas of Ouspensky, who purports to describe as literally as possible everything that Gurdjieff said to the group in Moscow in 1915, 1916 and 1917, and in the Caucasus in 1918. This description, given in *In Search of the Miraculous*, is much easier to understand. For this reason, this book has been much more widely read than *Beelzebub*. This Gurdjieff foresaw. When in 1948, Mme Ouspensky sent over the typescript of *Fragments of an Unknown Teaching*, as it was then called, and Gurdjieff had this read out in front of him, he constantly remarked that the presentation was not as satisfactory as *Beelzebub* and insisted that we should turn to the latter as the authentic source. Moreover, when the question of publication arose in 1949, Gurdjieff, to my knowledge, was very insistent that the publication of *In Search of the Miraculous* should be deferred until *Beelzebub* had appeared and had been on the market for a number of months. This wish of his was ignored after he died and the two books were brought out together.

It might have been supposed that Ouspensky, with his love of clarity and simple expression, bowdlerized Gurdjieff's more difficult presentation to express the ideas in terms more acceptable to the reader. But this does not seem to have been the case. Ouspensky was most concientious in his wish to convey just what he had learned from Gurdjieff, and, when he inserted views of his own, as for example, all his speculations about time scales in Chapter 15 of *In Search of the Miraculous*, he quite frankly says that these were his own ideas, and not Gurdjieff's. Rather it appears that Gurdjieff, having decided to throw open his ideas to anyone who chose to buy his books, wished to safeguard their real significance by making them accessible only to those who were prepared to make a very big effort. In doing this, however, he fell between two stools. On the one hand, he was very anxious that *Beelzebub* should be widely read. He took great pains to arrange this. Money was collected to pay for the printing so that copies could be sold at cost. He constantly asked his pupils to make sure that *Beelzebub* would be widely publicized, and read in public wherever possible. He certainly counted upon it making a very considerable impact in the world and he wanted to see it translated into as many languages as possible. On the other hand he was impelled to write more and more obscurely, and to break up certain ideas in such a way that it became possible to grasp them as a whole only by bringing together passages occurring in quite different contexts of the book. Sometimes it is possible to reconstruct only by referring to his other writings as well.

Gurdjieff was no doubt well aware that he was placed in this ambiguous position. His aim was to spread the ideas widely and yet to ensure that they would become accessible only to those who could use them properly and have the right respect for them. And the way in which *Beelzebub* was written was best calculated to serve this two-fold purpose.

We pass on to the years after 1931. He not only undertook the final revision of *Beelzebub's Tales*, particularly the chapter "Purgatory", but also did as much as possible in writing his final book. His second book, *Meetings with Remarkable Men*, is the least controversial. The only important omission from it, as published, was a chapter devoted to Prince Nijeradze, which, though several times rewritten, was never completed. There are two discordant translations of the original Armenian fragments, neither of which show the conclusion which he wished to reach. It seems likely that the omitted chapter contained a reference to Gurdjieff's search which he might have felt went too far towards disclosing the real nature of the source with which he had been and still was in contact.

We gather that Prince Nijeradze had been concerned in some embarrassing episode connected with the difficulty Gurdjieff came up against, through having broken some of the rules of one of the Brotherhoods where he had been receiving help and teaching. One who heard the chapter read in 1933, recounts that it produced a profound impression by its account of the state of a man who wakes up after dying and realizes that he has lost the chief instrument of his life, his body, and recalls all he could have done with it while he was still alive.

The book is notable for the fact that the most exciting and interesting passages are themselves absent. I refer to the three occasions when Gurdjieff said that he and the group who were with him received teaching of the utmost importance connected with the three bodies of man. In each case he promised that it would be included as a special chapter of his final work. On the first occasion the group, including Ekim Bey, was travelling in northern Persia and met a solitary dervish. In the course of a stay of a few days, the dervish gave them an exposition of the physical body of man and its needs and possibilities. On the next occasion they were in the mountainous region of the Pamirs and met a fakir who had formerly been an artillery commander in the Afghan Army. Here also, in a few days' stay, a special teaching was given to them on the astral body of man and its possibilities. Finally in the last published chapter, "Professor Skridlov", he describes a lengthy stay at a monastery in Kafiristan and the meeting there with Father Giovanni. Father Giovanni finishes his talks with an explanation about faith and its place in human life. This leads up to an account of the soul of man, how it develops and the conditions under which it is possible for man to possess his own soul.

So far as I am aware, none of these promised documents is extant and there is an indication that, if they were written, Gurdjieff destroyed them at some stage when he came to the conclusion that it would be unwise to let them become generally available. He had often threatened to destroy manuscripts and many of his American pupils believed that there had been a holocaust in which the missing sections perished. Presumably he judged that the information was of a nature that it could be misused if it got into the wrong hands.

So it comes about that his last work, *Life is Real Only Then, When "I Am"*, remains incomplete. It comprises a first section, or book, based on lectures given in New York in 1930 and 1931. The second and third books are entirely lacking; and the fourth book, consisting of the prologue and first two chapters, gives the most interesting disclosure of the inner world problems which Gurdjieff had to face and the process of his own spiritual evolution. The final chapter, called the "Inner and Outer World of Man" is incomplete, and it stops tantilizingly when Gurdjieff is about to disclose the secret which he had discovered for the prolongation of human life. Nevertheless, the secret of this is indirectly given for an attentive reader in the earlier part of the same chapter.

Paul Anderson writes on the loss of the missing books: "It became evident to us all that *Beelzebub* was the one significant document. All his secrets—or at least all those that he felt free to reveal—were preserved in *Beelzebub's Tales*, and the task that remained was to prepare people who would be capable of interpreting them. If *Beelzebub's Tales* were a legominism, he needed to teach initiates who could transmit the practical methods which the *Third Series* had been intended to indicate but not to teach. The two extant books of the *Third Series* are immensely important for anyone who wishes to undersand how Gurdjieff himself developed and how he worked: but they are not and were never intended to be practical text books."

A discussion of Gurdjieff's writing would be incomplete without a reference to the leaflet called *The Herald of Coming Good* which was published by him in 1933. It carried a note on the cover page: "Contrary to the established custom, I shall not only permit this first book of mine, as well as the books of the first series, to be reprinted in any country, but, if necessary, I am willing to subsidize it, on the condition of course that absolute accuracy is preserved." At first he instructed everyone to see that it got into the hands of all of his followers, with a view to raising further money in order to save the Institute. In a supplementary announcement, dated Tuesday, the 7th March 1933, written at the Grand Café in Fontainebleau, he said that he intended to lay the foundation stone of a new building which would be situated in the centre of the big park. There would be a new 'Study House' with lecture halls and theatres, three laboratories and an observatory. When I was at the Prieuré in 1923, he spoke to me about his plans in very much the same terms, so that evidently they were much more than fantasy. Either Gurdjieff intended to create something material or else it was a symbolical expression of something which requires to be specially studied; and it is clear that his three laboratories are intended to represent the different stages in the development of man, starting with the transition from the physical body to the astral or *kesdjan* body, the development of the reason in the kesdjan body and finally to the liberation of the third or higher-being body of the soul.

It is clear that all that is written in *The Herald of Coming Good* is not intended to be taken literally, but as a reminder that Gurdjieff was prepared to show to those who came to him the way of development. It is interesting here that he also refers to the booklet as the "Habardji", the Turkish word for 'town-crier'. This tendency to use Turkish shows how much he was steeped in the language from the time of his childhood: the only foreign language quotation in *Beelzebub's Tales* is a well-known Dervish saying: *"Dunyanin işi pakmazli pishi yeyen agizinda pusar eşegin dişi"*, meaning: "The affairs of the world are like a spiced dish, who eats it grows asses' teeth".

All that is written in *The Herald of Coming Good* is of profound interest for understanding the development of Gurdjieff's thinking; but, at the same time, it represents an unfortunate episode which he afterwards wished to bury. Only a year or so later he wrote in his last work that, if any of his readers had by their good fortune failed to read *The Herald of Coming Good*, he advised them not to do so and, if they had read it, to make sure that they would not pass it on to others.

The abortive attempt that was made in 1933 to resurrect the Institute was, it appears, the result of the very encouraging reception that *Beelzebub* had received among his American pupils; and with the improvement in the American economic situation came the hope that Gurdjieff might once again be able to obtain large sums of money from his American followers. At that time, around about 1934, Gurdjieff had gone temporarily into retirement. He was living with one of his old pupils, Fred Leighton, who afterwards repeated again and again the story how, after having had Gurdjieff with him for six months, Gurdjieff had said on parting from him—"There Fred, I have been with you all this time and you haven't made any use of me". It seems that Gurdjieff was neither engaged in writing nor was he prepared to do anything about the situation at the Prieuré. At times he has hinted that he went in 1932 on a visit to Central Asia in order to pick up threads of his former contacts, and returned to the U.S. determined to make one more attempt to resuscitate the Institute. According to another version, he attributed the journey to 1933, after the publication of *The Herald of Coming Good* and on his return completely dropped the project, repudiated the book, and set himself to complete his writings. So far as we know, he wrote nothing after "The Inner and Outer World Of Man", which was completed in 1935.

In May 1935, Gurdjieff finally abandoned his writing, leaving the *Third Series* unfinished. He explains in Book IV that he had been 'compelled to destroy nearly all that he had written' because he realized that he could not find people with the capacity to make use of it. After the death of Orage his hopes of re-establishing the Institute rested entirely upon the U.S.A. His American pupils had done what they could. Nick Putnam, who was like a son to him, arranged meetings with various rich people but nothing came of it. Paul Anderson succeeded in arousing such keen interest on the part of Senator Bronson Cutting of New Mexico that he asked him to meet Gurdjieff with a view to buying back the Prieuré and leasing it to a resuscitated Institute. Gurdjieff and Putnam went to Washington at the end of April. Senator Cutting had gone to New Mexico, and there was a ten-day wait which tried Gurdjieff's temper, already exasperated by the thoughtless reaction of hundreds of Americans to Orage's death. He asked Anderson to go to the Russian Embassy and ask if he could return to Russia and go on teaching his system.

On the night of May 6th, the plane carrying the Senator on his way to meet them exploded in mid-air and all on board were killed. Gurdjieff was visibly affected by the news. A few days later Paul brought him the report of the Russian enquiry. "We know about him and his activities," the counsellor had said. "He may return to the Soviet Union, only if he will accept work where he is assigned, but he must not teach anything." From that time for about ten days Gurdjieff disappeared from view. He did not go to any of the group meetings that had been arranged. Paul and Naomi, whom he saw privately, told me that his whole appearance was changing. He seemed to grow grey and listless and would talk only briefly. They saw him off on the train a few days later. He told them nothing: but it was evident that he had wanted to go to Russia and that the refusal had closed the possibility of something he wished to complete. Gurdjieff's passport, which I have carefully studied, shows that he went to Germany and returned to France in July. From what he said much later, I believe that he succeeded in going, during those two months, to the Caucasus and even into Central Asia. He certainly thought seriously of returning to Tashkent, but found that he would have little of the liberty of action he needed for his work.

He had to face the final and irrevocable downfall of his plans to set up his own organization. It is evidently significant for our assessment of Gurdjieff's connection with the Masters of Wisdom that we should know whether he did in fact go at that time to consult them. He drops strong hints to this effect in the fourth book of the *Third Series*.

8

Gurdjieff's Question

BORROWING from science fiction and space-travel fact, serious writers have introduced the term 'space-ship earth'; but who asks the question "If this earth is a space-ship and mankind is the crew, who is in command and where does he want us to go?" Suppose that a corporation, possessing a highly qualified scientific and technical staff, gets hold of a machine made by a competitor that is so entirely novel that no one has seen anything remotely resembling it. It is handed to the technicians and, after a time, they report to the management that they have discovered how it works. The comment might be: "That is fine, but what is it for?" They reply that this question has not occurred to them and they cannot be expected to answer it unless they know the competitor's plans. The management might legitimately retort that it is useless to know how a machine works if one does not know what purpose it is intended to serve.

Modern science is in this very situation. It is in process of discovering how the universe works but does not even ask what it is for. If the universe is too large a machine for us to think of as a whole, we have the solar system or even the 'space-ship earth' to study. Who asks the question: "What is this remarkable piece of mechanism for?" Man himself is another marvellously constructed machine closer to us than any other machine. Do we ask ourselves, "What purpose does this ingenious apparatus serve?"

Individuals and societies, scientific and non-scientific, are trying to pierce the veil that hides the future. It is obvious to all that mankind is in a serious crisis and some even doubt if we can survive. In all these studies, we can find scarcely anywhere recognition that the first question to ask is whether or not the existence of this earth and of mankind with it serves any useful purpose. This is strange, because we are constantly asking this question about subordinate entities, such as human organizations, activities and constructions. Indeed, we congratulate ourselves upon our utilitarian attitude and are ready to sweep away and obliterate whatever serves no useful purpose; and we are proud of man's ability to turn natural resources to useful account.

Life on this earth is a highly improbable state of affairs. It is a mechanism so ingenious in its capacity, not only to maintain its own existence but to evolve to more complex and improbable states, that it is really astonishing that no one asks what purpose it serves.

If Gurdjieff had done no more than direct our attention to the question, he would have been entitled to a special place among the pioneers of human thought. As we have seen in the earlier chapters, the question arose in his mind in his early youth and became the '*idée fixe* of his inner world' : *What is the sense and significance of life on the earth in general and of human life in particular?*

This should be a natural question, but when we ask why it does not occur to every thinking person, we penetrate to the depth of our human situation. We are so much concerned with our subjective problems that we do not stop to ask ourselves the objective question : 'What do I exist for?' For more than two thousand years, philosophers have been trying to answer such questions as 'What is Reality and how do we know it?' They have put aside the question, 'Who made it and why?', either taking it to be unanswerable or handing it over to the theologians to make good the deficiences of knowledge by revelation and faith.

Theologians agree that the first part of the answer has been revealed : life on the earth and man himself have been created by God. The second part, 'Why?', is put aside as inscrutable. A sceptic might echo the words of Anatole France : 'If God did it, he committed an act of supreme imprudence'. The comment seems even more relevant today than it was eighty years ago. Those outside the religious tradition, and especially those who doubt or deny the existence of God, are left without an answer and generally are satisfied to reject questions of origin and purpose as meaningless. If it is accepted that the purpose of creation must be tied to the existence of a Creator, God and Purpose seem to stand or fall together; yet, if God needs nothing, he cannot be said to have purposes either. There is something deeply unsatisfying here. If we turn to Eastern religions and philosophies, we find that they pay little atten-

Plate 8　The Prieuré from the Lime Avenue

Plate 9　Some of Gurdjieff's family at Le Paradou

Plate 10   Dervish Dance with Olgivanna Lloyd Wright, Mme Galoumian and
Irma de Schwung

tion to purposes and so do not think it necessary to account for anything whatever.

Buddhism, in all its forms, rejects such questions as futile and insists that the aim of existence is man's own need to escape from *duhkha*, which does not mean suffering so much as the conditioned state of the incarnated self. The one significant exception is the old religion of Zarathustra, which taught that both life on the earth and man endowed with intelligence were created to be allies for the Good Spirit Ahura Mazda in the struggle with the power of darkness. The Avestan hymns are full of references to the role man as a helper in the cosmic process. For example, Yasna 30.9 has the invocation: "May we belong to those who renew the world and make it to progress!" I have given my reasons for believing that Gurdjieff found that the Zoroastrian tradition lived on in Central Asia long after it ceased to be a state religion. For some reason, this important myth was forgotten and for a very long time the question 'why does life exist on the earth?' was lost to view.

Since the seventeenth century, European thinking has been occupied more and more with nature and less and less with the supernatural. When it began to be seen that nature is governed by laws that man can discover and turn to his own purposes, the pursuit of knowledge and power became an obsession. The question 'what is it all for?' seemed to be answered very simply. "It is all for man and for his satisfaction." The very word 'purpose' has come to mean human purpose directed to human ends.

At the end of the nineteenth century, when Gurdjieff embarked on his own search, science and religion were pulling man in different directions; but neither of them was concerned with his question of the sense and significance of human life on the earth. Each would have said that it knew the answer, but neither could have explained what it meant. Now, eighty years later, as the twentieth century is entering its last decades, we are faced with the consequences of neglecting the question. The very future of mankind is threatened by the sense of insecurity engendered by the suspicion that life has no purpose and man no reason to exist. Few people today can accept the doctrine that God created man to love and serve Him on earth and thereafter to live with Him in bliss forever. The naive ideas of heaven and hell that satisfied our ancestors mean nothing to modern man, even in the sophisticated forms evolved by theologians to keep pace with the progress of science. It is, therefore, strange that no serious attempt has been made to find some more convincing account of the significance of life on the earth. It is strange, because scientists are well aware that science cannot, of itself, provide answers to questions such as these, and know that there is a desperate need for a view of life that will restore confidence to a bewildered world. They marvel at the instrument and do not ask themselves what it is meant to be doing.

It would be wrong to say that no one asks the question: 'What is life all about?' On the contrary, we all ask it at one time or another: sometimes in despair but also sometimes in hope of an answer. Put in this way, the question subtly misses the point. Ostensibly objective, it is really a personal *cri de cœur*. We want our own personal lives to mean something and, if we are satisfied with our human relationships and our outward activities, we tend to forget that they have no bearing on the greater question. The suffering of the world remains, whether an individual is happy or wretched. The question: 'Why is the world like this?' is in the minds of all of us and, even if the answer misses the point, we must see how far the wise ones of the world can go towards a satisfying answer.

There are two main schools of thought. One is satisfied with the continuing search for causal laws which enable us to see 'how things work', and help us to 'make them work' to suit ourselves. They reject all questions of purpose—other than the purpose of advancing human knowledge and powers—as meaningless. Even if they do not reject religious faith on principle, they regard it as irrelevant to their own task. The other school tries to hold on to causal explanations in the natural order and yet retain belief in supernatural purposes. They are, in effect, dualists who accept two kinds of reality, one natural and the other supernatural, but do not feel either competent or obliged to search for a bridge from one to the other.

If we do not like such evasions, we must nevertheless recognize that religious people have made a serious mistake in attempting to give a reason for belief. The disastrous failure of the various rational arguments for the existence of God has resulted in the equally fallacious conclusion that failure to prove that God exists is the same as proving His non-existence. The 'argument from design' is still to be found in theological text books. Pious believers still say: "Look at the world, see how wonderfully it works, how finality and purpose breathe in every form of life. Can you doubt that this wonderful work must be the handiwork of a Supreme Artificer?" One by one, science has demolished each example: first by demonstrating how the physical world is governed by universal non-purposive causal laws, and secondly, by showing how life on earth can have evolved by natural selection from simpler forms, and these in turn by random chemical combinations from non-living matter. The argument from design has lost its cogency and with it—or so it seemed—the need to look for a Creator has virtually disappeared.

Neither philosophers nor scientists notice the trap into which they have fallen. The argument from design was anthropomorphic through and through. Man looked at natural objects, living and non-living, as he would look at human artifacts. He supposed a bird was fitted with wings because God wanted it to fly or a man furnished with reason because God wanted him to think. When it became clear that wings and brains can be accounted for as instruments of survival in the struggle of life, no further explanation seemed to be called for. It did not occur to people that there might be a purpose quite unlike any human purpose and yet not necessarily beyond human understanding. Science has widened man's horizons far beyond his earthly existence, and yet scientists do not notice that they have made possible a new way of thinking about the world, that would take account of the changes of scale that have put geocentric philosophies, once and for all, out of serious consideration.

How then did it come about that before the end of the nineteenth century Gurdjieff was asking his question that penetrates to the heart of the matter? Nothing that we have found in the teaching or the techniques of the Khwajagān and their successors justifies the suggestion that Gurdjieff found either the question or the answer among the Sufis. He himself emphatically asserts that it was his own question, and that, as stated above, it became the '*idée fixe* of his inner world'. If we accept this, then it follows that Gurdjieff was far more than a successful explorer who found and brought to the West 'fragments of an unknown teaching'.

Gurdjieff has his own clear message expressed in *Beelzebub's Tales* and especially the "Purgatory" chapter. The key passage reads: "the evolution and involution of active elements actualizing the Trogoautoegocratic principle of existence of everything existing in the universe by means of reciprocal feeding and maintaining each other's existence" (*Beelzebub's Tales*, p. 759).

Nearly all that has been written by Gurdjieff's admirers and detractors has referred to his psychological ideas and his manner of life.

These are both important, but they would not justify the dictum of Denis Saurat, referred to in Chapter 4 above, that there are unmistakable evidences that some of Gurdjieff's ideas are of 'extraterrestrial' origin. In the present chapter, I propose to examine some of these ideas and consider their place in a new *system of values* that could gain the assent and allegiance of all mankind.

Values and purposes are inseparable. If every state of affairs had equal value, we should have no purposes. If a state of affairs has value for me, I shall strive to achieve it with an intensity proportionate to its importance for me at this time. Strong and clear values arise from powerful needs. We need security and food for ourselves and our dependents, and our primary striving comes from the purpose that this need engenders. We are not clear about what we need beyond the means of preserving life and, in consequence, we are not clear about any larger purpose. If some state of affairs is presented to us as necessary or desirable—that is, as a value—and we are convinced or conditioned by the presentation, we strive to realize it and it becomes a purpose. In the past, men did not recognize how far their 'pupposes' were dictated by social pressures and animal instincts and shaped by custom and convention. One of the chief contributions of behavioural science in the last twenty years has been to demonstrate the extent to which human purposes are controllable by conditioning, suggestion and other social pressures. This has added to the general sense of unease, especially among very young people who have, so far, escaped from the conditioning influences of society.

A very serious situation has arisen in which great numbers of people find that they cannot accept value systems that no longer make sense but they cannot invent values of their own, for such a system is bound to be subjective and divisive. "One man's meat is another man's poison." We cannot believe that there is an absolute purpose in human life, as religion tells us, because we can see clearly now that such a purpose is both unverifiable and meaningless. We cannot accept our own personal purpose and nothing else: for this would set every man's hand against every other. We cannot find an overall human purpose that would not set man in conflict with nature as, indeed, he is in conflict already.

The only remaining possibility is to look for the meaning and purpose of life on the earth—and human life in particular—in the larger but not infinite context of the earth, the solar system and just possibly the galaxy in which our sun is a speck of dust. If there is a great and important purpose that goes far beyond the limits of human experience, our life and all life on the earth should be related to that purpose. If we could be sure of this, we should have a system of values that would be free from the defects of those by which we are trying to live today.

Some such argument must have occurred to Gurdjieff, and it seems likely that the problem took shape in his mind in about 1902, when he was twenty-five years old. This is a significant age when creativity reaches its peak in abstract thinkers such as mathematicians. Gurdjieff's startling precocity can account for his early grasp of the problem, but not for his discovery of a solution that goes counter to the modes of thought—religious and secular, philosophical and scientific—that were universal at the beginning of this century and dominant even today.

The answer Gurdjieff gives to the question—"What is the sense and significance of life on the earth?"—is radically different from any current views. Gurdjieff asserts in *Beelzebub's Tales* that the doctrine of reciprocal maintenance is derived from 'an ancient Sumerian manuscript' discovered by the great Kurdish philosopher Atarnakh. The passage quoted runs: "In all probability, there exists in the world some law of the reciprocal maintenance of everything existing. Obviously our lives serve also for maintaining something great or small in the world."[a]

This passage occurs in the description of a Central Asian fraternity called "The Assembly of the Enlightened", which had existed from Sumerian times and flourished openly in the Bactrian kingdom when Zoroaster was teaching. After Zoroaster, it disappeared for a hundred generations,[b] and only now has again begun to send out into the world its 'Unknown Teaching'. I have suggested that this is the Sarmān society.

What is this doctrine? Reciprocal maintenance in its special sense connotes that the universe has a built-in structure or pattern whereby every class of existing things produces energies or substances that are required for maintaining the existence of other classes.

[a] *Beelzebub's Tales*, Chapter XLIII, p. 1094.

[b] These twenty-four centuries correspond to what I have called the Megalan-thropic Epoch (*Dramatic Universe*, Volume IV, Chapter 49), characterized by the Master Idea that individual man is the ultimate value. With the transition to the new age of co-operation with the Higher Powers, that I call the Synergic Epoch, the ancient doctrine of Reciprocal Maintenance is due to regain its central significance for understanding human destiny.

Gurdjieff uses the terms involution and evolution to describe the process. Involution is the transformation process in which a high level energy acts on lower energies through an apparatus which provides the necessary environment and conditions. The human body is such an apparatus and so is any other living organism. The earth also provides an environment for high level energy—such as solar radiation—to act upon the more passive elements of the earth's crust and atmosphere. Involution is entropic, that is to say the over-all level of energy is always lowered in all involutionary changes.

Evolution is the reverse process. It is the production of high level energy from a lower level source. This also requires an apparatus, but of a different kind, for the 'up-grading' of energy is improbable and cannot occur at all unless some high level energy is present. Life is an evolutionary process that goes against the direction of probability. The work by which man is transformed is evolutionary. It goes against the stream of life. This is the meaning of Gurdjieff's saying, quoted by Ouspensky: "The work is against nature and against God."

Nevertheless, the work would be impossible without 'Help from Above' and this help is given "because such relatively independent formations are also necessary" (*Beelzebub's Tales*, p. 763). Within limits, the evolutionary process can start at a given point by a chance combination of favourable circumstances (Ibid., p. 762) but the promising beginning would come to nothing if the higher power were to withhold its intervention. This notion is very significant for understanding evolution in man both as a race and as an individual. In most cases, the initial move comes from some accidental combination which is sufficient to arouse the urge to escape from the stream of involution that ends in stagnation; but this urge is itself bound to involve and lose direction. It can, however, bring us under conscious and creative influences and a true movement of evolution is set going.

According to Gurdjieff's account, this is what happens on planets where formations capable of automatic movement accidentally arise (Ibid., p. 762). The Creator observes such events and only after they have occurred, intervenes to guide and help the process forward.

The accidental stage is within the field of possibilities set by the natural laws of the transformation of energies. The further stages require a supernatural action. This is not arbitrary, but depends on the relationship of entities, whereby each maintains the existence of others in a kind of universal mutual support system. Each order of beings is endowed with a form of energy that enables it to play its part in the cosmic process. An entirely new conception of value and purpose in life is thus established and is Gurdjieff's main contribution to a new master idea for the coming age.

The process can be seen in a very obvious way in the chemistry of the earth. The minerals of the earth's crust and the gases of the atmosphere produce the substances from which all living bodies are made. Green vegetation produces from carbon dioxide and water, with the help of solar radiation, oxygen and the carbohydrates without which no animal life could exist. Plants also produce nitrogenous compounds which are the key to the life processes of reproduction, regeneration and the transformation of energies of higher forms of life. If this were all that the doctrine of reciprocal maintenance was about, it would not be a revolutionary idea. The sting of the doctrine consists in the inclusion of man as a class of beings whose 'lives also serve for maintaining something great or small in the world'. Gurdjieff developed this theme by asserting that man, like every living or non-living thing, is an 'apparatus for the transformation of energy' and that he is specifically required to produce sensitive and conscious energy needed for maintaining the harmony of the solar system. He can produce this energy voluntarily, or involuntarily. The first way is by 'work on oneself'; that is, by striving for self-perfection. The second way is by dying. Hence the connection between reciprocal maintenance and war. Gurdjieff also connects the need for conscious energy with the population explosion (*Beelzebub's Tales*, pp. 1115–16). I have left a fuller examination of this law to the next chapter.

Under the primary law of conservation of matter,[a] the conditioned universe manifests loss of order and final dissolution with the passage of time; but Gurdjieff taught that high level energy is generated at an unconditioned level of being, as a corrective to to the process of entropy, and this energy makes evolution possible. The term *Trogoautoegocrat*[b] applies to the law governing this unconditioned side of creation, in no way violating the universal laws that are the conditions of existence in time and space.

[a] Gurdjieff calls this *Autoegocrat*.
[b] Which in the Greek vernacular means "I eat and so keep myself".

The other important concept Gurdjieff introduces, he names *Iraniranumange*, which "Objective science calls the common cosmic exchange of substances" or transformation of energies. The transformation of energies depends upon mechanisms of which the heat engine is the most studied example. In the heat engine, low grade energy-heat in the form of molecular motions—is converted into high-grade mechanical energy. In the electric generator, mechanical energy is converted into electricity. In living organisms, the the chemical energy in food is converted into mechanical energy exactly as in a heat engine. There are, however, more interesting, if less well understood, examples of energy transformation in our human experience. Sense perception converts the energy of electrical impulses of sight, of gaseous vibrations of sound, of chemical changes in taste and smell, into the energies of sensation, thought and feeling. These energies are produced by all animals, but man alone has the capacity for increasing, by his own voluntary effort, the quantity and improving the quality of the 'psychic' energies he releases. This is the second essential element in Gurdjieff's solution to the problem "What is the sense and significance of life on the earth and in particular of human life?" He makes the point perfectly clear in his account of the *Iraniranumange* (*Beelzebub's Tales*, pp. 762 and 764). The passage requires and repays very careful study. As the language is not easy, and the meaning apparent only by referring to many other passages, I shall interpret it as well as I can.

There is a remarkable convergence of two streams of thought of totally different origin. On the one hand, we are gaining a coherent picture of the origin of the earth, its atmosphere, oceans and the first appearance of life. Scientific cosmology and paleontology of the present day are very different from those of fifty years ago when Gurdjieff was writing *Beelzebub*. His stream of thought goes back thousands of years, but it anticipates many of the latest 'discoveries'. In Gurdjieff's scheme, those planets which acquired atmospheres became the scene of intense physical followed by chemical transformations, leading to more and more complex combinations that finally developed the property of self-renewal. The turning point came with the emergence of cells which are capable of aggregation to form multicellular organisms. This is the transition which occurred on this earth about a billion years ago from protozoa to metazoa, with the property of existing with some degree of independence of the environmental conditions (*Beelzebub's Tales*, p. 762, "the possibility appeared of independent automatic moving from one place to another on the surface of the given planets"). The conception is a striking anticipation of recent views on the origin of life on the earth. There is no suggestion in Gurdjieff's presentation of either *ad hoc* creation or of a pre-established plan. The new forms of existence arose spontaneously thanks to the organizing influence of the higher structures. When they were observed by *Our Common Father Endlessness*, "there arose in Him the Divine Idea of making use of it as a help for Himself in the administration of the enlarging world" (Ibid.).

Gurdjieff departs here from mechanistic theories of evolution. He propounds a scheme of consciously guided evolution that finally leads to the appearance of conscious and intelligent activity. Man differs radically from the animals, not by his origin, but by reason of his capacity for further evolution that he owes to the "special attention of the Creator whose own power works in them". This gives man and similar beings a threefold nature: body, soul and spirit and the potential for full individuation.

The entire system must be more carefully studied than is possible in this brief résumé. The effect is to present one with a threefold value system involving:

1. Man's concern with his own welfare in the light of his own mortality.
2. Man's place in nature and the obligations this entails.
3. Man's supernatural obligation to fulfil the purpose for which he exists.

Gurdjieff envisages the unification of these values through the natural operation of energy transformation in and by man himself. Man has the possibility, by his own choice, of accepting responsibility for transforming very high energies and thereby acquiring a 'higher-being body' or immortal soul, while at the same time, serving the process of reciprocal maintenance. The principle of the transformation of energies is expressed in the phrase: "The higher blends with the lower to actualize the middle". This implies a twofold source, that is the descent of the fine into the coarse in involution, and the refinement of the coarse by blending with the fine in evolution. The world is so made that energies are constantly involving and evolving and passing through various structures and systems. Life on the earth is such a system of energy transformation. Individual man also participates in this universal exchange, the totality of which is comprised in the term *Iraniranumange*. The πάντα ῥεῖ—everything is in flux—of Heraclitus acquires a new significance of which there is no trace in the fragments that remain of the speculations of the early Greek philosophers, and yet it reminds us very strongly that they were searching for some such key to the riddle of existence.

Gurdjieff thus offers a hope of reconciling material or mechanistic, with religious or spiritual views of man and the universe. The doctrine also suggests that man has a great responsibility. If the twin concepts of reciprocal maintenance and purposive energy transformation are valid, they provide us with a scheme of values that does not depend upon any particular form of belief. They answer the question of the sense and significance of human life by telling us that this depends upon our own decision. We can either transform energies mechanically until we die, when a higher energy will automatically be released but we ourselves as individuals will cease to exist, or we can transform energies by our own decision and live upon progressively higher levels until we become free immortal souls.

This doctrine is both heretical from the religious standpoint and unacceptable from that of scientific orthodoxy. The Christian and Muslim religions teach unconditional immortality of the soul which will be resurrected with a physical body. The Eastern religions also teach the unconditional immortality of the reincarnating principle. The destiny of the immortal principle in all cases depends upon moral conduct, that is, a pattern of behaviour regulated by Divine Decree or the Law of Karma. Gurdjieff asserts that the immortal principle in man is no more than a potentiality that becomes a full reality only rarely, and does so if the individual can bring about the complete transformation of his nature through his own 'conscious labour and intentional suffering'.

The doctrine just outlined is substantially that held by the Sufi schools of Central Asia and distinguishes them from the orthodox Islamic Sufis of the Arab countries. If we study the sacrificial hymns of both Iranian and Vedic scriptures, we can find clear references to the transformation of energies by food and fire for the very purpose of attaining immortality. Gurdjieff was probably familiar with such ideas from an early age, but could not connect them with 'the sense and significance of life on the earth' until he was admitted to the Sarmān monastery and initiated into the mystery of Reciprocal Maintenance. This is the key to a new and satisfying view of human life on the earth. If we can accept it, we have a touchstone by which all activities, great and small, can be evaluated. We can fulfil a three-fold purpose by our own will and acts : we save ourselves, we help mankind in its evolution and we lighten the sufferings of our Creator.

Universal causality is expressed by Gurdjieff in a subtly modified form in the formula 'everything arising from everything and enter-ing into everything'. There is no escape from the circular process that binds every event in the universe to every other event. Causality is the central principle of classical mechanics. Gurdjieff was well aware of the implications of this principle in his search for the 'sense and significance' of life on the earth. On the other hand, there is no evidence that either the Masters of Wisdom or their successors—or indeed any other Asiatic school—were aware of it in its scientific formulation. This does not mean that they did not recognize the problem in their own way. The orthodox Islamic doctrine holds that God's decrees are absolute and allow no exception. But it also holds that man's power of choice and hence his responsibility for the consequences of his actions is assured by the very decree that created him.

The Khwajagān held that God, by His presence in everything, en-abled all things to realize their own destiny, in spite of the implication that this was possible only if all is not predetermined by Divine Decree. There was probably a secret teaching, that does not appear explicitly in any of the Sufi literature, according to which the world harmony requires a contribution from man that he makes by means of his spiritual exercises and austerities. This is indirectly attested by the powers attributed to Sufis as a consequence of the performance of spiritual exercises. These powers are of two kinds : those acquired by work and those which are gifts of grace. The former are always associated with the acceptance of suffering and hardship.

Gurdjieff's solution to the problem centres on the discovery to which he refers as the 'Law of Sevenfoldness' or, as it is called in *Beelzebub's Tales*, *Heptaparaparshinokh*. Although he somewhat provocatively calls this the 'First Fundamental Cosmic Law', he never formulated it precisely. Ouspensky with his characteristic love of clarity and definition presents the law in his book *In Search of the Miraculous* as the rule for determining whether a directed process can be completed without loss of the original intention.[a]

In *Beelzebub's Tales*, Gurdjieff gives a variety of formulations. After many years of study, I have reached the conclusion that there is in nature an element of *hazard* that disturbs every process and yet also makes possible the attainment of purposes. This element of hazard is not arbitrary, for it enters, as Gurdjieff asserts, in two ways into any directed process. It is uncertain that *direction* can be sustained under the impact of the external random forces which are always present. It is also uncertain that *completion* can be attained without loss of form and content. Gurdjieff explicitly associates the ambiguity of hazard with the construction of the musical scale. The sequence of vibrations is said to exemplify the laws of sevenfoldness. We have here a decisive test of the originality of Gurdjieff's 'ideas'. The connection between vibrations and music was known to Pythagoras. The property whereby doubling or halving of the rate of vibration leaves the tone of the sound unchanged, and the discovery that there are intermediate tonalities corresponding to different ratios $1 : 2, 2 : 3, 3 : 4$, etc., was known both to the Greeks and the Chinese. Plato, in his *Timaeus*, set up an elaborate cosmology —the origin of which he explicitly ascribes to the Pythagoreans— based on the ratios of $1 : 2 : 3$. The resulting scheme has had an enormous influence on Western thinking. Under the guise of the music of the spheres, it was responsible for both successes and failures in the study of the Solar System. It guided the evolution of chemistry towards its present extraordinary power to transform the materials of the earth's surface.

Nevertheless, there is no trace anywhere in Plato or in the Neoplatonic philosophers and their mediaeval and modern successors of any recognition of the role of *hazard*. The transitions from one note to another were taken to be controllable and predictable. From the ignoring of hazard a fundamental misunderstanding of the

[a] Ouspensky interprets the law as follows in *The Fourth Way* (Chapter VIII, p. 191): "A succession of events proceeds according to the Law of Seven or the Law of Octaves. The Law of Seven must be understood . . . from the point of view of intervals. . . . No force ever works continuously in the same direction: it works for a certain time, then diminishes in intensity and either changes its direction or undergoes inner change. In every octave . . . there are two places where vibrations undergo a certain change, slow down and then start again. If an additional shock does not enter at these places, the octave changes direction."

limitations of the scientific method has resulted. It is only in recent times that the concept of causality has been questioned.

In the mid-1930's, I was one of a group of students who, under Ouspensky's guidance, tried to find sources of Gurdjieff's 'laws of three and seven'. We were able to find traces of the triad in all traditional teachings. The Chaldeans took the number 120 as basic— it is $1 \times 2 \times 3 \times 4 \times 5$ and is divisibly by 6, 12 and 24. This is how we have 360 degrees in a circle, and the numbers 60 and 24 in our measurements of time. But 7 is a maverick number. It will not divide exactly into any number and it seems to be connected with 'squaring the circle' for the ratio of diameter to circumference is almost exactly $22/7$. The belief that seven is a sacred number is traceable to Chaldean sources and the early development of arithmetic.

Such considerations led us to the conclusion that the 'law of seven' was probably formulated in Babylon and that it fitted very well with the Zoroastrian doctrine of the hazardous relationship of the universal forces. After the collapse of the Persian Empire, it was lost to the world, but probably was preserved by secret societies.

At that time, we knew nothing of the Sarmān Brotherhood, which, so far as I know, Gurdjieff first referred to in *Meetings with Remarkable Men*. It seems likely that Gurdjieff learned about the peculiar and unique formulation of the law in the same Sarmān monastery. The surmise is made very plausible by the reference Gurdjieff makes to the 'vesanelnian trees' which were used to teach the priestess-dancers the ritual movements (*Meetings with Remarkable Men*, p. 161). These are derived from the enneagram symbol which represents the overcoming of hazard by the interaction of three processes.[a]

It seems then, that we have further evidence of the extent to which Gurdjieff's cosmological and theological speculations were derived from Sarmān sources, and these in their turn from Chaldean and Zoroastrian origins. But he also drew on the Pythagorean tradition, through Neoplatonism and pseudo-Dionysius, in adapting the doctrine of 'different worlds' or cosmoses. Russian mystical theology accepts the doctrine of seven 'worlds' with God the Absolute Source, one, alone, inaccessible, beyond them all. These are much the terms in which Ouspensky presents Gurdjieff's 'Ray of Creation'. It does not fit into the Sarmān cosmology, but Gurdjieff does not wish to lose the valuable features of the Russian tradition. Gurdjieff's

[a] The enneagram symbol is discussed in Appendix II.

hierarchy of substances—the Table of Hydrogens—is almost certainly derived from the Neoplatonic and possibly also Gnostic speculations about 'emanations' from the suprasensible world.

It seems reasonable to conclude that Gurdjieff attempted to make a synthesis, bringing together, first, what he had learned from his early contacts with the esoteric Christianity of the Orthodox Church, and, secondly, the more powerful ideas of Reciprocal Maintenance and Universal Hazard taught in the Sarmān Brotherhood. He had found two cosmological schemes and attempted to reconcile them, without completing the undertaking. We shall see later that he also wished to integrate into his world picture the psychological teaching of the Masters of Wisdom with their roots in pre-Islamic, Buddhist and Central Asian traditions.

I believe that he asked his own question, but found the answer in the lost Zoroastrian tradition preserved by the Sarmān Brotherhood. Gurdjieff undoubtedly set himself to fill the gaps in what he had learned, and to interpret it in a form that would be acceptable to the modern world. He was not wholly successful in either undertaking; but his contribution remains outstanding. He alone has brought before us a line of thought that can lead to an acceptable answer to his own question. After half a century of contact with the notions of reciprocal maintenance, I am more than ever convinced that it contains the germ of a new understanding of man's place in the universe.

It must be understood that I have not attempted to interpret the whole message that Gurdjieff expresses in *Beelzebub's Tales.* If he had intended to make the message obvious to every reader, he would have done so himself. Those who find that his question is also their own question will search deeply for the answer. There is one passage, however, to which special attention must be drawn, for it throws a new light on Gurdjieff's understanding of the role of individuality in the cosmos. This is to be found in the strange but very significant picture of perfected individuals whose only aim is to serve their maker, and yet who, by the very fact that they are individuals, set up a tension that results in a problem not foreseen. So Gurdjieff not only rejects the doctrine of divine omnipotence, in the sense that the Creator is not able to overcome the conditions of the flow of time according to the law of entropy, but also in the further sense that there are limitations on his ability to penetrate into the future. On the other hand he accepts God as being unlimited ("Our Endless Creator"), all-merciful and wise, and allows an attitude of love, worship and confidence in the goodness of God. I think it is important to notice how Gurdjieff has thought out the theological implications of his doctrine.

The next basic idea is that everything in the universe is material, everything is energy, everything is undergoing processes of transformation, that in the existing universe there is no dualism of matter and spirit, just as there is no dualism of good and evil. Gurdjieff does not anywhere pick up the Zoroastrian doctrine of the dualism of good and evil powers. There is nothing in any part of his doctrine that corresponds to Ahriman, the wicked spirit who seeks to destroy. Instead he shows that in the limitations imposed by the conditions of existence in the universe there is present a denying force. This force is not of itself evil, indeed it is necessary to enable the divine purpose to be made manifest. This is made particularly clear in the most extraordinary passage in *Third Series* in which he describes his own dilemma, when he could not see the way out of his problem. Finally he saw the analogy between God and the Devil as the symbol of his own need to free himself of something dear and precious to him, in order that it should serve as a perpetual reminding factor.

The conception is of a creation which is not dualistic nor monistic either. The existing world is continuous interaction between different gradations of materiality and spirituality—twelve in all.[a] Each of these represents a different mode of experience, a different possibility of manifestation of the Divine Purpose, a different role in the entire scheme of things. Between these different levels of existence there is a perpetual exchange of substances. This cosmic exchange by which there occurs aggregation, disaggregation, the becoming more active and more conscious, the dissolving and becoming more inert, and even dissolution into the primary state is the universal process of energy transformation. This is all very much as it is viewed by physical science in our present day, with the all-important distinction, however, that the transformation of substances, for Gurdjieff, does not stop at the physical world or even the world of life, but goes all the way through to the experiences of thought and feeling and to the higher spiritual experiences of love, union, and creativity. All of these represent qualities associated with different states of the universal energy system of the world.

[a] See Appendix II for detailed account.

This is in itself not an idea for which Gurdjieff could or would have claimed originality; it was entertained by many people at the end of the nineteenth century. In the varieties of pan-psychism which philosophers have tried to introduce, there is some attempt to account for the coexistence of psychic or conscious processes with material or energetic processes by postulating one single substance. Where Gurdjieff's concept mainly differs—and it is an important feature of his system—is in presenting the different states of existence as each complete in itself and representing, as it were, a certain plateau or level which, while exhibiting inner variations, is still very different from the levels above and below. This is connected with his doctrine of cosmoses, or individualized states of existence, which are all constructed according to the same cosmic model and differ only in size and their external functions.

We have here a set of ideas that are essential for the whole of Gurdjieff's cosmology, but are distinct from the first group of ideas connected with God, the 'why' of existence, and the uncertainty and the hazard with which existence is surrounded. The second group of notions includes the common cosmic exchange of substances, and the individualization into cosmoses. Human beings are a particular example of this individualization that he calls the "fourth level of cosmic structuring", themselves being apparatuses or centres for the transformation of energy for the purposes of Reciprocal Maintenance. These notions are remarkable in themselves, and they deserve very special study. I do not propose to go into them at great length in this present book, because they are very adequately covered in Ouspensky's *In Search of the Miraculous* and in other books that have been written on Gurdjieff's teaching. The doctrine of Cosmoses is probably derived, as suggested above, from Gnostic or Neoplatonic origins. References to similar notions are found in Valentinus and developed in Rosicrucian writings. Gurdjieff introduced the idea of cosmoses with Ouspensky's groups in Russia, insisting that it is necessary to begin by understanding what is meant by a cosmos. He would not have repeated it in *Beelzebub's Tales* in the particular context of the "Purgatory" chapter, unless he had seen it as a link that unified the doctrine of Reciprocal Maintenance with that of a series of worlds.

It is essential at this point to examine what Gurdjieff means by the *Omnipresent Okidanokh*. This notion is first introduced in *Beelzebub's Tales*, Chapter III, "Cause of Delay", where the allegorical significance of space-ships is introduced. These refer to the 'ways' by which man reaches Objective Reason. Gurdjieff conveys that an improved Way, more rapid and effective than those of the past, is now available to mankind. The old ships were run on a cosmic substance which contained only two parts of the three present in *Okidanokh*, a reference to the concept of good and evil on which hitherto society has been regulated. It is not until *Beelzebub* has shown in Chapter XV the absurdity of trying to conduct human affairs in terms of abstract judgments of good and evil, that he comes back to the *Okidanokh* in Chapter XVII and gives a complete account of the 'new Way' that looks to the third force. There is still something not quite right and the experiments described in Chapter XVIII, "The Arch-preposterous", show that even the 'new Way' can be misunderstood, if people are led to believe that the Third Force can be introduced from the outside. The solution is given much later in Chapter XXXIII, "Beelzebub as Professional Hypnotist", where Beelzebub explains that "The learned members of the Akhaldan Society discovered that by means of the separately localized third part of the *Omnipresent Okidanokh*, namely, by means of its sacred neutralizing force or force-of-reconciling, they could bring every kind of planetary formation into such a state that it remained forever with all those active elements contained within it at a given moment: that is to say, they could stop and absolutely arrest their future decay." The significance of *Okidanokh* is further developed in the chapters on "Religion" and "Electricity". It is noteworthy that it is not once mentioned in the chapters "Purgatory" and "Heptaparaparshinokh", which contain the essence of Gurdjieff's cosmology. Gurdjieff evidently drew from several sources and was careful not to obliterate distinctions for the sake of a misleading consistency. He did this by using distinct terminologies for each of the sources and by putting the material into a different context. I am not concerned in this book to make textual researches except where it is of paramount importance to grasp Gurdjieff's intention.

We are faced with several conundrums typical of *Beelzebub's Tales*. The first, of course, is the meaning of *Okidanokh* itself. The second is its connection with the law of threefoldness. Another is its omission from the chapter "Purgatory". Finally, we have the role of *Okidanokh* in our own experience.

No solution to these and other conundrums can be 'authoritative', as Gurdjieff left it to the 'followers of his ideas' to find their own answers. As I see it, *Okidanokh* is the Creative Will by which the existing universe realizes and fulfils itself. The operation of the will can occur in several ways. There is first, the universal process of actualization in time and space. In this, there is no individualized or localized will. The laws of thermodynamics correspond to the operation of the *Omnipresent Okidanokh* in its primitive undivided state. Schopenhauer's 'will' and the development of theories of the unconscious from Schopenhauer to Freud and the libido doctrine and thence to various forms of behaviourism, are all illustrations of the primitive *Okidanokh*. It is the impersonal, unconscious urge by which the world is actualized 'according to law'. The second mode of operation occurs when there is a polar separation of forces. The ancient Greek notion of strife as the source of all activity, and the separation of affirming and denying forces, were the yang and yin and other male and female principles of the old world. The will is no longer blind and unconscious, for it separates itself from itself. From this separation comes sensitivity and the emergence of 'mind'. The 'new Way' comes with the discovery that the *Okidanokh* is really threefold and that true 'will' and hence true freedom reside in the neglected 'third force'. A being can be said to have will only if he can separate the third force. This is done by some kind of shock or tension.

Gurdjieff illustrated this perfectly in his own life and particularly in the two periods 1925–7 and 1927–9. During the first, he was working under the impact of the realization that his dream of setting up a world-wide organization to help mankind to be delivered from its central weakness—which is precisely lack of will—was not to be realized. When he saw that his decision to convey his understanding by writing was also going to fail, he realized that the old way would not do and created conditions in which the third force could be liberated.

A key passage occurs in the chapter "Electricity". Electricity itself stands for self-will, that is, those impulses of man which stem from his egoism and appear to him and to others as if they were acts of will. Self-will destroys the possibility of acquiring real will. The Saturnian sage, who has understood the true significance of will, declares that he had made it clear to his own reason that not only was the Omnipresent cosmic-substance *Okidanokh* necessary for the arising and maintaining of any form of existence, but also that the essence of every living or non-living object, including beings of every system of brain, depended on this substance. Finally comes the crucial statement; the possibility for three-brained-beings to perfect themselves and ultimately to blend with the Prime Cause of everything existing depends exclusively on it.

This statement in plain English means that it is our will alone that can make the free decisions that will lead us to final liberation. We may, under the influence of others, behave rightly. We may make the efforts needed for gaining unity and strength of being. All these may be done and yet we may remain imprisoned in our existential nature. To achieve the ultimate goal we must be prepared to renounce all lesser goals. The familiar conflict between dualism and pantheism is avoided. The dualists assert that the soul and God are two. God is 'outside', we aspire to reach His Presence which is in Heaven—or at least somewhere else than here and now. Sufism insists on the contrary, God is wholly here and now, within us, "nearer to us than we ourselves". God is All and Everything—*Deus est omne quod est*. The dilemma is well known to all students of religious and mystical experience.

Gurdjieff resolves it in the simplest way. It is not God that is omnipotent but the Universal Will, the *Okidanokh*, which is neither personal nor impersonal; it is one and yet it is divisible. It is everywhere and yet it can be localized. This is wholly compatible with the traditional teachings of the Khwajagān. We do not find it in the "Purgatory" chapter which is, I conjecture, derived from the Sarmān Brotherhood. If this surmise is correct, it gives us a most valuable clue to reconstructing the Sarmān tradition.

I have chosen only three out of the great range of ideas in *Beelzebub's Tales*, the *Trogoautoegocrat*, the *Iraniranumange,* and the *Omnipresent Okidanokh*, because they are perhaps the most original and surprising. They concern the three basic elements Function, Being and Will. There is a further most significant scheme that shows how the universal maintenance works in the Solar system: I will examine this in the next chapter. It is Gurdjieff's key to 'making a New World'.

9

The Law of Reciprocal Maintenance

I F the key to the problems of value and purpose that bewilder our generation is to be found in Reciprocal Maintenance, we should examine the doctrine more closely before proceeding. Gurdjieff left much to be unveiled, but gave the key to the riddle in a scheme that he showed to the little group that lived with him at Essentuki in the Caucasus at the height of the Russian Revolution. He called it the Symbol of All Life and said that it stood alone and could not be connected with what he had previously taught them. It is illustrated in Appendix II. Although it is concerned with food, it was not to be related to the transformations of food which concern the production of energy required for our work and our transformation. He explained, on the contrary, that he was concerned here not so much with cosmic events, as with cosmic balances and equilibria. The scheme was shown in a condensed form without explanation. When we studied it with Ouspensky in the 1920's, neither he nor we could make much of it, though we felt its importance. Since 1922, we have had fifty years to ponder over the scheme and have returned to it many times. I believe that it does contain the key to understanding the new world, and therefore make no excuse for giving here the results of researches that my colleagues and I in the Institute for Comparative Study of History, Philosophy and the Sciences have conducted over the past twenty years.

As Gurdjieff presents it, all modes of existence in the universe can be grouped into essence classes so that each of these classes provides for the maintenance of another and in its turn is maintained by a third class. Although man appears in the scheme, this does not refer to man as an individual being or even to all humanity, but rather to man as a being with a particular kind of essence able to transform energies of a corresponding quality and, therefore, to play a specific role in the universal maintenance. An essence class is not defined in the way a biologist would classify plants and animals. It is characterized by a pattern of possible experience. Gurdjieff's basic example is the division into one, two and three-brained beings; more or less corresponding to our invertebrates, vertebrates and man The one-brained being is wholly automatic in its behaviour and almost exclusively functions in terms of nutrition and reproduction. A two-brained being has a nervous system that enables its sensitive energy to be organized. It has varied experiences that we men can recognize as similar to our own. In particular, it is capable of feeling as we feel, but not of thinking as we men think. Man as a three-brained being belongs to a special essence class characterized by the potential for transformation. He can exercise a real power of choice which is almost entirely absent in animals except under direct human influence. From a few hints, which is about all that Gurdjieff left, we can construct a series of twelve essence classes corresponding to the twelve steps in Gurdjieff's diagram. This terminology I propose to use is given in the following table:

12. *Endlessness*	The Supreme Creative Will
11. *Trogoautoegocrat*	The spiritual working by which Creation is maintained
10. *Cosmic Individuality*	The Divine Will
9. *Demiurges*	The Angelic Host
8. *Man*	Three-brained Beings
7. *Verebrates*	Two-brained Beings
6. *Invertebrates*	One-brained Beings
5. *Plants*	Static Life Forms
4. *Soil*	The Sensitive Surface Layer
3. *Crystals*	Static Non-living forms
2. *Simples*	Primary combinations of matter
1. *Heat*	Unorganized energy

We have a strange propensity to look upon the human race as apart from the natural order. We have accepted man's evolution from the primates and the entire phylogenetic history of life from its first beginnings two or three thousand million years ago. We recognize our dependence upon the earth's crust for the raw materials and energies needed by our technology and upon animal and vegetable life for our food; but it does not occur to us that this dependence is mutual, that we are so closely integrated into the natural order that we cannot harm it without hurting ourselves. For this error, we have only our self-centred egoism to blame. It is otherwise with the deeper significance of Reciprocal Maintenance—the *Trogoautoegocrat*—which offers mankind a new and realistic approach to life's problems. This is by no means obvious.

Hitherto there has been no satisfying answer to the questions "Why do we men exist?", "What purpose does life serve?", "Why was the Universe brought into existence?" To reject such questions as meaningless, simply because we do not know how to answer them, or to accept meaningless answers such as "God created the universe for man and man for Himself" are equally unsatisfying. They give no foundation for building a new world. Gurdjieff offers an answer that can be translated into a way of life for mankind now and in the future.

The world was brought into existence because 'being' and 'time' are mutually destructive. Everything separate and closed within itself must perish for lack of a principle of renewal. There is partial renewal by borrowing energy from outside, but this is not enough. Full renewal requires full mutuality. It is by Universal giving and receiving of energies that Cosmic Harmony is maintained. This, in turn, requires an organized structure which is given by the interaction of the different classes of essence. This is the meaning of Gurdjieff's scheme. In the Symbol of All Life each essence class has three independent characteristics:

1. It is what it is. This is its quintessence whereby it stands at the heart of its own five-term system.
2. It has a range of possible manifestations limited by the essence classes above and below it.
3. It enters uniquely into the *Trogoautoegocratic* Process, maintaining and being maintained by essence classes outside its own limits of existence.

In Gurdjieff's scheme the process of evolution begins with formless energy. This is the same as the Vedic *Tapas* or warmth that hatched the world-egg. From random energy, simple combinations and states arise, from these come the first enduring forms, crystals which are the precursors of the world of solids, liquids and gases which form our material environment. The emergence of form from formlessness, permanence from impermanence is required before there can be identities, objects capable of independent existence.

The next stage sets the scene for the arising of life. It is the emergence of high concentrations of surface energy in colloidal materials. This produces the surface layer of active substances that becomes in the course of millions of years the soil that is the sensitive coating of the earth. The first complete self-renewing system comprises the five essence classes of plants, soil, crystals, simples such as air and water and, finally, heat and random energy. These essence-classes occupy places and fill a role in the cosmic harmony without which the whole structure would collapse.

These three characteristics are found in the crystal essence. It is the simplest form of existence that possesses its own pattern in space and time. It has the cosmic property of enabling a great number of identical atoms to be concentrated in one place for a long time. Without this, the transformations of life would be impossible. Because we are constantly surrounded by solid masses, we fail to notice how extraordinary a phenomenon they present. It is a phenomenon exceedingly rare in the Universe. Not one-millionth part of the masses of our galaxy is in the solid state and the proportion in the entire universe is very much smaller. Alone among the inner planets of our solar system our earth has this unusual combination. We are unique among all the planets in the immense quantity of water that maintains our extraordinary stable conditions of temperature and climate.

These considerations should make us pause to ask ourselves whether there may not be a good reason for our presence on a planet with such rare properties. The crystalline essence has a decisive influence on our lives by its power to concentrate the elements. In the course of hundreds of millions of years, the minerals of the earth's crust have been concentrated in huge deposits that we now draw upon relentlessly with little thought for the consequences. At most, we are concerned that our grandchildren may find themselves deprived of sources of energy and raw materials of manufacture. The truth is that the great mineral deposits play a vital part in maintaining the balance of forces acting upon life on our planet and particularly upon mankind. We are already encountering strange results from the disturbances we are causing. We find as we study the entire series of essence classes that there is an amazing set of interwoven activities that provide the most convincing evidence of a very high Intelligence involved in creation. The concentrations of elements in the earth's crust are themselves strange enough to provoke the question "by what Intelligence and to what end was this work done?".

The strangeness increases as we pass to the next essence class which is the intensely active thin layer of colloidal matter that covers the surface. This includes what we call *soil* which has the special property of allowing matter in the three states, solid, liquid and gaseous to interact with high concentration of energy. The soil is less than one millionth part of the earth's mass and yet, with the equivalent surface layer of the oceans, it is the scene of nearly all the transformations upon which life depends. The soil essence ranges from the crystalline to the vegetable. At one extreme it is little more than disintegrated rock and at the other it is almost alive.

The soil essence is dynamic. It is in a constant state of transformation. It grows from all kinds of breakdown products: silt eroded from the crystal rocks, dust deposited from the winds, the remains of vegetable and animal bodies. It feeds on simple substances and in its turn maintains the germinal life of the earth. We know that our life is dependent upon the soil. The deserts produced by the 'rape of the soil' are a constant reminder of the precarious hold that we have upon life. Without life, soil degenerates and loses its dynamic character. Without simples: air, water, carbon dioxide and salts, the soil perishes. When the soil is 'treated' with substances incompatible with its essence pattern—such as various chemical agents that we are now using on a large scale—its place in the universal maintenance is disturbed, and it gradually ceases to liberate the energies that are needed for the evolution of our planet. We are already beginning to observe the consequences of creating an ecological imbalance on the level of the soil essence. If we look more deeply we would discover that we are violating the laws of our own existence and perhaps understand that this must bring its own retribution.

Modern man ignores cosmic laws even when they are revealed to him. He does not see that he is already involved in the retributive consequences of his irresponsibility. We cannot plead ignorance, for even if we are unable to grasp intellectually the universal scheme, we can be sensitive to its working by the prompting of conscience. Hundreds of thousands of men and women are deeply distressed by what is being done to our Mother Earth. They may interpret this distress in superficial terms, but they do make great efforts to preserve our heritage. They half understand that by poisoning the soil, we

introduce psychic poisons into ourselves. It is an observed fact that all
countries which use a maximum of artificial fertilizers are subject
to the maximum of psychic disorders. People refuse to admit that the
connection is more than accidental. This refusal to face reality enters
at every stage of our involvement in the world process.

The next class is that of the plant essence. This is static. It produces
an extraordinary range of substances. Not only do all the chemical
elements enter vegetable life in the form of crystalline salts, but some
plants have the power to synthesize substances with a powerful action
on the human psyche. All life on the earth, all the possibilities of
experience, depend upon the substances produced by the vegetable
essence. We have an obligation towards this marvellous bio-chemical
system which maintains the balance of air, earth and oceans and
provides us with all our chief needs. While we recognize that the
destruction of forests and the loss of vegetable plankton due to
pollution of the seas—to cite but two examples—are threatening all
life on the planet; we do not see that mankind is going to pay the
price of all this destruction. We make the terrible mistake of treat-
ing nature as an alien power, instead of recognizing that we are
wholly involved in the well-being of the plant life of the earth.

The sixth essence class is that of the invertebrates or one-brained
beings. It is shown in Gurdjieff's scheme as food for man. This is
far from obvious, because of all forms of life on the earth, invertebrate animals play the least part in our diet.

We have several clues. Gurdjieff asserts in *Beelzebub's Tales* that
on all normal planets, the staple food of three-brained beings is
'prosphora' or the wheat germ. Grains and fruits are natural foods.
We also need vegetable and animal tissue in varying proportions according to our conditions of existence. In all cases the food stuff is
associated with reproduction. Sexual reproduction is a very complex
affair among the invertebrates which release great quantities of
sexual energy. This is on the same level in the cosmic scale as the
creative energy which is the highest characteristic energy of the human
race. We see in this way a special affinity of man with the one-
brained beings whose role in the cosmic harmony is not otherwise
easy to discern. Apart from a few 'useful' species, we regard the invertebrates as enemies and destroy them on a vast scale. The sole restraint
comes from realizing that the reproduction of all the higher plants
depends upon invertebrates to transfer the pollen from one flower
to another. We do not even guess at the more significant relationship

of Reciprocal Maintenance that binds man and the germinal essence in all its manifestations.

The seventh essence class includes all the chordate animals that Gurdjieff describes as 'two-brained', which means that they are capable of emotional experiences. The animals are the final result of natural evolution. Lacking creativity they are of necessity subordinate to man, but they concentrate a wide range of sensitive energies that are needed for the cosmic harmony. This is why we find in the animal kingdom sensitive experiences resembling the whole range of human emotions. This agrees with the rule that each essence class ranges all the way from the one below to the one above it. We are 'animals in our lower nature'. Our 'emotions' of fear and excitement, anger, curiosity, timidity and courage, irritation and contentment are the same as those we see in the animals. The truly 'human' feeling impulses of love, faith, hope and conscience are possible only in creative beings. Unfortunately, we have lost the ability to experience normally the 'positive' emotions and have substituted for them the lower animal passions. This is bad for our humanness, but there is another serious consequence of our wholesale destruction of animal species, inasmuch as the energies they should release have somehow to be made good. Since man alone has the required range of emotions, it follows that the human species has to replace the energies needed for the cosmic harmony that animals should be furnishing. Mankind thereby unwittingly condemns itself to a quasi-animal existence. This partly accounts for the terrifyingly inhumane behaviour that has become so prevalent in our time. Fear and anger lead us into bestial cruelty that bewilders those who believe in the nobility of the human essence. Gurdjieff's Reciprocal Maintenance may be hard to accept in all its details, but we must admit that it makes sense of much that is otherwise unaccountable.

The crucial test is the account given of Man himself and his destiny. We live in an age that can no longer accept either of the two extreme doctrines of the West represented by dialetical materialism and by 'heaven and hell' theism. The East offers the creed of 'liberation' which denies real values to the material world and rejects even the promise of immortality. The Buddhist version emphasizes liberation from existence and the Sufi version promises 'Union with the One'. But neither of these gives a satisfying meaning to our earthly life. If we reject all other wordliness, we are left with naturalistic 'humanism'. The trouble with any world view that seeks to derive all values and all meanings from human experience alone is that it fails to make sense. The world is too large and too obviously exciting in itself to be treated as a backcloth for the human drama. The enormous significance of Gurdjieff's scheme is that it shows us how we can give a coherent account of 'All and Everything'.

According to Gurdjieff's scheme, there are three entirely different kinds of being that take human form. The first are Incarnations, or 'Cosmic Individuals sent from Above'. The second are men and women who have learned how to live in harmony with nature by fulfilling their obligations. They are exempt from the hazards of ordinary life. They have become Individuals in their own right. I have called them *psychoteleios* to express the notion of a perfected psyche. Sufism calls them *Insan-i-Kamil*—the Perfected Man. The third comprises the vast majority who live a quasi-animal existence, or more exactly who live as mechanical toys moved almost exclusively by forces outside themselves. These are the psychostatic class; but they have the potential for self-perfecting. Gurdjieff is emphatic in his assertion that man who does not fulfil his cosmic duties by his own 'conscious labours and intentional sufferings' loses his immortal soul and after death is 'destroyed forever'.

The first category is much the same as the Hindu Avatar. The doctrine of *Resulallah* or messenger from God is the Islamic version. It finds an echo in the fourth Gospel: "There was a man sent from God whose name was John." The doctrine expresses Divine concern with the predicament of humanity. Gurdjieff explicitly shows how this concern is manifested through creative ideas, rather than by supernatural intervention. There is nothing startlingly new here, until we turn to the second category and relate it to the Reciprocal Maintenance. Gurdjieff constantly insists that the same service and sacrifice by which we play our part in the Reciprocal Maintenance transforms our nature from thinking animal to free individual and creates on earth a society that is in harmony with Nature. Man's nature is dynamic: in order to be, he must become. In order to become, he must pay the price of his existence. When he has done so, unlimited vistas of cosmic realization open to him. He can become the trusted ally of the Supreme Power by which the world is governed.

The man 'of the way' is a familiar concept in all religions. The elect are 'called to be saints'. The Buddhist *Marga*, the Path of

Liberation, once entered will be followed to the attainment of perfected being. The Man of the Way in Sufism is the *Salik* or Seeker of the Truth. In the West, we have lost touch with this supremely important prerogative of man. We have sold our birthright for the illusion of material power. This is commonplace. The unique feature of Gurdjieff's teaching consists in the connection he makes between self-perfecting and fulfilment of a cosmic obligation. Conscious labour and intentional suffering can be very simply expressed as 'Service and Sacrifice'. These two are the instruments whereby man is transformed. By them he liberates the energies needed for the *Trogoautoegocratic* Process, he acquires his own imperishable being and he prepares a better future for his descendents. Those who repudiate the obligation incurred by our existence in human form, lose their human nature and 'perish like dogs'.

Beyond Man is the ninth essence class that Gurdjieff calls 'Angels' and that I have named 'Demiurgic' to avoid theological associations. In *Beelzebub's Tales*, three-brained beings who are immortal and do not evolve into a different order of being, play an important role as the custodians of the world order. To do their work, they require the whole range of energies liberated by the animal essence and by man. The difference is that animals produce sensitive energies by living and dying, whereas man can do so by 'conscious labour and intentional suffering'. Herein lies the distinction between conscious (*Foolasnitamnian*) living and mechanical (*Itoklanoz*) living. We must make our contribution to the needs of the Reciprocal Maintenance whether we are willing or not. We have the choice of doing so consciously and thereby 'gaining our own soul' or of living an automatic existence gaining nothing for ourselves and giving nothing to the world except by our own dissolution.

The choice before us is as stark as that of Deuteronomy 28: "behold I have set before you life and death, blessing and cursing, choose therefore life that you and your seed may live!" The difference is that the 'life' we are required to choose is not our own or even that of our fellow men, but all life. The commandment becomes: "Fill your place in the Cosmic Harmony or perish."

Gurdjieff's scheme does not end with the Demiurgic essence. In *Beelzebub's Tales*, he cites different gradations of Objective Reason attainable by beings. We can form some mental image of the Demiurges, because man in his higher nature touches the Demiurgic essence. The stage beyond is incomprehensible for it is free from the conditions of space, time and number. Distinctions like 'here' or 'there', 'then, now or in the future', 'one, two, many, a great number' are all inapplicable. The difficulty can be seen in the Apostle's Creed where one translation says: "Born of His Father before all worlds". Another says: "before time began". The long disputes as to whether Christ has one or two natures, one or two wills, one or two persons are all the consequence of using concepts that apply on our level and are meaningless on that level. In Islam, it is said that all the Messengers of God are the same and yet they are many, that God manifests in His Messengers, but that they are not God. Buddhism teaches that the Buddha neither exists nor does not exist, that Buddhas are both one and many. Gurdjieff does not attempt to find a better formula; but refers only to the Incarnated Individual who lives as a man among men. This does not help us to understand the cosmic significance of the Individual Will. Gurdjieff does, however, make it clear that the 'Most Sacred Individuals' are not to be identified with the Supreme Creative Power.

The Cosmic Individuality is directly associated with the Creation and Maintenance of the World. In Gurdjieff's symbol this is called the Eternal Unchanging: In *Beelzebub's Tales* it is the *Trogoautoegocrat*, which in some passages Gurdjieff personifies as the Holy Spirit. This is the eleventh and penultimate stage in the creation and redemption of the world. One can sense Gurdjieff's difficulty in conveying the picture of a cosmic process that is also a state of being. The *Trogoautoegocrat* is not a part of the Creation, but a manifestation of the Divine Will whereby time and eternity are reconciled. I shall not attempt to interpret further.

The Ultimate Stage is that of the Endless Creator who is also called the Father and Saviour of the World. His Reason is infinite and enables him to achieve the impossible task of creating a world that is in time and space and yet not subject to decay and dissolution. Not only this, but the world is such that independent wills can arise in it and provide the one missing element, a mode of being that, though finite, can respond perfectly to the Infinite Being and Will.

10

Gurdjieff as Teacher

B Y 1934, Gurdjieff had completed his writing career; he had abandoned the hope of establishing an organization which could bring his work before the world on a large scale. For a year or two he did very little. The time for publishing his books had not yet come and he could not return to the past. From 1935 he began to work with relatively small numbers of people. The third and final phase of his life's work, beginning in 1934 and finishing fifteen years later with his death in 1949, was his work as a teacher. Of course, this does not suggest that he undertook no teaching until he had finished writing. On the contrary, he was, and was regarded as, a teacher as far back as his time in Turkestan; but there is a very great distinction. From all we can read of his work in Tashkent and Turkestan generally after 1910 or 1911, he was engaged in demonstrating the power of the Work and of preparing himself for his mission. He was undoubtedly convinced that he had a mission to bring before the world a new understanding of human life, and to help people to liberate themselves from their fundamental blindness and egoism. To do this he intended and hoped to set up an organization, his Institute for the Harmonious Development of Man.

Gurdjieff does not present himself, in the prospectus of the Institute, as a teacher. He rather is the one who has organized a great teaching process, making use of instructors whom he has prepared for the purpose, and himself looking upon the whole process from a different vantage point, projecting into it the power of his own *Hanbledzoin*, and his own knowledge, and yet not wholly involving himself in it. He did, however, of course, become very deeply involved on account of the material question and the troubles which plagued him from the moment he set himself to fulfil his mission, troubles mainly concerning the sufferings of his own physical body —by illness and accident. During his writing period, he specifically says he gave up his contacts with people. These began to be resumed from 1927 onwards, when he certainly gave very significant personal instruction to those who went to him with the right attitude and who were able to help him in his own work, mainly by their material resources and their ability to serve. Nevertheless, it still remains true that only during these last fifteen years of his life was he predominantly devoted to preparing those who could interpret his ideas.

During the transition from writing to teaching, he lived alone, first in America and then in Paris. The two men who took care of him during the eighteen months in 1934 and 1935 have given me vivid accounts of their experience. Fred Leighton, a wealthy young American who had been with Orage and at the Prieuré in 1927 and 1928, told me that Gurdjieff, "did very little, but thought a great deal", while staying with him. Fred thought he was exhausted from his efforts to keep the Prieuré going and needed the rest. Fred did the marketing and Gurdjieff cooked a scintillating variety of dishes from all over the world.

In April 1935 Gurdjieff came to a major decision; or perhaps it was forced upon him by events. He hints at it in the last chapter of his writings, "The Inner and Outer World of Man", when he describes what happened after the death of Orage. He went to Washington in the third week of July 1935, in the confident hope of raising the money required to reopen the Institute. The death of the prospective donor in the air crash described in Chapter 7 smashed his hopes. He reacted very strongly.

Gurdjieff had to face the final and irrevocable downfall of his plan to set up an Institute. He may have thought of returning to Tashkent and beginning again where he knew that he would be accepted. The information from the Soviet Embassy that he would not be allowed to teach closed this door. The death of the Senator in whom he had pinned his hopes was balefully reminiscent of his own accidents, and of the death of Orage a few weeks earlier just when he too was on the point of returning to Gurdjieff. Everything pointed to the need for a great decision. It is most important for our assessment of Gurdjieff's connection with the Masters of Wisdom that we should know whether or not Gurdjieff went to consult them before he abandoned his writing and resumed teaching.

From what Gurdjieff said once or twice in 1949, it seems that in 1935 he made a visit to Asia—he said 'Persia', which might include Turkestan. It must have been a short trip and presumably the purpose was to consult with persons he trusted about the next phase of his life. In conversation at dinner, early in 1949, he said that a critical phase of history had started when Hitler came to power and that he had been obliged to wait until the way mankind would react to it became clear. He refers to this in *Life is Real Only Then, When "I Am"* as a time of maximum periodic tension in relation to the earth. The cosmic law of periodic tension is mentioned several times in *Beelzebub's Tales*, especially in the chapter "Russia", where it is said to be "one of the two factors that bring about war and revolution". Gurdjieff ascribed his own external inaction to the general state of the world, but emphasized that the same state which arouses in people a 'need for freedom' is also the most favourable for self-perfecting. The world situation between 1934 and 1939 was one of the strangest in history; neither people nor governments were willing to look at the situation as it really was. Religion fell to its lowest ebb: opportunism in authority and indifference among the laity was a common feature of Christianity, Judaism, Islam, Buddhism and Hinduism. Gurdjieff's own work was in its least active phase; with the death of Orage and Ouspensky's withdrawal into his country retreat at Lyne Place, expansion ceased. Ouspensky himself abandoned hope of making a new contact with the source of Gurdjieff's teaching.

From the perspective of more than a third of a century since that time, we can see that Gurdjieff was preparing a new phase of his work. In *Beelzebub's Tales*, he emphasizes the importance of legominisms as a means of transmitting important knowledge from generation to generation, verbal formulations to be interpreted by initiated beings who are able to penetrate to the essential meaning. *Beelzebub's Tales* was the legominism that Gurdjieff had prepared and his final task was to train people to fill the role of initiates when the time should come for the ideas to make their impact on the world. One of the chief requirements for such a task is perception that is both sensitive and objective. It is also necessary to be free from self-seeking. Gurdjieff looked for people with the potential for developing the required qualities. I draw upon the recollection of one of his own family to illustrate his procedure.

From 1936, Gurdjieff was living almost continuously in Paris. His

Transliteration:

Always remember that you came here having already understood the necessity of contending with yourself only with yourself and therefore thank everyone who affords such opportunities.

Plate 11   One of the Study House Aphorisms

Plate 12   Gurdjieff in later life

brother Dimitri had died. The Prieuré had been sold and the pupils and family dispersed. He took over his brother's apartment at 6 Rue des Colonels Renard which was to be his home for the next fourteen years. His sister Sophie was nursing her dying husband and her son Valentin went to live with his uncle for nearly a year. He has described the training he received from Gurdjieff. He was required to run the house and prepare meals for the pupils who often did not eat till midnight. He had to learn at a moment's notice every kind of practical skill. He describes how Gurdjieff expected him to know what was needed without being told. He had to foresee the number of people who would come for a meal and what kind of food was appropriate. He had to be so well 'tuned in' to Gurdjieff's intentions that he could go in and interrupt a conversation just when Gurdjieff required it. He had also to maintain his serenity in the face of Gurdjieff's violent onslaughts which were frequent and terrifying. Those who have witnessed Gurdjieff's rages can understand what it means to be exposed week after week to them. His entire body would shake, his face grow purple and a stream of vituperation would pour out. It cannot be said that the anger was uncontrollable, for Gurdjieff could turn it off in a moment—but it was unquestionably real. I am not sure that it was always beneficial or intentional; but in Valya's case, the final outcome was remarkable; for his ability to keep calm under stress has carried him through great difficulties and now, as the oldest surviving member of Gurdjieff's family, he is a worthy example of what Gurdjieff's training can achieve.

From 1935, Gurdjieff undertook a variety of teaching experiments. His aim throughout was to leave behind him people who would be capable of interpreting his work. He almost invariably coupled his teaching with the reading of *Beelzebub's Tales*.

Before discussing specific experiments, we shall examine Gurdjieff's methods, and endeavour to relate them to those of the Khwajagān. There is necessarily something arbitrary in dividing Gurdjieff's life periods, but it is permissible to speak of six periods: the preparatory stage, up to about fifteen years; his search up to about 1907, when he was thirty; then when he established himself in Central Asia and later moved to Russia, which was his first period of manifestation; the founding of the Institute; the writing period; and, finally, the teaching. During what I call the manifestation period, when he was proclaiming his mission to give mankind a means of liberation, he did not do very much individual teaching. His work was mainly with groups, described in considerable detail by Ouspensky in *In Search of the Miraculous*. Similar descriptions occur in other personal records such as the de Hartmanns' *Our Life With Mr. Gurdjieff*. Although these indicate relationships, they were clearly not those of a teacher and pupil in the way that this is understood in India or among the Sufis. Gurdjieff was not a guru or a sheikh, for he had set himself to work on a very much larger scale than teaching individuals. His work with groups was of an exploratory kind to prepare the way for work on a larger scale. Up to the time of his accident in 1924, he was very insistent that the aim of his work was to establish branches of his Institute all over the world in order to train teachers and instructors; to these he was going to delegate the task of realizing his mission. People who wrote about their work with Gurdjieff at this time did not see that he was more concerned with advancing his own great undertaking than with working with individuals; in nearly every case their reports give the impressions that he was occupied with them personally, even to the exclusion of others. I believe, however, that this is something that he did with many people, perhaps, with those who in some way could be useful to him, and he continued to do this till the end of his life.

From the start of course, Gurdjieff wished to communicate his ideas. He developed the ideas in the groups in St. Petersburg and Moscow, and relied on Ouspensky to express them in written form. Perhaps the time had not yet arrived for the complete development of some of the notions, which still remain fragments even in Gurdjieff's last book. However, it is clear that Gurdjieff intended that his cosmological ideas should be published. The fragment, "Glimpses of Truth", which Ouspensky heard on his very first contact with Gurdjieff contains 'The Ray of Creation', 'The Notion of Cosmoses', and what we have come to call 'The Table of Hydrogens' embodying the same number system with its platonic sesquialteral combination of two and three that was afterwards developed by Ouspensky in *In Search of the Miraculous*. From the very start, therefore, Gurdjieff was concerned with the transmission of his ideas, but this must be distinguished from teaching in the strict sense of the word.

Gurdjieff certainly employed the group as a teaching technique. This at once suggests an affiliation with Sufism, where the *Khalka* is one of the five recognized ways (see Chapter 2), in which a sheikh works with this disciples. Gurdjieff made the notion of the group quite central, as Ouspensky indicates. He spoke of three lines of work —work for oneself, work for the group, and work for the teacher or work for the Work. Gurdjieff constantly used substantially the same group methods.

The second method used by the Sufi sheikh is that of *Sohbat*, directed to awakening the understanding of the pupil. It is somewhat different from the group teaching method of the *Khalka*, where there are exercises and tasks. The *Sohbat* teacher communicates not through his words but through his presence, more akin to the Indian *Darshan*, by receiving blessing through the sheikhs presence alone. The *Sohbat*—communication by mastery is probably the literal meaning—is associated with the transmission of *baraka*, the 'enabling energy' by which the Work of the pupil is greatly enhanced. This he refers to in another terminology as 'higher-emotional energy' or, as in *Beelzebub*, as *hanbledzoin*. This transmission of a higher energy that can be assimilated to the energy of the pupil is a vital part of the whole process, and in this sense it certainly can be said that Gurdjieff, at all times, was a teacher. Everyone who met him reported the sense of mastery, of a power which acted upon them, in much the same way as those who have been in the presence of the great Indian or Zen Masters, of whom it is said that by their presence alone the pupil had been transformed.

The particular methods which are transmitted from teacher to pupil are basically of two kinds: in Sufism they are called the *vazifa* and the *zikr*. The *vazifa* is an exercise that is given to an individual as a duty to be performed. The word *zikr* literally means 'remembering', which in Gurdjieff's presentation is the means of 'remembering oneself'. The special characteristic of the Sufi *zikr* is the invocation of the Name of God. It is a directing of the intention and the will towards the Diety within. It is not clear whether Gurdjieff practised this very much with individuals in the early stages of his work. He certainly gave group tasks or required his pupils to carry out certain individual kinds of work. As recorded in Chapter 5, he bound himself by a 'special oath' in his conscience to lead in some ways an artificial life which involved refraining from placing himself in a positive relationship to people, but, on the contrary, antagonizing them by every possible means. This would be incompatible with the use of the *Sohbat* which requires sincere mutual acceptance between teacher and pupil. It may account for the observation that the methods used by Gurdjieff up till 1932 or later were different from those which he employed in the last seventeen years of his life. It was only after 1933 or 1934 that he was able to employ more positive and gentler methods in his dealings with people.

In some, but by no means all, Sufi schools of Central Asia, meditation is taught and practised. It goes under the name of *muraqaba*, which literally means 'waiting and watching'. This was not something that we learned from Gurdjieff. He would never have styled himself a meditation master, either in the Zen tradition or in the sense in which meditation is now currently taught in many Western countries. For a Sufi, meditation is a very intense process whereby man is able to penetrate through the veil of his own personality, by getting beyond his own mental associations and becoming aware of the forces that are acting behind the screen of his ordinary awareness.

It would be possible to say simply that Gurdjieff taught meditation, but in the form of self-remembering, and that he associated it with the process which assists the assimilation of higher energy from the air we breathe. The connection between meditation and breathing affects the intimate working of the organism. Gurdjieff warned all his followers that breathing exercises are dangerous and he quotes with approval the warning of the Persian dervish (*Meetings with Remarkable Men*, p. 187) who says that great harm can come from them. As a result, some of Gurdjieff's followers have advised against breathing exercises. But, in fact, Gurdjieff taught many to me and to many other of his pupils throughout his teaching period. (He explained the principles of right breathing in general lectures at the Prieuré in 1923).

Gurdjieff's understanding of meditation and exercises that accompany it was thus very different from that which is customarily taught, especially in Western countries at the present time. It seems very likely that he himself learned at practical schools in Central Asia, where meditation with breathing has been taught for many centuries —as one could recognize from the teaching of the Khwajagān to which reference is made in Chapter 2.

Distinction has been drawn between meditation or *muraqaba*, and the invocation exercises or *zikr*, which serve a different purpose. The use of invocations or *mantrams* has been known for thousands of years. It is practised by people of all religions and in all spiritual ways. It is well known in Eastern Christianity in the form of the 'prayer of the heart'. It is well-known in India in the *mantram* and in Buddhism by the various invocations and repetitions. The *zikr* is obligatory for all Sufi communities: it is part of the initiation process by which a seeker is received as pupil. The sheikh gives him the appropriate *zikr* at the time of his initiation, at the same time communicating the *baraka* or energy that enables the *zikr* to be fruitful.

There are schools which practice the *zikr* with breathing exercises, with the retention of breath—the *hafs-i-nefes*; others who practise the *zikr-bil-lisan* aloud, and others again, silently, *zikr-bil-qalb*, that is, in the heart. There is, in fact, a great literature on the different *zikrs* employed by all the different Sufi schools, just as there is in India and Buddhist countries connected with the *mantrams*. The *mantram* is, substantially, the same thing as the *zikr*, consisting of an invocation of a few words that is repeated rhythmically or, in some cases, non-rhythmically, sometimes in time with the heartbeat, sometimes in time with the breathing, sometimes according to some externally imposed rhythm. Gurdjieff was well aware of all these methods but he taught them comparatively seldom and did not bring them into his public teaching.

In Sufism, and especially in the teaching of the Khwajagān, exercises alone were never regarded as adequate. All the masters taught the necessity of *riyazat* and *inkisar*, which is discipline, austerity and voluntary suffering. Gurdjieff translated these as "conscious labour and intentional suffering". In *Beelzebub's Tales*, the word is *partkdolgduty*, which is the word obligation in Armenian, Russian and English. No Khwaja could have spoken more emphatically than Gurdjieff about the need for labour and suffering on the path of self-perfecting. Gurdjieff in one of his lectures explained that intentional suffering means to expose oneself to painful situations in order to help others, especially situations caused by the negative manifestations of those one is trying to help. Almost all the heroes of *Beelzebub's Tales* are said to have undertaken *partkdolgduty* in order to acquire knowledge that would help mankind, especially future generations. Gurdjieff himself regarded the sufferings he incurred in his decisions, first, to establish the Institute and, later, to write his books, as means of paying the debt of his existence. It is true that Gurdjieff made things hard for his pupils, and they often took their sufferings as *partkdolgduty*. The Khwajagān also could be extremely hard on their pupils in the early stages of their training, but neither Gurdjieff nor the Masters of Wisdom continued this beyond a few years. By that time, they expected pupils to have found the way to create their own *partkdolgduty* and to find their discipline and austerity in the work of helping others. There are very profound secrets connected with the transmutation of suffering: I intend to say what I can about Gurdjieff's procedure in the next chapter.

An extraordinary manifestation of Gurdjieff's teaching is what were called at the Prieuré 'the exercises' and later came to be called 'the movements'. Gurdjieff himself describes his own status in the first chapter of *Beelzebub* as that of a teacher of temple dancing. He often repudiated any other role. This, of course, was not meant to be taken seriously, but it was for many the most attractive part of his work. It was through his sacred dances and movements that he made his first impact in America in 1924. I myself was first deeply impressed when in 1920 I saw a demonstration of the movements in a building close to the Grand Rabbinate in Constantinople. Gurdjieff's introduction to the West of the series of Temple Dances and Sacred Rhythms was a unique contribution.

Gurdjieff embodied teachings connected with the use of the body even in Tashkent, where sacred dances were known to the local inhabitants. He continued them with a selected group in St. Petersburg. During the revolution years they were temporarily abandoned, but taken up again when he went with his group to the Caucasus, and firmly established when he opened his Institute for the third time in Tiflis. He continued to use them in a very significant way for the propagation of his ideas, first at the Institute in Fontainebleau, then in Paris and in the United States in 1924 before his accident. Movements were abandoned after the accident, during the intensive period of his writing, but they were resumed in 1928 and were taught to the groups in America, though not in a very satisfactory way. Some of his pupils taught them in England. He resumed them in Paris during the war and continued himself to teach them, and to develop new numbers, to within a few weeks of his death in 1949.

Gurdjieff explained that, in ancient times, movements of the human body occupied a very important place in the art of the Asiatic peoples. They were also used in Africa and in the Far East.

Movements were used in sacred gymnastics, in sacred dances and in religious ceremonies. "The Seekers of The Truth", which included specialists in archaeology and oriental religions, established that these sacred gymnastics had been preserved in certain parts of Central Asia, particularly in the area from Tashkent eastwards towards Chinese Turkestan.

Even as late as the beginning of the present century, sacred dances were still widely in use in temples and monasteries. I myself have witnessed them in recent years and am certain that a great deal has been preserved. The significance of the sacred gymnastics were always known by those who practised them. Traditions have been preserved in certain monasteries and brotherhoods not accessible to the ordinary traveller. Others are easier of access, some very well known, for instance, the movements of the Mevlevi dervishes, and those of the Rufa'i whose weekly ceremonies are open to visitors including Europeans. Others, such as those of the Halwatis, whose name means secluded, are accessible to those who are accepted as true seekers. The most significant of the sacred dances, those of Central Asia, are not connected with any single religion. They have existed for thousands of years and the monasteries which have preserved them possess knowledge acquired in the distant past and transmitted from generation to generation by these very same sacred dances and rituals.

The ability to interpret the meaning of the sacred gymnastics and dances cannot be acquired without long study. In fact, as much work has to be put into watching them as to performing them. He who wishes to understand and interpret them must himself work to master the art in which they consist. In the past, movements, executed to the accompaniment of music or of singing by the participants were much more usual. Many of these sacred movements were accompanied by the *zikr*. The Halwatis have a reciter whose chant reminds the dancers of the meaning of their act. Country dances were formerly the principal forms of aesthetic experience among all races, and their decay is comparatively recent; but attempts at preservation and reconstruction have, for the most part, been made without knowledge of their original significance. The modern dance, whether ballet or rhythmic exercises, has no connection at all with sacred gymnastics as they were in the past. We think of the dance, even at its highest, as the expression of an aesthetic experience. It is shared by the choreographer, the musicians and the dancers. Rules for the construction of dances and ballets of recent origin are accepted by some and rejected by others: they originate in the fashions of each passing decade, and are subjective as a matter of personal taste. The only authority they carry is derived from the popularity and fame of the experts who have brought them into use.

In ancient times, the art of dancing had an altogether different significance. It was directly connected with the religious and mystical experience, but was also part of the scientific investigations of the wisest men of each period. In the course of his own research, Gurdjieff established that sacred dances are among the few vehicles still remaining, from among the various means used in ancient times, for the preservation of important knowledge and its transmission to succeeding generations. For this reason, sacred dances have always been one of the vital subjects taught in the esoteric schools of the East. Such gymnastics have a twofold purpose. They contain and express certain principles, or they record certain events regarded as so important as to make their preservation an obligation. At the same time, they serve as a means for those who participate in them, to acquire for themselves a state of being that is harmonious, and enables them to accelerate their own spiritual development.

The first of these principles is referred to in *Beelzebub's Tales* in the chapter "Art". In the passage referring to the dance, he describes the achievements of civilization before the beginning of history in the valleys of the Euphrates and Tigris and particularly the developments which took place at the height of the Babylonian period. These, as we saw in our study of the Sarmān Brotherhood, were transferred to Central Asia some time after the conquest of Babylon by Alexander the Great. While they have been quite lost in Mesopotamia, they continued to be preserved and transmitted in Turkestan. The schools of art which were established in Central Asia after the dispersion of the Babylonian schools, following the conquest of Persia by the Greeks, persisted and were found in the schools of Mithras and Manes up to Sassanian times.

According to legend, a society of learned men settled in the city of Babylon and undertook the task of preserving their knowledge in various ways. One was the use of sacred gymnastics. Gurdjieff's account tells how they "demonstrated with the necessary explanations every possible form of religious and popular dances, either those already existing which they only modified or quite new ones which they created" (*Beelzebub's Tales*, p. 475). Rituals, legends and teaching stories are the other means by which ancient wisdom is preserved.

In order to illustrate the way in which the preservation of know-ledge was achieved, Gurdjieff takes the Law of Sevenfoldness (*Heptaparaparshinokh*),[a] which he says was well-known to the Baby-lonian sages. There is the corroboration that the Pythagoreans are one of our main sources for the reconstruction of this law, and Pythagoras was among the sages taken by Cambyses from Egypt to Babylon in 510 BC. Not only the assembly of wise men, but also the people in general, were, at that time, aware that there was something mysterious about the way natural processes passed from one stage to another. They knew that man cannot achieve his aims by a direct attack upon his objective. As this very necessary knowledge was later lost, the world needs to find it again. It was with their remote descendants in view that the Babylonian sages set themselves the task of preserving the principles of the Law of Sevenfoldness in the various human arts and crafts. Beelzebub explains this to his grand-son by saying: "In order that you should have a better idea and well understand in which way they indicated what they wished in these dances, you must know that the learned beings of this time had al-ready long been aware that every posture and movement of every being in general, in accordance with the same Law of Sevenfoldness, always consists of seven what are called 'mutually-balanced-tensions' arising in seven independent parts of their whole, and that each of these seven parts in their turn consists of seven different what are called 'lines-of movement', and each line has seven what are called 'points-of-dynamic-concentration'; and all this that I have just des-cribed, being repeated in the same way and in the same sequence but always on a diminishing scale, is actualized in the minutest sizes of total bodies called 'atoms'.

"And so, during their dances, in the movements lawful in their accordance with each other, these learned dancers inserted intentional inexactitudes, also lawful, and in a certain way indicated in them the information and knowledge which they wished to transmit."

The programme of his demonstration of the work of the Institute for the Harmonious Development of Man in Paris and New York in 1923 and 1924 introduced some of the movements. The following are extracts:

[a] See Chapter 8.

GENERAL INTRODUCTION

"The program of this evening will be chiefly devoted to movements of the human body as shown by the art of the Ancient East in sacred gymnastics, sacred dances, and religious ceremonies preserved in temples of Turkestan, Tibet, Afghanistan, Kafiristan, Chitral.

"Mr. Gurdjieff with other members of the Institute pursued during many years, through the countries of the East, a series of investigations which proved that Oriental dances have not lost the deep significance—religious, mystic, and scientific—which belonged to them in far off ages.

"Sacred dances have always been one of the vital subjects taught in esoteric schools of the East. Such gymnastics have a double aim: they contain and express a certain form of knowledge and at the same time serve as a means to acquire an harmonious state of being.

"The farthest possible limits of one's strength are reached through the combination of unnatural movements in the individual gymnastics which help to obtain certain qualities of sensation, various degrees of concentration, and the requisite directing of the thought and the senses.

"As for the dancing itself, it has in that form quite another meaning to that which we of the West are accustomed to give it. We must remember that the ancient dance was a branch of art; and art in that early time served the purpose of higher knowledge and of religion. In those days he who had devoted himself to the study of any special subject, expressed his knowledge in works of art, and particularly in dances, just as we today give out our wisdom through books. Thus the ancient sacred dance is not only the medium for an aesthetic experience, but also a book as it were, containing a definite piece of knowledge. Yet it is a book which not everyone may read who would —which not everyone can read who will.

"A detailed study—extended throughout many years—of sacred gymnastics and sacred dances, gave practical proof of their great importance in connection with the all round development of man, one of the principal aims of Mr. Gurdjieff,—the parallel development of all man's powers. The exercises in sacred gymnastics are used in this system as one of the means of educating the students' moral force, and of developing their will, their patience, their capacity for thought concentration, hearing, sight, sense of touch, and so on."

In the programme much information was given about places that Gurdjieff visited and the origin of the dances and rhythms. He said that the inscriptions on some of the great buildings of Asia state that they were built to the accompaniment of music and dancing. This custom of building to music was still followed at the beginning of this century at the sources of the Pjandje River and in the Oasis of Keriya. He showed exercises said to be taken from the 'Temple of Medicine at Sari in Tibet' and from an esoteric school called the 'Seers' which had existed 'since time immemorial' in large artificial caves in the heights of Kidgera in Kafiristan. He also referred to monasteries at Maxari Sherif and Khavar in Afghanistan. Uchan-su —the flowing water—in Kashgaria was the centre of a Suhari *tekke*.

The programme concluded with an account of the important Sufi Stop Exercise:

"In this exercise, the pupil must at the word 'stop' or upon a previously arranged signal arrest all movement. The command can be given at any time or anywhere. Whatever he may be doing, whether at work, repose, at meals, on the Institute premises or outside, he must instantly stop. The tension of his muscles must be maintained, his facial expression, his smile, his gaze, must remain fixed and in the same state as they were in when the command caught him. The positions thus obtained are used by beginners for mental work in order to quicken intellectual activity while developing the will.

"The Stop exercises gives no new postures; it is simply an incipient movement interrupted. We generally change our attitudes so unconsciously that we do not notice what positions we assume between two attitudes. With this exercise the transition from one posture to another is cut in two. The body arrested by the sudden command is forced to stop in a position in which it never came to a standstill before. This enables the man to observe himself better. He can feel himself with new light. In this manner he may break through the vicious circle of his automatism.

"For the arbitrariness of our movements is illusory. Psychological analysis and the study of the psychomotor functions as laid down by the Gurdjieff system, show that every one of our movements, voluntary or involuntary, is an unconscious transition from one automatic posture to another automatic posture. The man takes from among the postures open to him those that concord with his personality, for you see his repertoire is by force very limited. And all our postures are a mechanical result. We do not realize how intimately tied together are our three functions, moving, emotional and mental. They depend one upon the other. They result one from another. They are in constant reciprocal action. One does not change without others changing too. The attitude of your body corresponds to your sentiments and to your thoughts. A change in your emotions will inevitably produce the corresponding change in your mental attitude and in your physical pose. A change of thought will start another current of emotional energy, which will naturally change the physical posture. So that, if we want to alter our ways of feeling and our forms of thinking, we must first change our moving postures, and at the same time, without changing our emotional and mental postures, it is impossible for us to acquire new moving postures. We cannot change one without changing the other. For instance, if a man's attention were concentrated on fighting, the automatism of his thinking processes and habitual movements would prevent a new way of thinking by producing the old mental associations. And not only are the thinking, feeling and moving processes in man bound together, but they are condemned to work, each and all, inside this closed circle of automatic postures. The Institute's method of preparation for the harmonious development of man, is to free him from automatism. The Stop exercise helps much toward that object. The physical body being maintained in an unaccustomed position, the subtler bodies of emotion and thought can stretch into another shape.

"It is however essential to remember that an external command to stop is necessary, in order to bring the man's will into operation, without which he could not keep the unfinished posture. A man cannot order himself to stop, because the combined postures of our three functions are too heavy for the will to move. Coming from another the command 'Stop!' plays the role of the mental and emotional functions whose state generally commands the physical posture, and in that case the physical posture not being in its habitual condition of slavery to the mental and emotional postures loses its strength, thereby weakening the other postures. And that enables our will to rule for a time over our functions."

If it had not been for his accident in 1924, Gurdjieff would no doubt have begun to use the movements in the traditional way as they were used in the ancient temples, for the principal purpose of transmission of knowledge directly to the higher centres without passing through the mind. As things turned out, the main use of the movements has been always for the second purpose, the inner development of those who directly participate in them. The body for Gurdjieff is not simply the physical organism, but this organism endowed with its three brains or three modes of perception. The three brains participate in everything that we do without co-ordination or harmony. One undoubted value of working at the movements is to bring about an awakening of the latent powers of the centres and to harmonize their working. But this is not a process that can be used for every stage of development. There has been a good deal of misunderstanding about Gurdjieff's movements in this respect. It is true that one of the first requirements for the attainment of the harmonious state of being is to achieve a proper balance between the three functions. Generally speaking, in Western man, feeling and organic sensation are not only undeveloped, but they play an unnatural and even harmful part in man's life. It is through the distortion of our feelings that we are subject to negative emotions and through distortion of our organic sensations that our bodily sensations are constantly interfering with the free working of our consciousness. Through properly selected movements, used in the right sequence and with the right understanding of the purpose, many defects—both physical and emotional—can be corrected and the pupil thereby brought to a more balanced and normal state.

It is also very necessary that we should develop the power of attention. This is brought into play in the gymnastic movements when it is necessary to be able to concentrate attention upon different parts of the body and know what they are doing without having to look at them or think about them. More advanced movements help to obtain certain qualities of sensation and produce a certain degree of control over the state of consciousness which is very hard for the ordinary untrained Western man.

Gurdjieff affirms that work on the movements also serves for developing man's own 'I'; that is, his 'will'. He comes to a stage where he is able to feel quite independent of his own body and, at the same time, in a state of mastery towards it. He is able to experience the feelings, even very refined feelings, that correspond to different gestures and sequences of movements and he can at the same time avoid being identified. All of this is of great value in the development of the will.

Although these uses of the sacred gymnastics, and all the training that accompanies it, make it a very important part of the whole of Gurdjieff's teaching, everything that Gurdjieff did was only directed towards the attainment of a particular result, a certain change, for example, in the pupil. He would give exercises which would be carried out for a certain time then abandoned or changed, and similarly with the movements. He did not intend those who were working on themselves, and who used the movements solely for this purpose, to continue to do the movements many years. Those however, who were intended to give demonstrations were serving the purpose of the Work, and in their case the movements was not so much a teaching as an act of service.

There is, of course, a tendency to look upon the movements as a spectacle. They are very beautiful and they produce a strong effect on the psyche of the onlookers. But their beauty is secondary and I think that Gurdjieff would agree with the dictum of the Indian Sage that "beauty does not lead us to God, beauty only leads us to beauty".[a] It is not through beautiful and harmonious movements that we achieve liberation, and Gurdjieff also taught ugly and discordant movements which helped to liberate men and women from obsession with their own appearance. In watching him teaching a class it was strange to see women unwilling to make ugly faces and discordant movements, in spite of the fact that they knew they were working on the movements for their own development and not in order to excite the admiration of the onlooker.

Gurdjieff, as a teacher of candidates for initiation, used different methods for different types and for the opposite sexes. He was constantly on the watch for those who had the potential for interpreting his message. He did not neglect those with small potential, but on the whole he taught them in a general way, whereas those who had great possibilities were subjected to the full force of his extraordinary powers.

There was a marked distinction in his teaching of men and women. In *Beelzebub's Tales*, Gurdjieff regarded women as having a passive role compared to the active role natural for men. A man who does not fulfil his active role, and a woman who on the contrary attempts to fill one, are both, according to him, members of the third sex for whom there is little prospect of transformation. All this is made clear

[a] cf. *The Long Pilgrimage* by J. G. Bennett, p. 164.

in very plain terms in the chapter "Russia" of *Beelzebub's Tales*. This apparently disparaging attitude towards women has been the cause of considerable difficulty for modern people who wish to put this distinction aside. But it is remarkable that many women were not only very devoted but also very successful pupils of Gurdjieff and attained perhaps more than most of the men. The main difference is in the kind of relationship which is possible between teacher and male pupil and what he can do with a female pupil.

At the Prieuré the roles of men and women were different. In the Study House men sat on the right and women sat on the left. On Saturdays, the men went alone with Gurdjieff to the Russian bath and there they heard many things that we were supposed not to repeat in the ears of women. After the Russian bath the men went privately to dine with Gurdjieff and the toasts, first of all, were given for men only—in accordance with almost all dervish practice. It was not until after his accident, when life at the Prieuré became more of a family affair than a work situation, that the segregation of men and women was modified. Several of the women nevertheless occupied very important and decisive positions. Mme Ouspensky, who at one time was in charge of the kitchen, was a very effectual and stern teacher. I learned unforgettable lessons in just one week as kitchen boy under her supervision. Mme de Hartmann was of decisive importance in the practical running of the Prieuré: without her it is hard to see how Gurdjieff could have kept it going. In later years, Mme de Salzmann became Gurdjieff's right hand without whom he could scarcely have launched his work in such a way that it would be able to continue after his death. These three women played a very important part. Nevertheless, Gurdjieff was insistent that it was not the role of women to take responsibility and make decisions.

Not many women succeeded in establishing a close relationship with him. As I said before, the three women who helped him most, Mme Ouspensky, Mme de Hartmann and Mme de Salzmann, also were separated from him but never in the same way as the men. They were always free to come and go and I think that they would have had no difficulty renewing their relationship. With other women pupils he had a different kind of relationship. With some there was no sexual element, with others a very strong sexual element. His sexual life was strange in its unpredictability. At certain times he led a strict, almost ascetic life, having no relation with women at all. At other times, his sex life seemed to go wild and it must be said that his unbridled periods were more frequent than the ascetic. At times, he had sexual relationships not only with almost any woman who happened to come within the sphere of his influence, but also with his own pupils. Quite a number of his women pupils bore him children and some of them remained closely connected with him all their lives. Others were just as close to him, as far as one could tell, without the sexual relationship. When we were in Paris in 1949, there was a tendency on the part of some of the women to convey the impression that only women could really understand him and only those women who had slept with him were really initiated into his Work. This is something on which I am not able to express an opinion, but it has to be recorded that for some women the Work relationship and sex relationship were inseparable. For others, it was not so at all. Gurdjieff could be 'all things to all women'.

When Gurdjieff's teaching period began in 1934, he set up a close relationship with a small group of remarkable women. These included Georgette Leblanc, who had been Maeterlink's mistress, Margaret Anderson who was one of the founders of *The Little Review*, Kathryn Hulme, who wrote *The Nun's Story*, and two others. Jane Heap had a loose connection with the group. With these women, he carried through for two or three years a very intensive and extraordinary experiment, making use of methods that brought them into remarkable psychic states, and developed their powers far more rapidly than had been the case with the pupils who had been with him during earlier years. Everyone of these women afterwards achieved considerable success, mostly as writers. The whole story is contained in the memoirs of two or three of them who wrote of their experiences—some of which I have been privileged to read but not permitted to quote from. I hope that they may see fit to publish what happened during those years, because it throws a very vivid light upon Gurdjieff's methods as a teacher and upon his use, for example, of drugs as a method of developing not only psychic experiences, but also opening the hidden channels of the human psyche. These ladies had a special relationship which continued right up to the end of Gurdjieff's life. When they came to visit him they were always treated as privileged people. This was true also of the English women, much more staid and I think probably without a sexual relationship, who included Miss Alexander, Miss Elinor Crowdy, and that remarkable woman, Miss Gordon, who died in Paris having never been separated from Gurdjieff and who had attained extraordinary results in her work upon herself. Miss Merston, after 1932, went to India and settled with Sri Ramana Maharshi at Tiruvannamalai; she had played an important part in the running of the Prieuré, possibly second only to that of Mme de Hartmann. There was also Mrs. Louise March who had come as a young German secretary to help with the German translation of *Beelzebub*.

Apart from these women, with whom Gurdjieff had in some way or another a special relationship, chiefly because they were able to help him in his work, there were great numbers of women pupils who aspired to a closer relationship. The story was always going about that Gurdjieff was seducing almost every woman that came to him and he himself lent colour to this. He used to say to a young girl, for example, coming to visit him for the first or second time, that she should stay behind after everyone else had gone or come back and knock at his door, and conveyed that this was the promise of a very special kind of experience. Sometimes girls were frightened and did not go. Others went but with some kind of wrong attitude, in which case they usually received a handful of sweets and were told to go away, Gurdjieff putting on the air of not understanding what it was they had come for. It seems that those who were discreet and who understood that by going to visit Gurdjieff they were not receiving any high spiritual benefit but simply a sexual occasion, were able to stay with him and have a relationship.

He was very insistent that sex should be separated from the intellectual and emotional life of man. Sex was sex and, if treated as such, was not only a legitimate but even a necessary part of the process of our development. It is, of course, clear from the chapter "Purgatory" of *Beelzebub's Tales* that Gurdjieff regards the sex energy, there called *exiohary*, as the main source of nourishment for the higher bodies of man. His teaching about the transformation of the sexual energy is very personal and he was emphatic that there are no general rules that can be given. In some cases he regarded abstinence as desirable, in others encouraged strong sexual activity; in some cases self-control, in others the devotion of one man and one woman to the creation of one single soul between them. In some cases, he demanded at least for a time a completely promiscuous sexual life in order to rid a man of obsession with sex. This variety of advice as regards sex leaves one with the feeling that Gurdjieff did not wish to give any rules that people would take to be universally valid and that could lead not only to misunderstanding but even to disaster.

Gurdjieff had a different approach for every pupil, but two main attitudes were discernible in his dealings with men. There was a comparatively small number of men whom he saw as possible independent sources for the development and transmission of the ideas and methods, that is, as potential initiates. With them Gurdjieff was very demanding and, in every case, at a certain point, he made it impossible for them to continue to work with him. The best known case is that of Ouspensky himself. Ouspensky was to the very end of his life devoted to Gurdjieff. He was convinced that Gurdjieff was no ordinary man. He knew that it was Gurdjieff alone that had given him hope that it would be possible to find a way out of the state of mechanicalness and confusion into which he saw the whole world plunged. He had no doubt that Gurdjieff had the secret of a method that would work and he had decided to devote his life to its propagation. Yet, within two years, Gurdjieff began to drive Ouspensky away from him. They met first in 1915, but did not start to work together until 1916; yet by 1918 Ouspensky had already made his first decision to separate from Gurdjieff and work on his own. Afterwards they came together again in Constantinople and worked together in the friendliest spirit. When Ouspensky came to London and Gurdjieff to Berlin, the relationship seemed to be full of promise, and we all regarded the two men as inseparable in the presentation of the Work. Yet the bombshell came in 1924, when Ouspensky informed us that he was severing all connection with Gurdjieff and told us that we had to make the choice, either to go back to Gurdjieff and lose all connection with him, or to stay with him and break off all contact with Gurdjieff. At first, it might appear that the decision was Ouspensky's, but, as the story has become clearer, it is evident that this was something that Gurdjieff himself did in Ouspensky's own interest: he put before Ouspensky a barrier which he had to surmount. He did this in such a way that it was impossible for him to surmount it immediately. Only by going away and coming to understand for himself the true nature of the situation could he reach the point where a decision to return could be taken. But with Ouspensky, this decision never was taken. Between 1924 and 1947, that is for twenty-three years, Gurdjieff and Ouspensky did not again meet and Ouspensky would not allow the name "Gurdjieff" to be mentioned in his presence. Gurdjieff, for his part, spoke always disparagingly of Ouspensky whom he even accused of sabotaging the Work by his failure to carry out the undertaking to write the system in a form that would be intelligible to all, so making it necessary for Gurdjieff to take the unaccustomed role of author. One of Ouspensky's most intimate friends and pupils told me of spending an evening with Ouspensky who, at that time, was drinking far too heavily. This was in the late 1940's not long before Ouspensky's final illness. When he was already in his cups, Ouspensky had broken down and cried, saying: "Doesn't he understand how much I love him? Why does he not let me go back to him? He knows that I need him and I know that he needs me." This cry of distress, which I know was authentic, shows the way in which Gurdjieff could make things almost impossible for those from whom he expected the most.

Reference has already been made to the circumstances under which Thomas de Hartmann was sent away in 1928. Orage, who had made the great decision to sacrifice everything, to break up his own work, and devote himself entirely to Gurdjieff in 1923, a commitment confirmed later when he signed the famous letter of renunciation in 1930, had parted from Gurdjieff by 1931 and decided to devote himself to propagating the Douglas system of Social Credit. The truth is that Gurdjieff made a demand of Orage which would, had he been able to respond to it, have set him free from his own central weakness. It was the inability to make the decision that made him return to London, and he was highly successful in his outward life, not so much in promoting Social Credit as in re-establishing himself as the leading literary editor with the *New English Weekly*. But he made up his mind to return to Gurdjieff at all costs, and told his friends of his decision. He gave his last broadcast on the B.B.C., and took steps to sever his connections with his own paper and with Social Credit. That night his heart failed and he died. Gurdjieff refers in *Third Series* to the extraordinary effect that this had upon him. In this case, I think that Gurdjieff himself counted upon his return and had not allowed for his premature death.

Dr. Stjernwal had been with him from the very earliest times of his starting his work in Russia. He had been with him through all the vicissitudes and dangers of the Russian Revolution and the escape from the Caucasus, travelled with him from Constantinople to Berlin, Brussels, London, and Paris and had helped him to found the Institute. Stjernwal was Gurdjieff's right-hand man in the visits to

America in 1924. He and his wife were old and close friends, and yet
in his case also Gurdjieff created a situation which made it impossible
for them to stay. He left the Prieuré and never renewed his contact
with Gurdjieff.

I remember with much feeling the case of two younger Russians,
Ivanoff and Ferapontoff, who were at the Prieuré in 1923. The
latter had been my teacher of the movements and I had known him
even earlier in Constantinople. It seemed out of the question that
either Ferapontoff or Ivanoff would be separated from Gurdjieff.
Ferapontoff was his secretary, the Russian pupil most fluent in
English. He did a great deal of the translating during the lectures and
he and Ivanoff were two of the leaders in the movement's demonstrations. Yet they also were driven away. They went first to Australia,
afterwards joining me in Athens, where I learned something about
the circumstances. I shall not go into the tragic sequel for those two
men were so full of promise who should have been points of expansion for the spreading of the ideas and methods. They were unable
to bear the treatment they received from Gurdjieff; they could not
understand that he did not allow them to understand.

The case of Alexander de Salzmann has already been mentioned. A
great stage designer, his brilliant lighting was partly responsible for
the extraordinary effect produced by the movements when I saw them
in the Champs-Élysées Théâtre in 1923. Salzmann was on exceptionally gifted man. I worked with him at the Prieuré in the forest
where it seemed that he must have been a forester all his life, but to
my astonishment, I later learned that he had had no experience of
forests except for a few weeks with Gurdjieff in the Caucasus. Salzmann and his wife, Jeanne, were the mainstay of Gurdjieff's opening
of the Institute in Tiflis and they meant a great deal to him in the
Prieuré. Yet Salzmann also was compelled to leave. His health broke
down and he died a few years later in Switzerland.

I do not not know how to place my own position. At our first meeting in 1920 I regarded him almost at once as my teacher. When I went
to the Prieuré in 1923, he made it clear that he accepted me as a
pupil and I was convinced that my life was thence forward linked
up with him. I counted on going back to the Prieuré to work with
him and eventually to become one of his helpers. Yet, after leaving
the Prieuré in August, 1923, I did not see Gurdjieff again till
I went to Paris in August 1948, exactly twenty-five years later. How
it came about that I lost my contact, how it was that I did not

understand what was happening, even now it is hard to explain. When I returned to Gurdjieff in 1948, I said to him that I felt that I had lost the best part of my life in the twenty-five years that I had been separated from him. He said: "No, it was necessary. Without this you would not be able to receive what I now can give you. You could not stay with me. Now you will be able to stay." And I stayed with him from that time until the end of his life. I felt that it was something very extraordinary that after twenty-five years I should be able to return; and in certain respects he continued the teaching almost as he had left it when I had last spoken to him, in Turkish at that time, in 1923. The experience, the successes and the failures of my life during the intervening period made the situation totally different: yet, I still felt like a child who was just beginning to learn what the world was all about.

I had been one of those who had the experience of being driven away and could not understand why or even how it happened to them. There were others who were able to stay with Gurdjieff and in effect become part of his family. They were more dependent upon him, more ready to be passive and he did not make the same demands upon them. There were some who went to him in trouble and he gave them great help and support. There were others whom he accepted to teach his methods, to teach the movements, to teach the exercises, to work with the new groups, but this all happened during the war years when planned activity was impossible. If he had not seen the end of his life coming, it is in my view probable that most of the men on whom he leant heavily in his last years would also have been sent away.

Before leaving Gurdjieff's role as a teacher, we must refer to the results of his activity during so many years. It seems that he had accepted pupils from 1909 onwards, and perhaps tens of thousands of followers had accepted his ideas. But not many of these met him, and still fewer had any kind of personal relationship with him. Yet, the number of those to whom he gave personal guidance at some time and who have regarded themselves as his pupils, probably run into a thousand or more. To my knowledge, only a small handful of men and of women have achieved something beyond the ordinary level, have come to 'realized being'. Though few, they are of great significance and, even if not all of them are widely known, they are playing a valuable role in the world at the present time.

To evaluate a process, we must know the aim to which it is

directed. Gurdjieff wished to show as many people as possible how to do the work of transforming energies that is necessary for the evolution of mankind. In this he succeeded to a moderate degree. He also wished to prepare 'initiates' who could interpret *Beelzebub's Tales* as a legominism and enable the profound knowledge the book contains to become available when the world should be ready for it. This concerns the future and I shall reserve discussion of it to the last chapter.

11

Man

IF Man, like everything living or non-living that exists in the universe, is an apparatus for transforming energies, what is there special about him? If we perform our cosmic function, to what can we aspire for our own personal fulfilment? In a public lecture given in New York in January 1924, six months before his accident, Gurdjieff said: "Man—how mighty it sounds! The very name 'Man' means the acme of Creation: but how does his title fit contemporary man? At the same time, man should indeed be the acme of Creation, since he is formed with and has in himself all the possibilities of acquiring all the data exactly similar to the data in the *Actualizer of Everything Existing* in the Whole of the Universe." He added, "To possess the right to the name of man one must be one." Two hundred years ago, Goethe wrote, *"Man sollt streben zu werden was er ist"*—"One must strive to become what one is". Gurdjieff's teaching about man could not be better expressed.

Our trouble is that we demand the status and privileges to which a real man is entitled without having paid the price of becoming true men and women. Since the seventeenth century, the Rights of Man have coloured our attitude to such an extent that even those who have been attracted to Gurdjieff's ideas have seldom paused to consider the full implications of the question why we should be here at all. We assess most things in terms of their possible usefulness to us, and yet it does not occur to us to ask whether we are not required to be useful for some purpose other than the satisfaction of our human desires, or at least our human needs. We do not take in the full significance of the assertion that the nobility of man consists in what he can become and in what he can give and not in what he is and what he has. One reason for this is our own egoism, but another equally serious obstacle is our ignorance. We do not know what we can become or what we can give. To know these things we need to discover the true link between our human nature and the universal nature. This is what Gurdjieff can help us to find.

The doctrine of Reciprocal Maintenance states that everything that exists serves some purpose, and that man's part in it is to transform energy. If this be true, then our entire attitude towards man and his destiny must be revolutionized. We can no longer think of ourselves as entitled to do what we like with the Earth and all that lives on it, providing only that we do not harm our fellow men or jeopardize their future—which is about as far as those who concern themselves with human problems are prepared to go at the present time. It is not only the attitude of modern non-religious man that is inconsistent with the idea of Reciprocal Maintenance. 'The world is made for man' (and man is made for God) attitude is characteristic of the Western religions, those that we call the Judaeo-Christian tradition. The Eastern doctrine that man's very existence on the Earth is an unnatural state from which he can liberate himself, is inconsistent with the belief that man serves a purpose which he must fulfil whether he likes it or not, insofar as the word 'existence' is taken as the only reality. The Buddhist Nirvana confuses those who cannot understand that existence is a state of limitation from which we can be liberated. Gurdjieff's assertion that we must 'pay the debt of our existence' is fully consistent with the belief that, by paying the price, we can be released from the limitations of existence. The real inconsistency arises from equating existence with reality, and from the assumption that man, by the mere fact of existing, has a place in the real world. Side by side with this assumption is the humanist doctrine of man's 'right' to live a secure and happy life. Everything turns upon our understanding of what is meant by paying the debt of our existence.

Ever since man's attitude towards life has been founded upon rights rather than upon obligations, we have lost touch with the sense and purpose of our existence. According to Gurdjieff, it was not so before the last Epoch. There was a time, that he connects with the Sumerian civilization, when people were aware that the purpose of life was not the satisfaction of our desires but the fulfilment of a cosmic purpose.

The whole of Gurdjieff's teaching and the example of his life contradict some of the most cherished beliefs of modern man. We believe for example, in unlimited material progress, coupled with the right to dominate nature and to impose ourselves to an ever greater extent upon the world in which we live. In recent times, this belief has even gone beyond the limits of our planet, and people have thought seriously of colonizing other planets and even of invading other stars. All this stems from an attitude that is deeply ingrained. Even if we put aside all the exaggerations, it is impossible to justify man's disregard of the rights of non-human existence and his view of all obligations in anthropomorphic terms. It is painfully true that man has created God in his own image and ascribes to him the same sort of demands as we people make upon the world. It is very hard to understand the extent to which we are imprisoned in an anthropocentric world. Not even the revelations of modern science that there are worlds into which man can never penetrate have brought us to our senses. These worlds are either too small or too great, or involve time periods so far exceeding those of human life that we disappear before them. It seems that almost the entire Universe must remain securely entrenched in his man-made, man-conceived world, and all that Gurdjieff did to try to awaken us to the absurdity of this attitude has been largely disregarded.

Those who come to Gurdjieff's teaching do so usually because they are aware of the inadequacy of other systems or ideas and the unsatisfactory quality of the life they are living. They can quite readily accept some of the basic teaching that man is 'asleep', that he does not know himself, that he has no 'I', that he has no 'will', and they grasp at the hope that by work upon oneself these defects in our nature can perhaps be remedied. But, if such an assessment of the goal of transformation goes no further than this, it still remains imprisoned within man-made concepts. To get beyond this, we need first of all to ask ourselves whether we are prepared to accept the doctrine of Reciprocal Maintenance. For this turns upside down the idea that the world is made for man, and asserts, on the contrary, that man is made to serve the world. Note that it is not God, but the world around us, that we serve by the *Trogoautoegocrat*.

I have started from this point because it is necessary, if we are to appreciate the importance of Gurdjieff's contribution, to understand that he does not simply offer us a system for improving ourselves, for bettering our lives, for overcoming the defects in our nature. He offers us, on the contrary, an entirely new outlook on life and a new understanding of the goal and purpose of human existence.

The basic description of the human situation is succinctly made in

Ouspensky's little book *The Psychology of Man's Possible Evolution*. He shows that we can easily test and verify for ourselves that we are not conscious in the way that we commonly suppose. The greater part of our lives is passed in the state of automatic movement and 'thinking', devoid of intention or even awareness. In the West, we believe that we are permanent individuals; we have accepted Descartes' plausible argument that "I think and therefore I am". Though this was refuted long ago by Hume and the other sceptics, Gurdjieff makes it a starting point of a new kind of understanding. While accepting the sceptical view that man has no 'I', he also shows that among the many 'I's that are constantly succeeding one another in the awareness, it is possible for a certain number to change their attitude, to recognize that they are in a state of slavery, and to set themselves to work to become free. Many of these ideas, revolutionary when they were first presented in 1921, are now being verified by modern behavioural research, and are being claimed as new discoveries. The conclusion reached by Ouspensky's study is that man is very seldom able to decide anything for himself, because of:

1. His inability to act on his own conscious intention.
2. His enslavement by habits formed in the past.
3. The extent of his influence by the external world.
4. The immutable characteristics of his own nature.

It is generally accepted that man is conscious of only a part of himself, and that very important processes concerned with his nature take place outside of his conscious awareness. The doctrine of the 'unconscious', which was introduced by Hartmann, and became the central feature of Freud's psychology, is now quite orthodox, though strangely, the nature of the unconscious is little understood, even after a hundred years of research. Therefore, in spite of the fact that Gurdjieff's attitude towards man is not acceptable to modern psychology, many people are now attracted to his ideas and methods.

We must, however, understand that this is only the first introduction to the ideas. As soon as we go beyond the diagnosis of man's deficiences and the demonstration that it is possible to do something about them, we enter into realms that are foreign to modern psychology.

The Harmonious Development of Man, as understood by Gurdjieff, is an extraordinary process that makes it possible for us to go beyond the limitations of our ordinary human nature, to enter different states of consciousness, to acquire new powers for understanding, and to go beyond the conditioning of our earthly existence. The best way of looking at this concept of man's possible development is to take Gurdjieff's division of human nature into seven categories. Man has a thinking, a feeling and an instinctive nature. These are not equally balanced in all people. The majority are dominated by their bodies, by their instincts, by physical habits, by sex. Men and women dominated by the physical body are called men or women number one. Man number one is not necessarily what we might call a 'physical type'. He may be intelligent and interested in ideas; but when his behaviour is carefully observed, it can be seen that he is dominated by material considerations. He is insensitive to the feelings of others and has not even much feeling for himself. He may appear to make intellectual judgments, but looked at closely they prove to be based on quantity rather than quality, on the visible and tangible rather than a sensitive appreciation of deeper values.

There are also many who are dominated by their feelings, though they are much less numerous than the first category. Their emotional states are more important to them than their bodily and mental states. These are called men number two. They are people who have strong feelings; whether or not they have strong bodies, it is the feelings that predominate. In the extreme case, man number two is emotionally exaggerated. His likes and dislikes are flamboyant, his enthusiasms irrational, his hopes and fears unrelated to the facts of the world. Not all men number two are obviously emotional; the real mark is that of trusting feelings rather than material considerations or abstract ideas. Man number two may love money and possessions but he does so to satisfy his self-love, rather than to find material security. He can feel for others, but only insofar as he is himself involved. Though more sensitive than man number one, he is usually more self-centred.

People of the third kind, men number three, are those whose thinking part predominates. They live by theory or assess everything in terms of yes and no, agreement and disagreement. These are the logical people whose minds dominate their bodies and their feelings. This is the smallest group which can be recognized by certain characterstics, such as lack of feeling and instinct, and the tendency towards abstraction and the desire to solve their problems by words rather than deeds.

According to Gurdjieff, all the people that we are likely to meet

belong to one of these three categories. They are what he calls
'contemporary people or men-machines'. So long as there is lack of
balance between the three sides of man's nature, his further development is bound to be lopsided.

One of the characteristics of man number four, is that there is
balance between his body, his feelings and his thoughts; but the most
important property is defined by the idea that man number four has a
'permanent centre of gravity'. This means a settled and final attitude
towards life, a system of values that is thoroughly accepted, so that he
will live by these values. In general, the value system which is required is that man accepts his twofold obligation, to serve the cosmic
purpose and to fulfil his own destiny. The principles to which anyone must be committed who aspires to be a real man were defined in
terms of the five strivings which Gurdjieff placed in the mouth of
Ashiata Shiemash (see Chapter 3).

These strivings are the consequence of his commitment to fulfill
his destiny on the earth; this gives him a power of decision that is
lacking in man one, two and three. Man number four has made the
first step towards liberation from his own egoism. He sees where he
has to go, and he is prepared to make the sacrifices necessary in order
to reach his goal.

The next stage, defined as man number five, is the first step beyond
the limitations of human existence. This is where Gurdjieff's teaching begins to be difficult to express adequately in words. By ordinary
standards, number four is what man should be. He is balanced, he has
sound judgment and he has a right and permanent system of
values; he knows what he must do with his life and he has committed
himself to doing it. He knows that it is necessary to make sacrifices
and he is prepared to make them. This, in ordinary terms, is what we
call a good man, and we do not ask more from him than that he
should continue upon his way. According to Gurdjieff, however,
man number four has not acquired anything that is beyond the
limitations of this life. There is an inner and a secret transformation
that can take place, whereby man acquires a different kind of being
which is no longer subject to the limitations of existence, where he
has passed beyond a certain threshold. He is now said to have a
second body, different from the ordinary physical body, though also
like the physical body formed of existing materials. In Chapter III
of *Beelzebub's Tales*, Gurdjieff introduces the Persian word *Kesdjan*,
meaning the 'vessel of the soul', to designate this second body. It is

much the same as the astral body of the theosophists, with the main distinction that Man one, two, three or even four have it only in an embryonic state.

This is the crux of Gurdjieff's anthropology—Man is not by nature an immortal soul nor is he a soulless automaton. He is a natural being with supernatural potentialities. The seeds of immortality are planted in him but their germination is not guaranteed. The first stage is the formation of the *Kesdjan* body, which comes about by a process that is subject to the laws of the existing world, but not subject to its limitations, particularly those of space and time. With the acquisition of this new dimension, man becomes different from ordinary people. Man number five is balanced between the material and the spiritual worlds. He has two bodies and his *Kesdjan* body can acquire 'objective reason'. Nevertheless, until he has acquired it, he still remains within the limits of his human nature. He has attained what is natural and right for man to attain. There is beyond this a transformation which goes beyond his own individuality.

Man number six is probably the same as the Bodhisatva of Mahayana Buddhism, or the great saints and *wadis* of Christianity and Islam. He is no longer concerned with his own personal welfare, but has committed himself to the salvation of all creatures. These definitions, made in terms of our ordinary experience can be very misleading. The real truth is that man number six is no longer confined to the existing world. He has been liberated from the limitations of existence. This is described in the words attributed to the Prophet Muhammad, *"Mutu kablen temutu"*, "die before you die". The meaning of this death is incomprehensible until man has had at least an experience of liberation from existence. We are left, therefore, with the difficulty that Gurdjieff points a direction for man's development which we cannot follow even in our minds. Man number six has a 'higher-being-body'. This is the seat of Objective Reason, which is the principle of immortality. Man number six has died and been resurrected in a transcendental mode.

The seventh level, the man who has reached ultimate liberation, has ceased to be constrained by any of the limitations even of his own individuality. Here we have another very great difficulty, that our own thinking cannot help distinguishing between the singular and plural, between one and many. We cannot understand the state of affairs in which number has ceased to have any significance, when it is no longer legitimate to count, for it is no longer possible to distinguish between this and that. This state of affairs is only one of the characteristics of the seventh degree of man. For that reason, we are reduced to an almost abstract scheme; but, nevertheless, it is very important because, in putting it forward, Gurdjieff shows that he himself has gone far beyond the religious or theosophical concepts of human perfection and he has also gone beyond the limitations of the mystical union.

The scheme of seven categories of man is a remarkable concept. This was the first presentation that I ever had of Gurdjieff's teaching: Ouspensky, taking a piece of paper in our flat in Constantinople in 1920, made the diagram showing the first three levels of man all parallel, and the fourth man still upon the same level, still confined within the limitations of existence. I could not grasp the full significance of the vertical column going in the direction of man five, six and seven. It was for me particularly significant to return to this after more than fifty years, and to look from quite a different perspective at the meaning of what was shown me then, when I was about to meet Gurdjieff for the first time.

One has to consider how Gurdjieff regards the question of the soul. In his account of the wise men who met in Babylon about five hundred years before Christ, Gurdjieff satirizes the controversy of the soul, and shows how impossible it is to discuss this question with any real significance so long as we think of it in terms of our ordinary experience. The possibility of the soul lies in the presence in man of a certain combination of substances which are without organization, but which carry all his potential for experience. These substances can be organized and, in the course of this, they are eventually transformed in the *Kesdjan* body which is the outer vehicle of the soul. Ordinary man in whom these substances have not 'crystallized' is not immortal, although there is a sensitive something in him that is able to survive the death of the physical body. This sensitive mass has no permanent form and eventually dissolves. Man becomes immortal only when he has created or built for himself his own complete soul. His immortality is not existential, for it is seated in his Objective Reason.

Another way of presenting the goal of human development is to take it as Union with God. This idea is very close to what in Christianity is called the Beatific Vision, and represents a very important group of beliefs about man and his destiny which are common to the southern Sufis (see Chapter 2), and in a modified form to Christian Mysticism. For the northern Sufis, the Union with God, *Tawhid*, is either an inadequate expression or a stage through which we have to pass. The real goal for the northern Sufis, as it is for the Buddhist, is liberation from the conditions of existence. The question is whether Gurdjieff himself holds the doctrine of *Itlaq* or liberation, which I think is rightly attributed by Hasan Şuşud to the Khwajagān and the Masters of Wisdom. This is a very important question which we only can answer when we have examined the Gurdjieff doctrine of man in greater detail.

We have already considered the simple presentation of man as having three types of experience: thinking, feeling and instinctive. These Gurdjieff associates with three centres which have an anatomical significance, being related to different parts of the nervous system. This is fairly straightforward and, when it was first presented to us, we made many experiments and observations in order to satisfy ourselves that the notion of three centres was valid. Gurdjieff, however, complicated the issue by distinguishing between the moving and the instinctive centre and adding a sex centre, making five in all. Then to these five centres were added two others: the Higher Emotional and the Higher Mental centres, arriving finally at a total of seven. These are represented in the diagram of which Gurdjieff made very extensive use, and which basically shows man as composed of three distinct parts, or which presents man as a three-storied factory. In *Beelzebub's Tales*, this picture is modified and the allusion is almost invariably to man as a three-brained being. The possession by man of three brains distinguishes him from other forms of life by making him similar in his essential pattern to the structure of the entire universe. This is the meaning of the passage quoted at the beginning of this chapter: Man can "acquire all the data exactly similar to the data in the *actualizer of everything existing*", because he can become an independent self-sufficing will through the liberation of his three brains from external influences. The potentiality is a central feature of *Beelzebub's Tales*, but it is not fully developed or explained. There has been in consequence a tendency to confuse the psychological presentation of man having three, four, five or seven centres with the cosmic presentation of man as being constructed according to the Law of Threefoldness.

This brings us back to Gurdjieff's question and the answer presented in the last chapter. Because man is able to be himself the bearer of the reconciling force, he is said to be made in the image of God. He is able to represent in himself the Cosmic Working whereby the spiritual and the material world are harmonized and the Divine Purpose is realized. The affirmation or positive force is in his head, in the brain. The denial or negative force is his body, his sensory-motor function. The third or reconciling principle is in his emotional nature, dispersed in various centres in the region of his breast. This doctrine, that the emotional nature of man is dispersed among a number of points, is of psychological significance; but it is equally important to understand that by this Gurdjieff intends to convey that the reconciling principle enters into and works through individual centres. It is a Universal Spiritual Power, as might be understood either from the Great Spirit doctrine, or from the Christian notion of the Holy Spirit as the Universal Love—whereby the Father and the Son are united and whereby the Godhead is united with the Creation. Nevertheless, once Gurdjieff's interpretation of the Law of Threefoldness is even approximately grasped, a wonderful light is thrown on the theological doctrine of the Holy Trinity. Gurdjieff clearly intended this because he designated the primary emanation from the Prime Source as the *Theomertmalogos* or Word-God. The passages in which this occurs have (see Chapter 8) been taken to indicate a Gnostic origin of Gurdjieff's ideas; but, gnosticism lacks the uncertainty of the working of the laws that is so important in Gurdjieff's presentation. If Gurdjieff discovered anything not known to scholars, it must have been with the mysterious 'Essene Brotherhood' that he claims to have visited in the 1890's.

It must be admitted that Gurdjieff's description of man as a three-brained being and his psychological teaching about the centres is somewhat confused. This confusion is partly deliberate, in that Gurjieff would take incomplete ideas, present them and then modify them, until gradually his pupils were able to retain a complex idea that would have baffled them had it been presented in un-garnished form. For this reason, perhaps, commentators on Gurdjieff have not grasped the significance of man as a three-brained being as presented in *Beelzebub's Tales*.

We should consider a transition from the idea of a three-brained man to man as having four parts. In the last chapter, "From The Author", of *Beelzebub's Tales*, man is compared to an equipage in which the coach corresponds to the body, the horse to the feelings and the mind to the driver. The passenger or the true Master and owner of the equipage is said to represent the 'I'. Gurdjieff in many places insists that man has no 'I' and no 'will'. Indeed, in the same chapter in which this passage occurs, he illustrates in a very telling way the abscence of the 'supposed will' in man. This often creates misunderstandings. It is necessary to understand that the fourth part of man, his 'I', is indeed his 'will' but, owing to the faulty conditions of education, man reaches adulthood without his own 'will', which is the same as saying without his own 'I'. The place of 'will' and the way by which the 'will' in man can be developed, is seldom discussed either in Gurdjieff's own writings or in books about Gurdjieff. It is worth noting however that in the various prospectuses of his Institute, the training of the will was always included. It is only the method that remains undisclosed.

Gurdjieff never failed to make it clear that the possession of one's own will is the mark of the real man. Consequently, the development of man should be conceived not in terms of knowledge and being only, but rather of the three elements of *knowledge, being* and *will.* Failure to recognize this has been one of the reasons why the practical application of Gurdjieff's methods has not always given the results that one hoped for. People have not believed in the possibility of 'will', the true possession of one's own 'I', and so they have not undertaken the work that leads to this with the persistence and intensity that is required. A careful reading of all the passages in *Beelzebub's Tales* referring to the *Omnipresent Okidanokh* will convince the reader that Gurdjieff has a profound and startling understanding of 'will'. The emergence of this understanding—as I tried to show in Chapter 8—was a decisive step in finding the answer to the question of the sense and significance of life on the earth. In one of his lectures at the Prieuré, Gurdjieff was asked the question: "Then has no one any will?" to which he replied, "Who has will has will, but you do not understand what that means. First understand that you have no will and then you can ask from knowledge, not from ignorance as you do today." He emphasized that to have one's own 'I' and free 'will' is a great achievement and even those who desire it sincerely may fail to reach it.

Many today have become sceptical of the promises that are held out for human development. If, indeed, man has within him the seeds of an immortal soul, and if he is destined to play a conscious part in the evolution of the world, how is it that we find him so remote from any such attainment? How, when we set ourselves to follow the path of self-perfecting, do we meet with failure after failure? Looking back over history we see how seldom men have attained what is said to be their legitimate destiny. This is closely connected with the question that for more than 2,500 years has tormented mankind, how to reconcile the belief in the Love of God with the observed facts of suffering, sin, disease and frustration. The question did not arise until it was first proclaimed that there was Cosmic Justice and that the Divine Power was beneficent, merciful and loving, at the time of the great change that occurred five hundred years before Christ. Before that time, the higher powers were regarded as capricious and indifferent to human suffering. It was regarded as capricious and indifferent —even hostile—towards man. It was accepted as in the order of things that man should be subject to want and suffering and that he should be unable to secure either happiness for himself or security for his descendants.

It would be easy to put aside the question by denying the existence of any purpose, and by asserting that man is self-sufficient; that he suffers because of his own immaturity and mistakes. Through learning not to repeat these mistakes he is ensuring his own limitless evolution towards ever better ways of life. This is the essence of the humanistic view of man that has in the last few centuries begun to prevail and is still gaining ground at the expense of the religious theistic view. Gurdjieff adopts a quite different conception. According to the myth that he develops in *Beelzebub's Tales*, at a certain period in the history of the earth it was perceived by the Higher Powers that a very undesirable and dangerous situation was developing on the planet Earth which could endanger the equilibrium of the entire solar system and, in particular, the evolution of the Moon. For this reason, the Higher Powers intervened and brought about the insertion into man's physical nature of an organ said to have been situated at the base of the spine and called by Gurdjieff the 'Organ Kundabuffer'. This prevented man from seeing the situation as it really was and led him to base his values solely on the satisfaction of his own desires and the pursuit of happiness. The organ had the effect of arresting the evolution of man and ensuring him a blissful though animal existence.

The 'Organ Kundabuffer' was referred to by Gurdjieff in his talks and lectures long before *Beelzebub's Tales* were written, and he certainly intended the account of its historical appearance and disappearance to be taken literally. There need be nothing supernatural or occult about such a phenomenom. We know that the frontal lobe operation removes nearly all unpleasant emotions without necessarily destroying the capacity for enjoyment. Very early man had a fairly erect stance, and so has modern man. Between them came Neanderthal man with a curved spine and the head differently placed in relation to it. Neanderthal man could enjoy life, but he could not speak as we do. About 35,000 years ago, he was suddenly displaced by the Aurignacian and other precursors of modern man. These facts are quite consistent with the account Gurdjieff gives in Chapter X of *Beelzebub's Tales*. Gurdjieff says that it was necessary to arrest human evolution and that this happened before the last Ice Age. He says that this was connected with the development of the Moon and 100,000 and 70,000 years before the present, when Neanderthal man appeared. The transition to modern man with the full power of speech and endowed with creativity occurred about 35,000 years ago and was complete at the end of the Ice Age about 12,000 years before the present. All this fits well into Gurdjieff's picture.

Admittedly there is no direct evidence of the intervention of higher powers, but we could not in any case verify this by the means at our disposal. Gurdjieff's account is as good as any other. It is a fact that the evolution of man stood still for nearly a hundred thousand years and started again with a bang thirty or forty thousand years ago. According to Gurdjieff this was done to ensure that the energies needed would be transformed. This state of affairs continued until the danger of mans ceasing to transform energies had passed. Then the organ was removed and man's evolution again proceeded. But a mistake was made. Those who were responsible for the operation had not foreseen that during the many generations when man was living according to the pleasure principle, he would develop a habit which would be transmitted by heredity to his decendants: this is what Gurdjieff describes as the predisposition to the properties of the 'Organ Kundabuffer'. The conclusion is drawn that although man is free to attain his own fulfilment—to pass through all the stages of development, from man one, two and three to man five, six and seven—he is nevertheless obstructed by his inability to see the situation as it really is. The position is described in the legominism, "The Terror of the Situation", attributed in *Beelzebub's Tales* to the prophet Ashiata Shiemash. Man, in order to realize his own destiny, must live by *conscience*; but this has been buried in his subconsciousness, and with his ordinary conscious mind he continues to live as if he were dominated by the working of the 'Organ Kundabuffer'. This is equivalent to the condition mentioned at the beginning of this chapter, that man lives by his rights and, in particular the right to pursue happiness, and disregards his obligations, in particular the obligation to pay the debt of his existence. The consequence of the properties of the 'Organ Kundabuffer' are described as all kinds of egoism, self-love, vanity, conceit, adulation and all that we regard as fundamental defects of character and at all times have agreed to treat as unworthy of man. In spite of this, we continue to live under the dominance of our own egoism and the other properties of the 'Organ Kundabuffer'.

Man was created with conscience and, because our true destiny is to achieve full being, something in us is not satisfied with life limited by the effeffcts of the 'Organ Kundabuffer'. Beelzebub explains to his grandson, at a very early stage of his education (Chapter XVI, "Time"), that there exist in the Universe two principles of the duration of life. The first is called *Foolasnitamnian* and is proper to man: it is possible only by the development of the will, through conscious labour and intentional suffering. Those who practise this are said to evolve their 'second-being-body-*Kesdjan*', through which when ultimately perfected by Reason, they will be able to have direct perception of the Cosmic Reality. The second principle, called *Itoklanoz*, results from the separation of the will into opposing urges. A person living this way is controlled by attraction and repulsion, likes and dislikes and the alternation of active and passive states. Such a state is normal for the lower and animal creation but it is abnormal for man. Although it is easy and requires no effort, a man living this way is cut off from conscience and, unless he is a lost soul, he feels a sense of discomfort. It is probable that everyone is aware that life is not as it should be; there are always people who awaken to the situation and look for a way out. This is what Gurdjieff calls the development of a 'magnetic centre', It works in the opposite way to the 'Organ Kundabuffer' by producing a state of dissatisfaction with life for pleasure alone, and a need to find a way from dream life to real life.

The notion that man's evolution has in some way been intentionally obstructed at a remote period in the past, and that the possibility has since been restored, makes sense of many of the absurdities of our present situation. However, many are confused by Gurdjieff's assertion that the obligation to transform energies is laid upon mankind because the evolution of the Moon requires it. There is no doubt that Gurdjieff was convinced that in some way there is a relationship between the Moon and the unsatisfactory conditions of existence on the Earth. In *Beelzebub's Tales* this relationship is made explicit by the intervention of the Archangel Looisos who, to avoid trouble, decided that the 'Organ Kundabuffer' should be implanted in man. In many other places Gurdjieff refers to the Moon as man's enemy. Some have mocked Gurdjieff's insistence that we are 'food for the moon', as if he was saying something really absurd. There is certainly something very strange about the suggestion. Orage's easy explanation that the Moon is to be understood psychologically suggests it is a synonym for the 'Organ Kundabuffer' and there would be no need to introduce an arbitrary notion of this kind.

Gurdjieff certainly got from somewhere the notion that man's destiny is linked with that of the Moon. For an understanding of human destiny, the whole notion is very instructive. We have, willy-nilly, to produce the subtle energy that is required. This can be produced either voluntarily or involuntarily, by our own conscious labour and intentional suffering or by the process of our own death. The first is the *Foolasnitamnian* and the second the *Itoklanoz* way of living. He suggests that the release of this energy through death is something which occurs with all living beings, not only man. The difference is between man and animal is that man is able to release it by his own conscious decision and, in doing so, liberate also, for his own purposes, the two complementary substances which are required for the development of his two 'higher-being bodies'.

This brings us back to the Doctrine of Higher Bodies and to the meaning of the higher centres and Objective Reason. Gurdjieff's teaching is that man has the possibility of developing three bodies. One is his physical body that develops by nature; the second is his *Kesdjanian* body which develops through its own conscious labour; and the third is his higher-being body, called the body of the soul, which develops through intentional suffering. Objective Reason cannot enter into the physical body of man. It is not possible for the ordinary centres—the thinking, feeling and instinctive and moving centres—to be instruments of Objective Reason. Man can begin to acquire it only when his second body is already formed though not necessarily perfected. And there is a higher gradation of Objective

Reason by which man is able to understand and participate in the grand Cosmic Process that is acquired only through the development of his highest-being body.

Similar notions of higher bodies are to be found both in the Buddhist and Tantric teachings of India and Tibet and also in the Sufi doctrines of Central Asia. It therefore seems likely that Gurdjieff developed this part of his system in the context that he found in eastern Turkestan, Afghanistan, Tibet and possibly India. It is well-known in the theosophical teaching that man is endowed with a number of bodies. It is said that these are present in him as part of his own nature, but they are dormant and require to be developed by exercise. Gurdjieff, on the other hand, says that these bodies are only potential and not actual until they develop by the work that man does on himself. There is not really as sharp a contradiction between these two views as might appear at first sight because, if the possibility of a higher-being body is present in man, this possibility must be in some substance or material which is capable of being organized; Gurdjieff probably intends us to understand that we have the material of a higher body in a disorganized fluid state but can bring it into coherence and organization through our own efforts.

There is a certain discrepancy here between the ideas that Ouspensky presents in *In Search of the Miraculous* and Gurdjieff's own teaching in *Beelzebub's Tales* and elsewhere. In the former, the emphasis was mainly placed upon the awakening to the higher centres making possible higher forms of perception, knowledge and understanding. The functions of these two centres are very clearly described and are an important part of the whole teaching. The higher-emotional centre is the organ by which man is able to know Reality as it concerns himself. It is the seat of his conscience, the seat of his 'I' and his decision-making. It is the organ of his personal individuality. It is always present in him. According to Ouspensky's report, the higher centres do not need to be developed, they are present in us all. It is only through the lack of development of the lower centres that we are unable to communicate with them. The higher intellectual centre (not very happily named), is the one by which we have contact with the Cosmic Principles. The use of the word 'intellectual', which tends to associate this with the work of the 'thinking-brain', has been a source of considerable confusion. The work of this centre is wholly outside of the mind. It is not a process of thinking or sense perception. It is timeless and immediate and, for this reason, we cannot describe it in terms of our thought, which is a spatio-temporal faculty.

Gurdjieff says that the higher-intellectual centre is the normal instrument of man number seven, the man who has not only passed beyond the limits of individuality, but beyond the limits of 'being' itself. He has reached the stage where he is no longer in his essential nature like people whom we can know. I have already quoted Meister Eckhart's extraordinary description of the 'man-divine'; it is said elsewhere that he perceives as God perceives. His perception is a direct Divine Perception and, therefore, quite incomprehensible to our ordinary thinking. Perhaps this is why Gurdjieff gave up the use of the word 'higher-intellectual centre' and referred to the higher gradations of Objective Reason. In *Beelzebub's Tales*, he distinguishes five gradations of Objective Reason, all of which imply high levels of development. It is said that, if three-brained beings lived normally according to the *Foolasnitamnian* principle, they would have the same duration of existence as all normal three-brained beings arising everywhere in our Universe. They should exist without fail until their second-being-body *Kesdjan* had been finally perfected by the awakening of the higher intellectual centre. When a man had reached this degree, the duration of his life no longer depended upon chance but was a matter of his own choice, so that he could continue to live on the Earth until his task has been completed. Elsewhere, and particularly in the chapter "The Results of Impartial Mentation", Gurdjieff distinguishes between four grades of Objecive Reason, of which the fourth represents the highest possible for an individualized being and is said to be only two degrees removed from that of the Absolute Reason of the Creator of the existing world.

The rather commonplace terms used in *Beelzebub* of higher states of reason are liable to suggest that these higher levels can be understood by analogies drawn from our ordinary experience. The metaphor should not be pressed too far, lest it encourages an anthropomorphic tendency. Even *Our Common Father Endlessness* whom Gurdjieff takes as the Sacred Power by which the Universe is brought into existence and redeemed is spoken of in very human terms. It is said that our *Endlessness* had to think very hard; he had to take steps because he was faced with a problem, which at first, seemed to be insoluble. All of this is very hard to reconcile with the absolute notions that were current among the Sufis, and particularly, the Khwajagān, so we wonder why Gurdjieff chose to present his ideas in this form.

In *Beelzebub*, Gurdjieff makes a distinction between Cosmic Individuals incarnated from Above, and men who had attained a high degree of Objective Reason during their life on the Earth and who were after death preparing themselves to be united with the Sun Absolute. This union converts them in their turn to Cosmic Individuals. I remember a conversation with the Shivapuri Baba in which he explained things in very much the same way. He said that, when a man had completed the cycle of existence on the Earth and attained absolute liberation, in other words, when he had passed beyond the limitations of being itself, he then returned to the Source and was under no further need to incarnate. Such a being would, however, return to the Earth, as Jesus Christ did, in order to help mankind. This is very similar to the ideas which Gurdjieff presents in his Messengers incarnated from above and Cosmic Individuals. In one place, Ouspensky reports Gurdjieff as having said that "If one were to place a measure on the Being of Jesus Christ, one would perhaps call him Man Number Eight". This implies a level for an individual man. As he treats Jesus as a Cosmic Individual in *Beelzebub*, presumably this is the doctrine which he wishes to convey: namely, that there can be beings who are already perfected and who come to the Earth in order to fulfil a mission. At the same time, they are transformed by their sojourn on the Earth, as it is said that Ashiata Shiemash had been Very Saintly, became the Most Very Saintly, and is now one of those Cosmic Individuals without whom *Our Common Father Endlessness* will not condescend to actualize any measures for the benefit of the Cosmos. I previously suggested that Gurdjieff was aware of the Khwajagān teaching of absolute liberation called *Itlaq*. It is repeated over and over again in the sayings of the Masters that *Itlaq* is attained only by intentional suffering. We must relate this to Gurdjieff's image of the Holy Planet Purgatory. Those who have in them the possibility of going to the end of the way of self-abandonment reach the same goal, by whatever name it may be called.

This completes the concept of man which was outlined earlier. It implies a very great difference between the kinds of being who have passed through the Ultimate Barrier and re-enter from the Source of

All-Being, and those who have attained the highest degree of perfection possible for a man, Man Number Seven. We must remember that when we are talking about such beings, we are talking of the rarest of the rare. This is constantly emphasized by the Sufis. For example, in many conversations that I have had with Hasan Şuşud, he constantly says that we must understand that those who achieve complete liberation do not appear even once in a century. Such beings are different—they are self-created beings; as Hasan Şuşud puts it, not merely God, but beyond God. In other words, here we are speaking about ineffable regions that have little resemblance to any mode that we can understand, limited as we are by the narrow perceptions of the existing world.

We may then ask—what is the thread that can connect our ordinary level of being through the various gradations, from the man who has passed through the early stages of his development, right up to the ineffable levels that are not only beyond existence, but beyond being itself? The answer to this is very simple. It is the Will. The Will is independent of being and of level. It is omnipresent. It is the *Omnipresent Okidanokh,* which, though One, is nevertheless capable of unlimited division through which it produces the different conditions into which the material world can enter. We cannot understand the transformations of man unless we take this into account. But when we come to man as a person, we have to recognize that his individuality, his will is out of sight. It is not only invisible to others, but also imperceptible to himself, to his ordinary awareness, his ordinary consciousness. There is, as the Shivapuri Baba called it, 'the Veil of Consciousness' that cuts us off from our own reality, that is, our Will.

The same is true of *conscience* which, as Gurdjieff insists, is present in every man, but situated beyond his ordinary consciousness, it has not degenerated as have the other sacred impulses of Faith, Hope and Love. We have to trace the connection between conscience and will. Conscience itself is an organized power in us; it is not only able to do but it is able to know, is the same true of will—can we simply equate the two and say that our conscience is our will and our will is our conscience? There is something here which is not quite right, and we must look at it more carefully.

In the chapter "The Organization for Man's Existence Created by the Very Saintly Ashiata Shiemash", he is said to have found two great initiates who had reached already the awareness of their own nullity; he explains to them in detail what Objective Conscience is, and how factors arise for its manifestation in the presences of three-brained beings. He says: "The factors for the being-impulse conscience arise in the presences of the three-brained beings from the localization of the particles of the 'emanations-of-the-sorrow' of our *Omni-loving and Long-suffering-endless-Creator;* that is why the source of the manifestation of genuine conscience in three-centred beings is sometimes called the *Representative of the Creator.*" He adds that the sorrow is formed from the persistent struggle in the Universe between joy and sorrow. In all three-brained beings, without exception, among whom we men are included, "the-whole-of-us" and the whole of our essence are, and must be, only suffering. He goes on to explain that this is necessary, because without it the impulse of conscience cannot become apparent. It depends upon a constant struggle of two opposite functions, one from the desires of the planetary body and the other from our aspiration towards higher levels of being. This explanation of conscience is typical of the more profound conception which pervades *Beelzebub's Tales,* compared with the relatively simple description of conscience that we find in Ouspensky's *In Search of the Miraculous.*

It is very likely that Gurdjieff himself came to understand conscience differently when, in 1927, he passed through the great crisis that enabled him to complete his writing. Prior to this he had not seen the human situation in these stark terms. It must be remembered that conscience is one of the sacred impulses which Gurdjieff earlier calls a 'positive emotion', which every three-brained being must be able to experience. This is the birth of the Objective Reason which marks the transformed man. Although the Doctrine of Conscience is emphasized in *Beelzebub* and elsewhere in Gurdjieff's teaching, we must not forget that the impulses of Hope, Faith, Love and Joy are also inherent in man's nature. The goal of our striving is not an unmitigated state of unrelieved suffering, as might appear at a first reading of these passages. Those of us who followed Gurdjieff's teaching were too much inclined to look at the gloomy side of life and to suppose that the work itself was essentially a matter of denial of rejoicing, a denial of the good things of life. We should have known better by looking at Gurdjieff himself who was as fully capable of joy as he was capable of suffering. Seeing Gurdjieff at the end of his life, one was struck by an overwhelming compassion. Here was a man whose face was lined with suffering. He was relieved only by the strength of the love shown him by all those who surrounded him and who had profited by his teaching.

The truth is that it is not possible to speak adequately about those who have gone beyond the limitations of existence. I quote from Meister Eckhart in the sermon "Young Man, Arise!" "Pity them, my children, they are from home and no one knows them. Let those in quest of God be careful lest appearances deceive them in these people who are peculiar and hard to place; no one rightly knows them but those in whom the same light shines."

12

Making a New World

A HUMAN child passes through a long period of helplessness followed by partial dependence upon others. Finally he reaches responsible age when he must find his own way in the world. Human life on the earth has similarly passed from helplessness through a million years of dependence and must arrive at a moment when it will have to be responsible for its own progress and perhaps even for its own existence. There are many indications that we are entering that moment and are not prepared for it. We do not even know what kind of life on this earth is right for mankind. We do not see that hitherto our needs have been provided by Great Nature and that we are squandering recklessly the little that remains of what she had prepared. Resources accumulated over millions and hundreds of millions of years are disappearing in centuries. The self-control that is required in an adult is almost totally absent from the human race as a whole and even from great nations and societies of people. As a race, we have no control over our appetites: sexual, emotional or merely habitual and conditioned. We are behaving like spoiled children which indeed is just what we are.

All this and much more is being said by individuals and societies concerned with the state of the world, but as the Russian proverb says which Gurdjieff was so fond of quoting, it is all "pouring from empty into empty". We do not have the knowledge and understanding required to enable us to see what a responsible humanity upon this earth would now be doing. The reality of the situation can be reached only through Gurdjieff's question: "What is the sense and significance in general of life on the earth and in particular human life?" We cannot be responsible unless we know for what we are responsible. In the absence of an answer, nothing remains except childish human egoism.

Having come so far with Gurdjieff, we must see if he has left us a convincing answer as to the needs of the future. In October 1949, in the last weeks of his life, I gave a series of lectures in London with the title "Gurdjieff—The Making of a New World" and it was for sentimental reasons that I chose the same title for this book. I was already convinced at that time that mankind was to pass through a period of unparalleled crisis in which only an intervention by supraterrestrial influences could enable us to survive (*Crisis in Human Affairs*, 1948, last page). At that time, no one could foresee how the crisis was to come upon us. We did not perceive that the old world was already dead and that willy-nilly we were going to live in a new one. In my last talk with Gurdjieff, just before his death, he spoke of the future. I told him that in lectures I was saying that *Beelzebub's Tales* contained the key to understanding what mankind needed. He nodded agreement and went on to say that there was, indeed, now a war between the old world and the new. He added characteristically: "I must make the old world chik or else it will make me chik. From now on, I need soldiers who will fight for me for the new world."[a] I promised him that I would devote my life to this. Gurdjieff was clear and specific in his demand: The publication of *Beelzebub* must be accompanied by a drive to get it widely read and understood. I did not grasp at the time that he was thinking of it as a legominism and that his 'soldiers' had to be initiates who could interpret it. He was not concerned—as his manner of speaking might have suggested—with the immediate future, but with the longer-term transformation by which mankind could be brought to a new understanding of human destiny that all people would be able to accept.

Let us look at what Gurdjieff left behind him. Three generations have passed since he began his search; nearly a generation since he died. In seventy-five years, the entire world situation has been turned upside-down, and it is not too much to say that the old world has died. Only on the material plane have predictions made at the end of the nineteenth century in any way been fulfilled. Though the technology of the last twenty-five years could not be foreseen, great advances could be and were predicted. What was unforeseen, though predictable, was the human failure. Gurdjieff, growing up in the

---

[a] The phrase 'to make chik' was a favourite one of Gurdjieff's. It imitates the sound made when a louse is squashed between the nails of our two thumbs and it means to destroy completely something which has to be removed.

midst of war and revolution, could see perhaps better than Western Europeans and Americans how things were going. A war that to us was not even a war—The Younghusband 'Expedition' of 1902 in Tibet—was in Gurdjieff's eyes a precursor of disaster. He referred to it again and again in his writings and conversations as a crashing blow to the hopes of mankind. It is a fact of history that from 1903, the world situation has progressively deteriorated, but it was not until the end of the 1960's that mankind began to awaken to the full extent of the impending danger. We had been so accustomed to think of war, and especially atomic war, as the ultimate disaster that we did not notice the other threats creeping up on us until it was almost too late. Man has lost even the semblance of control over his destiny. One short generation ago when the United Nations Organization was set up in San Francisco, it was assumed that, with goodwill on the part of the great powers, world progress could be resumed and assured. Fifty years ago, when Gurdjieff came to the West saying: "Man is a machine. He is asleep. He can do nothing. He can control nothing. Everything controls him", it was hard to take him literally. Today, the same is being said by professional students of human behaviour, by philosophers, by popular writers. There is no doubt that Gurdjieff has contributed to this change of attitude, though the grim sight of the human world disintegrating, while three billion men and women watch helplessly or occupy themselves with their own petty egoistic concerns cannot be ignored. An even greater number of people, especially among the young, refuse to continue living in the past and search diligently for some better way of life than meaningless 'progress'.

There is a growing realization that technology can no longer save mankind and that the problem is beyond the power of government or even world agencies to solve. If the combined threats of population explosion, exhaustion of resources, pollution of land, air and ocean and—perhaps gravest of all—the revolt of the deprived billions, are to be averted, there must be a change in our attitude towards life. This change must come not only on the part of a few spiritually-minded souls, but among the effectual majority of those who 'enjoy' the benefits of modern civilization.

Here Gurdjieff's account of the situation departs decisively from that of the wise men of our time. Here also the interpretation of his account given in the present book departs considerably from that adopted by those who have written about him and his work. I have distinguished between those who look at Gurdjieff the man and treat his "system" as no more than the expression of his genius, and those who look at the "system" and treat Gurdjieff as no more than a link in the chain of transmission. These latter also are inclined to suspect that the link broke at some point and left us with no contact with the source. I have rejected both these interpretations in favour of the hypothesis that Gurdjieff was in contact with a source that may have been the Sarmān society or, at any rate, was a brotherhood of people with the capacity to survey the world on a great time scale. I believe that Gurdjieff has brought in *Beelzebub*, a message that we have to convey to mankind in language that the people of the world can understand. In doing so, we shall be co-operating with agencies that we cannot perceive with our senses or even know with our minds— the agencies that I have called the Demiurgic Intelligences. This hypothesis is partly derived from the evidence, admittedly scanty, that there is a group of people who have preserved ancient knowledge now being offered as an answer to the question how mankind is to be redirected into the way of evolution. More convincing reasons for believing that mankind is being guided towards a new world are to be seen in the events themselves. The traditional knowledge, hitherto kept out of sight, is now emerging in multitudinous forms all over the world. There is a widespread sense that great events are on the way which will be favourable to mankind rather than precursors of our extinction.

I am convinced that Gurdjieff had a mission connected with the re-introduction of the traditional knowledge into human life. He worked in three phases. The first was his attempt to set up his own organization—The Institute for the Harmonious Development of Man. The second was the creation of a legominism in *Beelzebub's Tales*. The third was the training of people who could interpret his work through the preparation of initiates.

If *Beelzebub* is a legominism, what is it that we have to learn from it? It is an insight into the human situation as it really is and not as we imagine it to be. There are three main elements in the appraisal.

1. Man as a three-brained being is capable of unlimited evolution. He can become a free, conscious individual capable of understanding the workings of the Creation and of being a helper in the Creative process.

2. Man's destiny has gone wrong. He bears the consequences of errors made not by him, but by 'Higher Powers' at an early stage of his earthly evolution. Though later corrected, these have left him with a legacy of egoism and a reluctance to face reality that condemns him to a miserable state, compared with that of normal three-brained beings of the Universe.

3. Man must play his part in the Reciprocal Maintenance of all that Exists. He may do so by his own Conscious Labour and Intentional Suffering or he may do so passively as an animal does. In the first case, he becomes an immortal soul and an active participant in the fulfilment of the Cosmic Purpose.

This picture of man differs radically from any of the well-known religious creeds, philosophical or scientific systems of the West or those of India, China or the Levant. The more one examines it, the more remarkable does it appear. On the one hand, man is presented as a potential ally of the Creator of the World, able to make a contribution in his own right as an independent creative will. To become what he is destined to be, man must be transformed, but an almost inseparable obstacle blocks his way : *he cannot and will not face reality.* He prefers to live in illusion and eventually to be destroyed entirely, rather than accept his situation. The really extraordinary feature of the whole presentation is that the way to liberation is not by virtuous living, but by fulfilling the obligation to transform of energies needed for the Cosmic Purpose.

Beelzebub needs to be interpreted, but it would be an intolerable pretension were I to claim that I can offer the interpretation which Gurdjieff would have given. Among his closest pupils there has been no unanimity as to how we are to understand his intentions. He made many confusing and contradictory statements that could not be attributed either to carelessness or to caprice. We are so accustomed to expect stable meaning and unequivocal statements from wise men, that we find Gurdjieff hard to 'take'. He was well aware that the sense of satisfaction that overtakes man's thinking apparatus that comes when he recognizes a formula that fits his mental patterns, is a barrier to any real understanding. All real truth appears to our minds under a guise of contradictions and antinomies. *Beelzebub* is a closed book to those who have not grasped this. Gurdjieff makes sweeping statements that readers either reject or take literally.

It is unnecessary to interpret such passages for those who have grasped the Chapter "Form and Sequence". In this, Beelzebub explains to his grandson the plan of his tales, specifically distinguishes between the 'reason of knowing' and 'reason of understanding'. The second alone can be man's inalienable possession and lead him beyond the limitations of earthly life. He uses the word 'contemplation' to denote the penetrating action by which we face and live through the deeply felt contradictions of human experience. The power of contemplation can be acquired only by those who are totally committed to the task of discovering and fulfilling the sense and aim of their existence. This work is incumbent upon us all and no one can do it for us, for it is no less than the creation of our own being. Gurdjieff was quite certain that this task has been delegated to us by our Creator: he calls it 'paying the debt of our existence' or 'acquitting ourselves with Great Nature'. We are mere shadows of men and women until we have created ourselves, which means not only to transform our essential nature by the formation of the higher-being bodies, but also to establish in them the Objective Reason that will enable us to understand the purpose of Creation and to make our independent contribution to its fulfilment.

The extraordinary picture of man which this evokes is scarcely to be found elsewhere. To make sense of it, we have to accept the corollary that we are needed in an objective sense, which means that each of us has something to contribute that the Creation needs and that we alone can give. As I remarked earlier, alone among the revealed religions, Zoroastrianism ascribes man's creation to the need of the Good Spirit (Ahura Mazda) for help in overcoming the onslaughts of Ahriman. The Jewish tradition accepts Satan, but does not regard man's role as concerned with the conquest of Satan, which is the task of the Angelic Host. *Beelzebub* contains no adversary, no Ahriman, no Satan, no principle of evil. All that is said is that 'certain most high Individuals' have committed an act of unpardonable unforseeingness, that has landed mankind in endless trouble. This is a significant departure from other accounts of the fall of man.

If Gurdjieff invented this cosmotheology, he was a prodigious original genius. His power was in his quest and his determination to fulfil his mission. That he was not a trained thinker is quite clear from the unfinished state of so many of his speculations. Ouspensky was not far out in describing Gurdjieff's system as 'fragments of an unknown teaching'. Gurdjieff discovered, or perhaps more accurately was permitted to discover, some very important knowledge with a profound bearing on the future of humanity. We are now passing through a critical transition which demands that this knowledge must be made available to those who can use it, as an obligation that overrides personal considerations.

I have given my own interpretation in the *Dramatic Universe* and need not reproduce it here. The key is to be found not in *Beelzebub's Tales* directly, but in a diagram or symbol that Ouspensky briefly describes in *In Search of the Miraculous* and that Gurdjieff developed with some remarkable extra detail in lectures he gave at the Prieuré in 1923. These diagrams and concepts are illustrated in Appendix II.

The doctrine: "God created Man for Himself and the world for Man", though specifically Christian, is common ground for all religions and it has been taken into atheistic materialism by omitting the reference to God, and thereby losing even the implication that man is responsible to God for what he does with 'His world'. This doctrine, harmless in its origin has become the bane of mankind. It is the chief cause of man's irresponsible attitude towards nature and his selfish insistence upon his own welfare to the exclusion of all else.

'God created Man for Himself' suggests an equal selfishness on God's part, particularly when we survey human suffering and try to understand the problem of evil.

Few people still believe that obedience and love are all that God demands from man, especially when the demand is made with the promise of eternal bliss for the obedient and damnation for those who rebel. The universal cry is not for a creator who has no need of his creation, but for a convincing answer to the question: 'Why do we exist at all?' Most people, especially among the young, are convinced that we must be and are responsible for our destiny and not helpless puppets of an 'inscrutable Providence'. These attitudes express themselves in the 'revolt of youth', whether this be violent or non-violent. They show themselves in the cynical exploitation of power by which every group, nation, state or superpower plays the game of 'each for himself and the devil take the hindmost'. We have returned to the crude and cruel power policies of the Assyrians and the Romans, aggravated by the vast scale of our operations.

The complexity of life has made mankind dependent upon institutions. These range from pressure groups and youth organizations through industrial corporations to trade unions and international agencies. By a strange anomaly, all the subordinate institutions use power to attain their aims. Only the international institutions like the United Nations, the World Health Organization or the World Council of Churches are without power. These institutions which could perhaps put an end to conflict are singularly powerless to do anything effective. An impartial observer from another world, such as Beelzebub is represented to us, would be excused in concluding that mankind wants conflict and will not allow anything to prevent it. Beelzebub's reiterated expressions of horror and amazement that men should periodically set out on an increasing scale to destroy other men's existence is more than a protest against war. It draws attention to a fundamental lack of purpose in human life. Beelzebub finds that we kill one another aimlessly, without rhyme or reason. This is not how it looks to the combatants; but it does appear so to an increasing number of people especially among the generation that was born after the last World War.

There is now in the world a growing division between the institutionalists and the anti-institutionalists. The latter are very numerous but unorganized. The common man throughout the world feels that he is being trampled upon by a herd of juggernauts. If he seeks to protect himself, he creates the very institution from which he wishes to escape. Those who join the institutions are, for the most part, unwilling slaves of a situation upon which their way of life depends, but which is deeply repugnant to them.

This strange division may seem less significant than the world-wide disparity between the 'haves' and the 'have nots', and less dangerous than the conflicts of the super-powers or the reckless exercise of power by every kind of pressure group. In reality, it is a most serious symptom of the world malaise. If great and well-meaning institutions cannot save us, where are we to turn except to a sterile anarchy?

Gurdjieff's solution is first indicated in the early chapter of *Beelzebub's Tales*, in which he shows by a variety of illustrations that mankind is influenced decisively only by ideas that all can share. The task Beelzebub undertakes of diminishing animal sacrifice is accomplished by disseminating ideas that appeal to the common man. The uselessness of seeking to impose reform from above is satirized in the story of the earnest young devil who rebelled against the forcible collection of taxes in Atlantis. Ashiata Shiemash finally succeeds in setting up a non-violent society by introducing the idea of conscience. He does so because he observes that it is useless to appeal to man's 'better nature' in terms of Faith Hope and Love.

It is unlikely that the promise of becoming a 'Son of God' by the awakening of conscience will appeal to the majority of people in the world today. There is however, a very real 'Terror of the Situation' that faces us in the threat of population explosion, food shortage, exhaustion of resources, pollution and the revolt of the deprived billions. As we look at these portents of disaster, we can see how they all come under the heading of abberation from the principle of Reciprocal Maintenance. Presented in conventionally moral terms, we can be told not to be selfish and lacking in compassion for the deprived. We can be told not to be self-indulgent in sex or in the satisfaction of our desire for possessions. We can be told that without generosity, tolerance and self-restraint, mankind will perish. It is clear that such moral injunctions without sanctions do not work. The old sanctions have no coercive power and, as they go, the old morality goes with them.

Herein lies the great underlying problem of the world. We have lost all sanctions except that of survival. But this concerns the whole race. It scarcely touches the individual, who sees that he can continue to get what he wants if he or the group of which he is a member can exercise the necessary power. Against power, there is no sanction except that of an accepted idea.

We are faced with the need to make real present sacrifices in order to serve a future in which we may not even be alive. Not one man in ten thousand is capable of such self-denial. Gurdjieff's message bridges the gap: our own immediate welfare is bound up with the entire life of the earth and its future. We cannot fulfil ourselves even to the extent of achieving happiness or security, unless we play our part in the Cosmic Drama. In all appeals to the conscience of mankind to combat pollution, the squandering of resources and the destruction of our plant and animal genera, there is a missing link. They do not answer the question: 'But what does all that mean to me personally more than my own welfare and that of my family?" Gurdjieff shows us how and why our personal well-being no less than our prospect of achieving 'real being' depends on the way we serve all life on the earth.

If we look objectively at human life, we can see that our real desire is for enduring well-being for ourselves and those with whom we are identified; our family, our friends, but above all ourselves. We have learned from Gurdjieff as from all the real teachers that this can be achieved exclusively by 'conscious labour and intentional suffering' for the good of others. Once this truth is established in us beyond all doubt—and this comes only by repeated experiences of success and failure—our attitude to life and our life itself changes irrevocably. To reach this point most of us need support and encouragement. These may be the chief contributions of a teacher. Gurdjieff supported us by his own spiritual energy, *hanbledzoin*, and he encouraged us by demonstrating to us again and again that real change of our being is possible. Without such help and encouragement, how are people to be brought to the conviction that 'unselfish work' alone makes life worth living?

We have reached a moment of history when the threat of disaster, if not the extinction of mankind, is beginning to become so serious that millions are taking it seriously. This is more true of young people than the older generations can quite grasp. The feeling of 'no future' is producing an attitude towards life that, with an awakened understanding, is prepared to undertake conscious labour and intentional suffering. There are hundreds of thousands of people who would be prepared to submit themselves to the process of transformation, if they could be convinced that it will work, and that it will lead not only to their personal salvation, but to the betterment of the lot of their fellow men. There is also a remarkable awakening to the horror of the wholesale despoiling of life on the earth, and indeed of the very substance of the planet on which we live. Those who have felt but not understood the extent to which modern man has betrayed his destiny respond to Gurdjieff's message in a way that was scarcely possible when he came to the West fifty years ago.

There is also a growing awareness that the specialization that gives man his power over inanimate nature is totally unsuitable for solving our real problems. 'Divide and rule' has been a successful maxim for two thousand years. It has created empires of the mind no less than of the body. We can exercise power locally at the expense of slavery elsewhere. This is a universal law that derives from the very nature of existence in time and space. We cannot grasp the full significance of *Beelzebub's Tales* unless we see that Gurdjieff meant what he said in describing the human situation as one of progressive and even accelerating deterioration, that must not be confused with moral degeneration ascribed by 'do-gooders' to the younger generation. The *Third Series* makes it clear that Gurdjieff's concern is with the increasing mechanicalness of human life, with mass hypnosis and the lost capacity for independent judgment. Mankind is floundering, and though many people know it, they do not see the cause.

Gurdjieff is not basically pessimistic for he insists that man like all other 'three-brained beings of our Great Universe' has an unlimited potential for self-perfecting. He goes further and says that our Creator has set his hopes upon men as aids for Himself in the administration of the enlarging world. Our great destiny is essential, our disabilities are accidental. Moreover, at no point does Gurdjieff suggest that the blight on the human race could go so far as to threaten our existence. He even suggests that time is on our side. When Hassein asks Beelzebub what can deliver mankind from the blight of egoism, he replies, "if this property of terrestrial beings is to disappear from that unfortunate planet then it will be with Time alone, thanks either to the guidance of a certain Being with very high Reason or to certain exceptional cosmic events' (*Beelzebub's Tales*, p. 1118).

The key to understanding the paradox of human degeneration and progress is to be sought in the dualism of man's nature. What one side of our nature sees as the triumph of man over brute nature, another side mutely shrinks from as an enslavement of spirit by matter, yearning for imperishable values of the spirit and distrusting the attractions of the material world. We oscillate between the two and find no rest. At the present time, the lure of material progress has reached its highest intensity and the reaction is beginning. We cannot turn back to the naive other-worldly beliefs of our forbears, and we see humanity in desperate need of new foundations on which to build a bridge between the two worlds, but know not where to turn.

When we look at Gurdjieff's message from this standpoint, we can see that it is indeed a message of hope. The unexpected answer to the question: 'On what are we to build?'' is that we shall not find it either in matter or spirit, but in the creative work of Reciprocal Maintenance. Our refusal to face Reality is due neither to wilful ignorance of facts, nor to callous indifference to values, but rather it is the consequence of our unwillingness to accept the task laid upon us as three-brained beings to make our contribution to the evolution of the solar system. This is where atheists and believers have both gone wrong. They have seen the issue in reconciling the concrete facts of the knowable world with the abstract values to which we give lip service without knowing why. They do not see that man's unique creative power carries with it an immense obligation to disregard which is to forfeit our birthright.

Gurdjieff tells us clearly that our personal salvation, the welfare of mankind and the evolution of the earth and solar system, are intimately linked together in the universal transformation upon which the maintenance of the world depends. As he does not tell us very much about the way this process works, this is all the more reason why we should seek for clues in the legominism of *Beelzebub's Tales.*

The key to understanding human life is given by the doctrine of Reciprocal Maintenance. This alone breaks down the artificial barrier that man has erected between himself and his Mother Nature. Man is in the full sense a natural being, but he has a supernatural destiny which he cannot achieve without fulfilling his obligation towards Nature. Man belongs to the highest class of living beings; but he is non-existent in the world of universal essences until he liberates himself from the conditioning of his animal existence. In former times, as for example by the Buddhists, this liberation was understood as being away from nature and even 'out of' Nature. For Christians and Muslims, man's spiritual concern was solely with God and they also disregarded man's obligations to Nature or rather treat them as secondary. The result has been to set up a totally false and most dangerous relationship which is the main cause of the present troubles of mankind.

The only way to redeem the situation is by a total re-alignment of our attitude towards nature. This has been recognized intuitively by good men such as Albert Schweitzer and Peter Scott, but they have not seen the objective basis for their belief. The result is that their case has been based either on humanitarian or 'aesthetic' grounds which appeal only to those whose feelings are already open. Moreover, no campaign for the preservation of nature has gone far enough to reach the core of the matter. This can be done only if we can see the entire nexus of relationships by which the universe is created and maintained. One real merit of Gurdjieff's presentation is that it is simple enough for anyone to grasp. "Everything that exists maintains and is maintained by other existences and this must apply to man also." We can now apply the scheme developed in Chapter 9 to the task of converting the principle into a realistic programme for the future.

In the relationship of the twelve great essence-classes, we can see what obligations are associated with every form of existence. We can use the scheme as a model with which to compare human life as it is now and as it might be. The true purpose of human existence is to ensure the conscious and creative evolution of the earth, and all that it contains non-living and living. The task is a prodigious one and its fulfilment should be the chief glory of mankind. There are many who have seen that if evolution is to continue, it must be with the conscious co-operation of mankind, but few have seen the task as a whole and what it implies. Evolution at every stage since life began has required sacrifice of existence for the sake of essence. Hitherto, this has taken the form of the succession of new phyla and orders dominating for a period and then suffering eclipse. If we men are not to meet the same fate, we must learn to accept service and sacrifice as our way of life. Gurdjieff's scheme shows us what this implies. The points of responsibility: the earth's crust and its minerals, the soil, the vegetable kingdom on land and in the seas, the invertebrates and animals and man himself, are just those very situations that are now causing great anxiety on the score of depletion of resources, of soil impoverishment, disease, over-population, famine and war. When Gurdjieff propounded his scheme sixty years ago, these anxieties seemed remote. Now they are urgent. Today, we can look at Gurdjieff's Reciprocal Maintenance and see it in a final warning and also a supreme hope. It is a picture that can be put over to the world.

This is the task to which Gurdjieff called us for which he prepared people in the last period of his life. It falls primarily on those who are able to look beyond outward appearances and see essence behind existence. But it also calls for much expert knowledge, for authority and organization.

Most of all it calls for a fundamental change in values which will consist in putting Nature first and man second. This is a bitter medicine to swallow, but unless we take it we shall perish. There is a little time left, but not very much. By the end of this century the New Epoch must have been established in the sight of all.

Appendix I
Gurdjieff's Style and Terminology

MANY who encounter Gurdjieff for the first time in *Beelzebub's Tales* are disconcerted by the style, and by his use of strange neologisms which often seem quite unnecessary for conveying his intention. There are several reasons why Gurdjieff decided to create his own literary style. In the first place, he was well aware that clarity and consistency in speech and writing nearly always result in the sacrifice of flexibility of expression and depth of meaning. When he spoke or lectured he paid no attention to the rules of grammar, logic or consistency. After he had learned some French and English, he mixed them indiscriminately, regardless of the linguistic limitations of his hearer. All of us in speaking disregard the rules that we follow in writing; Gurdjieff went further and put all rules behind him.

His manner of speaking and writing was not due to indifference. Like most orientals, especially Armenians, he was intensely interested in the use of words. He revelled in philological discussions. This was not strange to those of us who were familiar with scholarly Indians, Arabs and other races who seriously discuss the most fantastic etymologies, and in doing so convey meanings that would be incommunicable in straight speech. As Gurdjieff's ideas derive their significance far more from their breadth and depth than from logical consistency or even factual accuracy, he was almost compelled to express himself in new and startling terms. In the first chapter of *Beelzebub's Tales*, called the "Warning" he states his intention of abandoning the "bon ton literary language", but does not give his reasons. It was certainly not from inability to write well and clearly. He showed in *Meetings with Remarkable Men* that he could write in a straightforward narrative style, but this was deceptive for every chapter conceals hidden messages that few readers have been able to discern. In the *Third Series*, we have everything from clear and simple accounts of personal experience to deeply obscure passages said to be transcribed from ancient manuscripts, the meaning of which emerges only after many readings and much experience and meditation.

Beelzebub's Tales belong to an entirely different category. They are an experiment in a new literary form that combines the allusive character of Eastern fables with the pungent flavour of Western satire. It includes another element that is to be found only in sacred literature, such as St. Matthew's Gospel, the *Tao Teh King* or the *Bhagavad Gita*. This consists in the presentation of a teaching that itself is clear and consistent so as to allow the reader to glimpse the deeper meanings that defy logic and which lose their essential character if expressed in plain language.

I have read *Beelzebub's Tales* forty or fifty times and pondered over them deeply, and have never failed to discover new depths of meaning each time I have read them. In a way, this makes it more difficult for me to help those who have not seriously studied these ideas. I tend to assume that the reader is already convinced that there is a hidden treasure to be found and is therefore willing to commit himself to do some hard work in order to find it. In my experience, people who hear or read about Gurdjieff often start by reading *Beelzebub's Tales* and even follow Gurdjieff's advice to read them thrice, but I have never met anyone who has been able without help to penetrate deeply into the meaning of the crucial passages.

After Gurdjieff died, I was asked by some of the old pupils to write a commentary on *Beelzebub*. When I had written a few chapters and sent them round for comment, almost all agreed with my view that it would be a mistake to publish them. If Gurdjieff had intended his meaning to be readily accessible to every reader, he would have written the book differently. He himself used to listen to chapters read aloud and if he found that the key passages were taken too easily—and therefore almost inevitably too superficially—he would rewrite them in order, as he put it, to "bury the dog deeper". When people corrected him and said that he surely meant "bury the bone deeper", he would turn on them and say it is not 'bones' but the 'dog' that you have to find. The dog is Sirius the dog star, which stands for the spirit of wisdom in the Zoroastrian tradition.

It is true that to achieve this purpose, the secrets of *Beelzebub's Tales* must be unearthed by our own understanding. In this book, I have referred only to some of the basic principles that Gurdjieff wished everyone to understand. The finer points will not survive translation into plain English and must be seized directly by the combination of past experience and immediate awareness that Gurdjieff (in *Beelzebub's Tales*) calls contemplation, the sole means of attaining the reason of understanding. His aim is to lead the student towards this contemplation, and it would hinder rather than help this process to make things easier.

There are many stories in *Beelzebub's Tales* that on the surface appear to be little more than rather dated satires upon the culture of the early twentieth century, but which contain very significant insights into the process by which man can find his way out of the confusion of modern life. Some of the most violent and apparently irrelevant attacks upon human stupidity are to be read as directions for self-observation and self-discipline.

Apart from the allegorical and parabolic mode of writing, Gurdjieff makes use of the device of introducing the picture of the human predicament through the eyes of a being, who though like man, a three-brained mortal, comes from the distant centre of the universe and has been exiled to our solar system for reasons that have no connection with human affairs. Mr Beelzebub does not understand all that he observes, although he claims to have unveiled many of the minutiae of the human psyche. Other characters in the story include angels and archangels whose nature is not divided and who therefore find it hard to enter into the feeling of ordinary mortals. They make mistakes because they cannot make allowances. There are also men "incarnated from Above." These are cosmic individuals both historical like Jesus, Mohammad, Buddha and Moses, and also mythical like the very Saintly Ashiata Shiemash. Other men attain the stature of saint by their conscious labours and intentional sufferings. Such are the founders of brotherhoods and great scientists like Choon Tro Pel who discovers the law of sevenfoldness. Female characters play no significant roles in *Beelzebub's Tales* and very little is said about the lives of ordinary people. The result of this unusual *dramatis personae* is to place the reader constantly in the unaccustomed perspective of an extra-terrestrial observer.

To strengthen this feeling, the language used is interspersed with artificial words, neologisms, onomatopoeic contrivances and uncouth syntax. This device is trying to the reader until he gets used to the jargon. There are more than two hundred words that do not belong to any language. Some of these have a simple and obvious derivation such as *Kesdjan*, in Persian 'vessel of the soul' and *triamazikamno*, as in Greek 'I put three together'. Other words such as *Heptaparaparshinok* have a mixed derivation. The Armenian roots, with which Gurdjieff was familiar from boyhood, are unrecognizable for most Western readers. Other words are taken at random. When I was with Gurdjieff in Vichy in 1949, he pointed out of the restaurant window at the sign over a shop opposite and said "that is where I took the name Boulmarshano".

There are only about twenty fabricated words that have special and deep significance and I have discussed most of them in an appropriate chapter. For me personally, the most important of all is the *Trogoautoegocrat*. The derivation is simple enough : but the meaning is subtle. The words *trogo* I eat, *auto* myself, *ego* I and *cratizo* maintain are taken from the modern rather than classical Greek usage. There is the further sense of the *Autocrat* which is one of Gurdjieff's names for God, alternating with *ego trogo* which is a very human expression. In the cosmic sense, God feeds on the Creation and the creation feeds on God. For this they must have distinct and separate natures. Consequently, God has rendered Himself for the most part independent of the Creation by making it relatively independent of Him. The finite human mind cannot grasp the mystery of the relationship between the one Infinite Will and the multiplicity of finite wills. It is hard to see how they can share in the working of one and the same world. Gurdjieff makes his own faith clear by his reference to the hope which from the beginning our all loving Father Creator has placed in man, as in all other three-brained species, as potential helpers for himself in governing the expanding world. In *Beelzebub's Tales* Gurdjieff designates Ashiata Shiemash as the perfect exemplar of a Cosmic Individual, who has now reached so lofty a development of objective reason, that the Creator will not undertake any major action without consulting him. As I showed before, Ashiata Shiemash stands for the *Trogoautoegocrat*. The word *Shiem* also means sun and suggests that Ashiata was a solar incarnation. Even such a being is born neither perfect nor infallible. He is in the process of evolution towards the point where he can be charged with the greatest cosmic responsibility.

The *Trogoautoegocrat* is variously described as a principle, a law, an emanation of the Sun Absolute and as a means or method of stabilizing the Creation. Such a use of words is disconcerting in English or in any Indo-European language which distinguishes the parts of speech as belonging to different logical categories. In Turkish, there is no such distinction and Gurdjieff was clearly at home in Turkish : to such an extent that we may suspect that his contact with his Sufi teachers was made in the Turkish language. He shows no sign of having known Persian.

Gurdjieff uses all kinds of imagery to convey his intentions. He was well aware that descriptive writing is deceptive. When he makes use of it he usually apologizes to the reader, as for example in his description of dawn on the Amu Darya in the last chapter of *Remarkable Men*. The personages of *Beelzebub's Tales* are all images that show us some aspect of human or even superhuman nature that Gurdjieff wishes to portray. Even the Remarkable Men of the Second Series are highly stylized. Pogossian represents the man who works on himself through his body, Yelov through the mind and Bogachevsky through the feelings. The characters of the later chapters of the *Second Series* stand for the different types of seeker and show the transformation that they can achieve. For Gurdjieff the people in his books were themselves images, symbols or expressions of the essence values that he wished the reader to understand. They were not 'real' people, not even 'types'. The incidents, even when historical, were not inserted for historical reasons but to evoke pictures of situations.

The apparently slipshod use of words extended into general terms. He would reify abstractions, use concrete expressions in an abstract sense, personify laws and principles. This requires that in reading him, one should set oneself to seize the intention and substance, which calls for a considerable change from our usual ways of reading. It is hardest of all for professional philosophers and students of language.

To illustrate this let us look at the word "Law" which he uses in a sense that diverges to the point of absurdity from our modern usage. For him, laws are not abstractions or even generalizations, they are the actual workings of the world. He says of *Heptaparaparshinokh* that 'this law is a force constantly evolving and involving.' The 'force' is the 'flowing of the line.' The law is said to 'exist' in various situations. On a superficial reading all these references seem to betray woolly thinking and careless expression. When we begin to see that Gurdjieff is referring to the world of essence, we understand that whereas we see 'things' as real and 'laws' as the description of their behaviour, for Gurdjieff the laws are the essential reality and things and even beings are no more than manifestations of the working of essential laws. This may help us to understand why it is that Gurdjieff refers so often to the 'laws of world maintenance and world creation', and why he says that one of our basic duties is to seek to understand them more and more.

The widely held belief that the world and man are made on the same model was taken by Gurdjieff as a self-evident axiom. He extends it to a series of seven worlds or cosmoses all constructed according to the laws of three- and sevenfoldness. The cosmic model is represented by a symbol that has come to be identified with Gurdjieff's teaching, largely because it was made the emblem of the Institute for the Harmonious Development of Man and has been widely adopted by Gurdjieff's followers. This is the enneagram, or figure of nine lines, discussed in Appendix 2.

We should seek to understand the world because this develops in us the 'objective reason' which is an integral part of the aim of our existence. This must be our own inalienable property transubstantiated in our being. It is not acquired by way of knowledge, particularly not by verbal knowledge, which can be learned with comparatively little effort on our part, for modern education lays much store by devices that make learning easy. As Gurdjieff's aim, and therefore his methods were entirely different, I should do the reader no service by offering him a fictitious ease of comprehension.

Nevertheless, I believe that it can be useful to give some hints as to the ways in which the inner meaning can be found. On a superficial reading Beelzebub appears to be implacably critical of all attempts to improve the conditions of mankind. For example, in the chapter "India", he heaps contempt on the notion that one can bear the unpleasant manifestations of others by immuring oneself in a dark hole until death ends one's miserable existence. As he mentions monks and monasteries, this might be taken as an attack on the monastic life. A more careful reading makes it obvious that he is referring to psychological self-immurement. Those who seek salvation by avoiding temptation, and pride themselves on keeping out of harm's way miss the whole point of life. Gurdjieff makes no direct attack on any particular way of life, but shows the absurdity of the attitudes by which most ways of life are inspired.

He does not say outright that he offers mankind a method simpler and more effective than those of the past. He conveys this discreetly in his account of the various designs of space-ships. The older space-ships worked by attraction and repulsion and required incessant care and constant refuelling. This refers to the 'old law' of reward and punishment. The improved space-ships of Saint Venoma worked by attraction : Man could be saved by faith and love. He required only to trust himself to the medium. It is not hard to recognize in this a description of the Pauline account of the Christian gospel or Mohammad's doctrine of salvation by hope. The defect of these doctrines is that they do not allow for the hazards of the existing world. The atmosphere refers to the short range field of force that surrounds every entity. A human being has such an atmosphere, and when two people interact, forces that they do not understand are released. One can love one's neighbour so long as he keeps his distance. I can be a good Christian or a good Muslim so long as no one treads on my toes. The latest system of space-ships invented by the archangel Hariton takes account of the realities of existence. The very cause of trouble, the irritation caused by the behaviour of others, can be turned into a transformative force. Gurdjieff's methods of work on oneself abound in examples of turning negative forces to positive account.

This is illustrated by another story, this time easily recognizable as an allegory. It occurs in the chapter "Beelzebub's Last Sojourn on the Earth". The hero is an amiable Jewish pharmacist living in Moscow. Beelzebub sees him taking Dover's Powders, a popular remedy containing a small dose of opium but substitutes it by quinine and burnt sugar Beelzebub protests that such a blatant fraud can not go undetected. The details of the subsequent conversations are a remarkable expression of Gurdjieff's views on the true and imitative ways of spiritual development. Gurdjieff was, more than anything else, a Sufi and he wishes to convey that one cannot recognize the Sufi path by outward appearances alone. The true way transmits a spiritual power, *baraka* or *hanbledzoin*, which enables the seeker to do what is quite beyond his unaided strength. But it is also possible in an imitative way to have the illusion of receiving such help. This comes from belief in the method, which combines bitter and sweet experiences, as the fictitious Dover's Powders combines quinine and burnt sugar. Opium stands for the *baraka* or higher energy which becomes indispensible to the true seeker as opium cannot be given up by the drug addict.

Many other stories in *Beelzebub's Tales* appear on the surface to be little more than rather naive satires upon the culture of the early twentieth century, but, on more intuitive reading, carry valuable insights into the way the seeker after the truth can find his way through the confusion of the modern world. Very often violent and seemingly irrelevant attacks upon human frailty are to be read as practical directions for self-discipline.

With Gurdjieff, the three elements of communication; speech, language and meaning were always integrated into one whole. This was achieved by applying the principle of threefoldness developed in all his writings, but especially in the chapter "Purgatory" of *Beelzebub's Tales*. The anode-beginning, or force-plus, or masculine element, was always the intention from which meaning derives. The cathode-beginning, or force-minus, was language. Language for Gurdjieff, was passive, the feminine element in discourse. Speech, or the medium of communication, was the reconciling principle or neutralizing force. This is one reason why it is important to hear Gurdjieff's writings read aloud and it probably explains why Ouspensky said that he was a magnificent lecturer but a poor writer. Speech reconciles the poverty of our language with the exuberance of our intention. Gurdjieff's power of speech was extraordinary. He could hold our attention for hours in a smoke-laden crowded room when we had eaten and drunk more than we wanted. The required effort of attention came only partly from our confidence that he might at any moment make utterances of great significance that we might never hear again. It was essentially his own 'being' which inspired his speech with the power to penetrate below the surface of our personality. In his written word he set himself to achieve an equal penetration. He did not always succeed, but there are passages in all his writings that have no less force than that of the spoken word.

This force was attenuated for some listeners by the use of unfamiliar words of his own invention. I have referred to the *Trogoautoegocrat* and its importance for understanding Gurdjieff's cosmology. The central idea is that the Creation of the world has occurred in stages. The first stage was that of a totally unconditioned state of being within which the Absolute will established the field of its own activity. This corresponds to the Vedic doctrine of a primal state in which the Creator and his creation were undivided. According to the Sānkhya interpretation, the emergence of the three *gunas* was subsequent and resulted in all the diversity by which the world is maintained. Gurdjieff expresses the same idea in his Fundamental Law of *Triamazikamno*, or, as it was written in the earlier version of *Beelzebub's Tales, Triamonia*. In the version which Gurdjieff had read to his American groups in 1929 there is a remarkable passage which runs : "He directed the action of the laws of Triamonia and Eftalogodiksis which had been in the Sun-Absolute itself from within the Sun-Absolute without, and from this resulted what is now called the Word God or emanation." This passage, so reminiscent of Gnosticism and Neo-Platonism, has been cited as evidence that Gurdjieff's cosmology is entirely of Gnostic origin. This theory breaks down in view of the succeeding passages which introduce ideas that are not to be found in

Neo-Platonic writings or Gnostic fragments. The Logos issued from the Absolute Being, but it proved sterile. This was because it did no more than set up a state of polarity. "When our Creator directed the forces of the Sun-Absolute from within out, the emanations obtained from this had not at first the possibility of containing all three forces of the Triamonia in a vivifying state. Only two of these were vivifying namely the positive force and the negative force." Here we have the primitive conflict of yang and yin, of the male and female principles. Then Gurdjieff introduces the idea of a third force in a most significant form: "Our Almighty Endlessness was therefore obliged to vivify the third force, the Neutralizing force, during the first creation by the force of his Own Will." It can be seen that this departs from accepted Christian theology and is indeed quite different from any of the heretical views put forward between the third and eighth centuries. The conception reverts unmistakedly to the middle Babylonian period of Zoroastrianism. The Merciless Heropass— the Babylonian Zervan—is beyond the power even of the Creator Himself and he must resort to a stratagem to ensure the permanence of His place of Being, the Sun Absolute.

The Third force was called *fagologiria* which presumably means the reversal of forces by eating and being eaten. For some reason, in the final revision of *Beelzebub's Tales*, the word was entirely removed and there is not even the statement that Our Endlessness was compelled to vivify the neutralizing force by His Own Will.

Such changes were certainly not due to an oversight. They illustrate Gurdjieff's way of 'burying the dog deeper'. I would not have seen what he means in his account of the law of threefoldness in the published version, if I had not compared it with the more explicit statement in the earlier one. Gurdjieff attached very great importance to his account of the Laws of World Creation and World Maintenance. He did not wish this account to be analysed and criticized by philosophers and theologians, so he wrote in language that learned beings would not trouble to read, but he did not write so obscurely than an ordinary intelligent reader might not catch the intention if he were prepared to take the trouble.

If one looks at the language and terminology as a whole, one can see that Gurdjieff was consistent and had a clear purpose. He created a legominism and sent it out into the world in a form that would ensure its preservation. He intended to prepare initiates who could interpret it; but died before this part of his work was completed. We have now to carry it forward as well as we can.

Appendix II

The Great Laws

OUR customary way of thinking and talking about the world is in terms of objects and events, both of which are abstractions. Gurdjieff saw the world as the universal process of transformation of energies, regulated by two fundamental laws and various 'second-grade' laws arising from their interaction. The two basic realities are *relations* and *transformations*. The first are governed by the Law of Threefoldness variously called *Triamonia* and *Triamazikamno* and the second by the Law of Sevenfoldness called *Eftalogodiksis* or *Heptaparaparshinokh*. The interaction of these two laws is represented by the Enneagram symbol and by the Diagram of All Living referred to in Chapter 11. It is also noteworthy that Gurdjieff refers in the Purgatory Chapter to a scale of energies of different 'degrees of vivifyingness', which is divided into twelve steps or stages. We find on close examination that all the first twelve numbers are associated with various laws or principles of the relationships and the transformations of substances. With the exception of the numbers five, seven and eleven, these are all obtained by combining two and three, as Plato does in his exposition of the Pythagorean doctrine in the *Timaeus*. Gurdjieff himself ascribes this knowledge to the Masters of Wisdom of Atlantis, again reminiscent of *Timaeus*. He departs however from the platonic tradition in his description of Reciprocal Maintenance which has no place in Greek cosmology and did not enter European thinking until Gurdjieff came to the West.

Nevertheless, it must have been known in some form, because we can find traces in the Rosicrucian literature of the sixteenth and seventeenth centuries; that is just when the Khwajagān had finished their work in Central Asia and were handing their knowledge on to various Sufi brotherhoods, and probably also to European societies with the same fundamental aim. The Rosicrucian symbol of the pentad which appears in Dr. Fludd's *Systema Universi* corresponds exactly to the 'Diagram of All Living' and hence to the structure of the *Trogoautoegocrat*. The same work contains the doctrine of the quintessence and transformation. Every cosmic manifestation has its higher and lower natures, the interaction of which produces the quintessence. This is also Gurdjieff's teaching expressed in the statement (*Beelzebub's Tales*, p. 763) "The Higher blends with the Lower to actualize the Middle". The pentad symbol is :

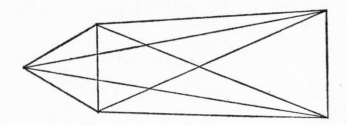

By placing the five terms at different levels in the diagram, we indicate the five nodal points. Reading from left to right, we show three kinds of relationships :

1. What it is in itself; the quintessence.
2. The essence classes from which and to which it evolves.
3. How it enters into the *Trogoautoegocratic* process.

We can illustrate these by reference to man. The quintessence of human nature is consciousness. Man is created a conscious being. He is endowed with the power of choice and because he is a three-brained being, he is 'made in the image of God'. Nevertheless, consciousness is not his highest attribute. Concealed in his nature is the creative power which God has shared with him : this makes him potentially a demiurgic intelligence. He has also an animal nature from which he has evolved but that still makes it possible for him to live unconsciously by sensation alone. Man is one in his essence and threefold in his nature. All men are aware—some strongly, some dimly—of their creative potential and of their animal instincts, and know that their consciousness forbids them to identify with either. It is much harder for us to see that we feed on the germinal essence, and are destined to become food for the Cosmic Individuality. We will examine this *Trogoautoegocratic* relationship for each essence class in turn.

The pentad is the basic value system. We require a pentad in order to answer questions such as Gurdjieff's "What is the sense and significance of this existence?" An essence class in Gurdjieff's system comprises all entities that occupy a specific place in the cosmic order, by what they are, by what they arise from and are transformed into and by what they eat and what they feed. This gives five independent terms and this is why a pentad is needed to define an essence class completely. So that Gurdjieff's scheme—if we can make it work—should provide us with a comprehensive yet simple system of universal values and obligations.

The first essence class which I have called heat is the substance out of which the universe has been created. It is the same as the Hindu *tapas*, which in the Vedic hymns is the first creative urge. In physical terms, heat is the formless energy that can be converted into other energies only by means of heat engines and generators. All forms of energy in their conversions liberate or absorb heat. All this is consistent with what is written in *Beelzebub's Tales* about *Etherokrilno*. Heat like every other essence class has upper and lower limits. The upper limit is approached at very high temperatures where heat can be directly converted into matter; for example, in the fusion reaction by which hydrogen is transformed into helium. Here temperatures of tens of millions of degrees are involved and the concentration of energy is so great that heat is materialised into atoms. At the lower limit, heat merges into a state of zero entropy which is the same as Gurdjieff's, 'absolute firm-calm'. It satisfies the conditions for being an essence class. Heat is omnipresent and it has been intuitively understood from a most ancient time as the condition for evolution towards higher levels of existence. This is why the same word *tapas* is used for heat and also for austerity and sacrifice.

The second essence class, that I have called 'simples', comprises all states of matter which lack any coherent structure above the molecular level, but are nevertheless identifiable as entities. Simples include the chemical elements, but also other entities such as electrical and magnetic fields and radiations. Air, water, sunlight are all simples. The earth's core beneath the rocky crust is composed of simple substances. So we can picture a primitive state of existence in which all was simple. This state could not manifest any values and was therefore not a level of being. It did not have any food, for according to the *Trogoautoegocratic* principle, food comes from a class once removed from one's self. Gurdjieff expressed this by calling it a "hydrogen without the Holy Ghost", one of his pregnant utterances that say so little and yet convey so much. Another way of putting it is that the simples cannot evolve but can be the means for the evolution of others.

The third class, which I call 'crystal', is known to us as the solid state in which there is a recognizable pattern and corresponding bulk properties. The rocks of which the earth's outer crust is composed were originally crystallized from the simples of the primitive earth matter. All rocks have a regular structure, even when there are no visible crystal forms. The oceans too have the structure of salt-bearing water that is very different from the simple state of water vapour that existed in the earth's atmosphere before the oceans condensed. We have thus the picture of an essence class that forms a layer many miles thick covering the whole earth with water, ice, rocks and air. This has grown mainly by the action of heat, light and gravitation upon the primitive state of the earth. It is, therefore, plausible to say that 'heat and random motion' is the food of the earth's crust. Without heat, this earth would be a dead planet; but heat must be absorbed according to a definite pattern to maintain the balance between land, water, air and ice which makes life possible. The earth's crust is a complete essence class, ranging from simple states of matter to the mountain scree and valley detritus which are so close to the soil essence that they can support vegetable life. The five terms of the crystal essence can be represented with our symbol:

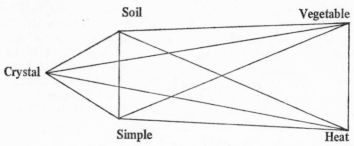

We have here the basic state of Reciprocal Maintenance. The variety of existing forms and their complex interactions are placed in the essential relationship of mutual support. The 'spiritualization of existence' consists in the organizing of lower forms by assimilation into higher forms. The 'realization of essence' consists in the manifestation within the existing world of higher patterns of value. That is why the entire system is called one of 'reciprocal maintenance'. Each essence class derives its cosmic significance from the three properties: First of being what it is, second of being food for a higher essence and thirdly, feeding upon the lower essence. By this, the relationship of eating and being eaten acquires universal significance and the importance attached to it in Gurdjieff's presentation is explained in a way that is by no means clear in *Beelzebub's Tales*.

I would like here to draw attention to the understanding of the place of life on the earth that we can derive by contemplating this essence class of the crystals. We can see that this is no chance process of aggregation, but also no predetermined and precreated world, but the universal exchange of substances, the *Common-Cosmic Ansanbaluiazar* and the *Trogoautoegocrat* in action. We human beings are involved in this, not directly but because we have the power to influence it for better or for worse.

The planet on which we live is not a dead mass moved only by gravitational and thermal stresses. It is a cosmos with its own essence pattern and therefore its own destiny. We are involved in this destiny, but it is unfolded upon a time-scale so vast that a hundred generations of man see no visible evidence of change. Gurdjieff, in one of his lectures at the Prieuré, spoke of "Rocks, winds and waves" as having their own life which we can feel but not share in. Out of this life comes the Biosphere that transforms and concentrates the energies by which the earth and moon evolve towards the fulfilment of their cosmic destiny. This destiny is both involuntionary and evolutionary. It is a combined process of realization and spiritualization. By 'realization' I mean the action whereby spirit acquires a body, and by 'spiritualization' I mean the process whereby body acquires a spirit. The two are inseparable. This is the sense of the Greek saying— *odos ano kato*—the way up is also the way down. It is called in *Beelzebub* the *common-cosmic-Ansanbaluiazar*.

We can see this in the history of the earth. As the earth was differentiated into layers from the core to the atmosphere, it was transformed into a body capable of responding to spiritual influences originating in the Sun. This is explicitly stated in the "Purgatory" chapter of *Beelzebub's Tales*.

The next stage in the spiritualization of existence occurs at the very surface of the planet in the layer of soil, the average thickness of which is only a few feet; that is, about one ten-millionth of the earth's diameter. This intensely active skin which surrounds nearly all the land surface of the earth and continues in the plankton layer of the oceans, plays a vital role in the whole life and evolution of the earth. The soil's volume is about 500,000 cubic miles, one thousandth the volume of the crust and only one millionth part of that of the earth. I quote these rough figures to illustrate Gurdjieff's point that quantity diminishes enormously whereas quality increases at a corresponding rate as we go up the scale of being. And yet, the structure remains similar throughout.

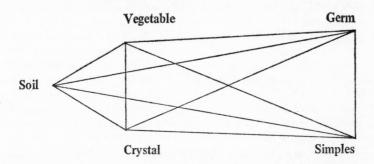

The soil has the crystal as its lower nature and vegetation as its higher. This agrees with what soil science tells us. It is also well established that soil feeds on simples. The only new and surprising features of the diagram is the soil's relationship to the germinal essence. Gurdjieff dropped a hint when he said that worms are the typical one-brained beings. The intimate connection between the annelids and the life of the soil is well known.

We should feel a very close affinity with the soil which is the womb of all life as the earth itself is its mother.

The soil essence is in a constant state of transformation. The particular mechanism of transformation is very instructive for our understanding of the *Trogoautoegocrat*. The soil grows on all kinds of breakdown products : the silt carried down by the mountain streams is eroded from the crystal rocks, the dust deposited from the winds, the remains of vegetable and animal bodies. All this is expressed in the symbol which shows simples as the food of the soil. The soil is a dynamic essence : its significance lies in what it can become rather than in what it is. Without life, the soil degenerates and reverts to the state of the crystalline crust. When the soil is 'treated' with simples incompatible with its essence pattern—such as certain chemical agents that we are now using on a large scale—it loses its dynamism and can no longer provide a healthy source of nourishment for the germinal essence. The observed facts of ecological imbalance speak for themselves. We, however, should look more deeply and see that in raping the soil, we violate a cosmic law and this must inevitably bring its own retribution. Modern man ignores cosmic laws even when they have been revealed to him, and does not see that this is the cause of many of his troubles.

Even if we do not know the laws; by the working of Conscience, we can be sensitive to them in the depths of our being. There are hundreds of thousands of people who are deeply distressed by what is being done to the soil and to the germinal essence. They interpret this distress perhaps in superficial terms, but they do make great efforts to preserve our heritage. If they could see more deeply, they would understand better what needs to be done and how to do it. We need to accept the soil as an essence class having its place within the cosmic harmony. We have no right to injure its essential pattern which is that of a generator of a transformation that links the non-living and living states of matter. In this transformation, energies are produced and liberated that are needed for cosmic purposes. This process is more important than we can imagine and we interfere with it at our peril. In the past, many civilizations have perished because they violated cosmic laws, which are inexorable and cannot be twisted to serve illusory human purposes.

Man has a special affinity with the soil, because he too is a dynamic essence through which cosmic transformations are proceeding. Man also is a 'soil' which links unconscious and conscious states of matter. He does not see that he cannot evade his destiny.

The vegetable essence is static. A plant is a being, though not—in Gurdjieff's terminology—spiritualized, possessing a brain. Gurdjieff calls vegetation thoughout *Beelzebub's Tales* 'Surplanetary Formations' and he divides it into three main classes. The first class, which he calls *Oonastral-*

nian serves only for the purposes of the earth itself. This is the primary function of maintaining the equilibrium of earth, air and water upon which all life depends. Vegetation fixes carbon and liberates oxygen, it synthesizes carbohydrates, proteins and fats. These are primary cosmic functions that no other essence can perform. Vegetable life existed on the earth long before the arising of organisms with brains. Nearly a thousand million years were needed to set the scene for the emergence of animal essences. During this time, the soil slowly developed on the land area, oxygen was concentrated in the atmosphere, plankton proliferated in the seas, climates were regulated and stabilized. In this immense preparatory work, flowerless vegetation played the central role. When this task was accomplished, vegetation began to diversify. Flowering plants appeared. With this came the second class of vegetable essences that Gurdjieff calls the *Okhtatralnian*. These serve not only for the purposes of the earth's maintenance but also to permit evolution of higher forms of life, the energies of which Gurdjieff specifically says in the chapter "The Law of Heptaparaparshinokh" have their origin in the Sun and other planets of the solar system.

The third category of vegetable essences is called *Polormedekhtian* which means that it is able to concentrate energies that originate "beyond the solar system" and are associated with higher states of consciousness. They include the grape vine from which wine is made and the tobacco plant, opium poppy, hemp and certain mushrooms—all of which have specific actions on the human psyche. All are included in the Avestan *Haoma* or Sanskrit *Soma* and have been used for thousands of years for inducing states in which people can be aware of cosmic realities. They have a special connection with man on whom their use places a sacred responsibility.

The structure of the vegetable essence is shown in the diagram :

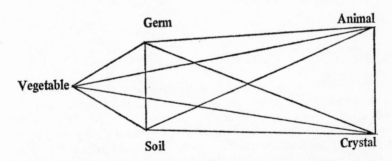

The vegetable essence comprises a range of potentialities from soil to germ : The vegetation has evolved from pre-living forms and in the course of evolution it has given birth to the germinal essence. At first sight, one might say that it feeds upon the soil. It is more accurate to say that it makes the soil by its own metabolism, life and death. Its nourishment is more primitive than the soil essence : all the elements of which the earth's crust is made, all the crystalline forms created during a thousand million years enter into vegetation through which they are dispersed, concentrated and enter into the soil. There is an endless cycle of materials and energies between the four essence classes—heat, simples, crystals and soil. This is the lower tetrad of the *Ansanbaluiazar*. Vegetation is the lowest member of the tetrad of life. In Beelzebub's language, it is individualized but not spiritualized, for it has no brain system. The first spiritualized essence is the germ which is called "Invertebrate" in the 'Diagram of All-Living' and one-brained being in *Beelzebub's Tales*. Like the vegetable essence, there are three categories of germinal essence. One is the invertebrate phyla which enter into the energy transformations of the earth and though not directly connected with man, do indirectly support his very existence. The activity of the invertebrates such as worms and insects and animal plankton in the seas maintains the conditions for our life. The second category includes the micro-organisms that produce substances that act upon the bodies of animals and men : the bio-chemical agents. The third category has always been represented by the wheat-germ that Gurdjieff calls 'Phosphora' and says that it exists on all planets where there are three-brained beings and serves as their principal essence food. The germinal essence is particulary associated with sexual reproduction and is dynamic by nature.

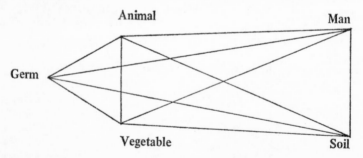

The germinal essence as shown in this diagram derives its nourishment from the soil and is food for man. These are three dynamic essences that are concerned in the process of transformation. The soil, the germ and man, are all in a state of becoming. The soil is not a ready-made finished product but has incessantly to be regenerated, and the same is true of the germinal essence. There are energies that are liberated in this way of which we can have some experience and they are the ones that give us our characteristically human life. In so far as we also have animal bodies, we, like the animals, derive our food from the vegetable essence, but the earthly significance of man is in his relationship with germinal essence. This also helps us to understand why the sexual activity occupies such an important and powerful place in human life and why Gurdjieff says that the sex energy, to which he gives the name *Exiohary* is the means provided for man's self-creation and for the development of his higher bodies. The germinal essence and not the vegetable was the starting point of animal evolution.

The sixth class includes all the chordate animals, but particularly the mammalia which have a fully developed two-brained system. The cosmic significance of the animal essence is also threefold. Animals concentrate sensitive energy in almost all its possible varieties. This is why we find in the animal kingdom sensitive responses that have such a strange similarity to the whole range of human feelings. According to Beelzebub, these energies are required for the *Trogoautoegocrat* of the entire solar system. If the energy that is liberated by the different species of animals is required, then these species of animals are also required. Then, if we destroy a species of animals, we men will be required to produce the corresponding energies. Not understanding this, we allow whole species to become extinct or even deliberately destroy them for our own profit as we are doing, for example, with the whale. Many of us have a deep feeling that there is something terribly wrong about this. There is, in fact, a serious threat to the future of the human race if we allow these processes of destruction to go too far. It may be that this has been foreseen and that the 'animalization' of humanity is one of the possible results of our present way of living.

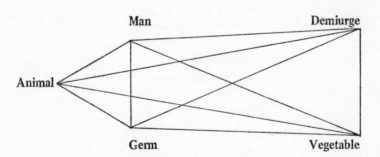

It will be seen from the diagram that the animal essence serves as food for the Demiurgic essence. This strange idea is referred to many times in *Beelzebub's Tales*. The point here is that without psychic energies derived from the animal essences, the Demiurges cannot perform their work. This is constantly emphasized in *Beelzebub's Tales* and it is given as an explanation of the occurence of war and the reason for animal sacrifices. It is also very clearly said that the time when the destruction of other forms of life was needed has passed and indeed the time when war was unavoidable has also passed. If we are to enter into a new age, we must understand that we cannot destroy animal essences any more than we can destroy human essences without reaping the consequences.

The diagram suggests a static equilibrium of the vegetable and animal kingdoms in their relationship with the Demiurgic Intelligence responsible for the orderly progress of the solar system. Once this idea really comes home to us, we begin to see that a totally different attitude toward nature must replace that now current, according to which the balance of life and power on the earth has mankind for its pivot.

This brings us to the seventh essence class; Man. First of all, we note that man himself can have very different essence natures. It is probably right to say that there are three modes of humanness. The first is the man who lives according to the *Itoklanoz* principle. The second lives according to the *Foolasnitamnian* principle. The third consists only of those most rare individuals who are incarnated from Above. They, like the Demiurges come into the existing world fully developed with a mission to perform. In man's threefold modality, we can see a parallelism with the other essence classes. The true human essence is the man who lives according to the *Foolasnitamnian* principle. This is man in the process of transformation destined to arrive eventually at union with the Cosmic Individuality. It is in this sense that man is said to be 'food' for the Cosmic Individuality. The *Itoklanoz* man has emerged from or perhaps has reverted to, the animal essence.

The pentad symbol applied to man shows in succinct form the whole significance of human destiny which we studied in Chapter 2.

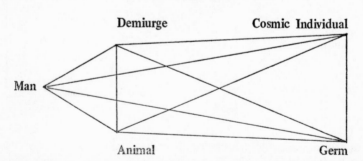

Man is, by nature, poised between animal and the Demiurgic essences. This is reminiscent of the saying of St. Augustine: "Little higher than the animals, little lower than the angels." It is right to say that there is in man on the one hand the property of passive acceptance of a quasi-animal life and on the other hand the creative power to transform the world. Man is both an animal and a creator. This is implicit in *Beelzebub's Tales* and at this point, Gurdjieff's scheme coincides with the fundamental teaching of all religions. Man is placed before a threefold choice. He can resign himself to living as a 'thinking animal' seeking pleasure and avoiding suffering. This is *Itoklanoz* living. He can also exploit the Demiurgic powers that are part of his nature, but do so for egoistic and self-destructive ends. This is the Hasnamuss Individual of *Beelzebub's Tales*. Man's true destiny forbids him to surrender to either extreme. Because he is a man, he must work and suffer to serve the Cosmic Purpose and to equip himself with the vehicle of Objective Reason. This will eventually bring him into union with the Cosmic Individuality: the *Tawhid* of the Sufis. Even this is not the end; for the path of Absolute Liberation will lead him beyond being into that state that Gurdjieff calls our *Common Creator Endlessness*.

Man has an unlimited potential for evolution, for he is endowed with the capacity to go beyond the limitations of the existing world. Nevertheless, his path is not *out of* this world, but *through* it. Gurdjieff makes the tremendous claim that our Creator looks to man for 'help' in the administration of the enlarging world'. This seems to contradict the doctrine that the ultimate goal of human evolution is beyond existence and even beyond Being.

There is an ineffable mystery in the doctrine of liberation. For ordinary thinking, freedom is 'from' some state of constraint. Essential liberation is the annihilation of conditions, but not the abandonment of obligations. Our Creator needs man no less than man needs Him; but this is anthropomorphic language. Man in the very core of his being is already the Creator. He is beyond the distinction of one and many, of great and small. When all limitations are transcended, nothing remains but the One Will which is 'I'. The *Trogoautoegocrat* thus reveals itself as Cosmic Love. Everything gives and receives life and the willing, free acceptance of the relationship of mutual fulfilment is love. In the revelation we can see how the Christian Eucharist is itself a representation of the *Trogoautoegocrat* and also how it is descended from the Zoroastrian love feast. The sacrifice of the Mass, is not a one-way traffic in which the Cosmic Individuality is sacrificed for man. It is also man's own sacrifice of his separate existence. Some years ago, I served the Mass for the Father Abbot of St. Wandrilles-Fontanelle. While giving thanks, I was overwhelmed by the awareness that as Christ had entered into me, I had also entered into him. I saw that the distinction of eating and being eaten had disappeared and that I was as truly God as God was truly myself. Since that moment, I began to understand the *Trogoautoegocrat* as the Being and Becoming of God himself manifested in the Creation.

The creation is both dynamic Will and static Being. Man by his essence belongs to the dynamic mode. The Demiurgic essence is the highest individualized essence in the static mode. The Demiurges are the class that corresponds to Beelzebub's sacred individuals from the 'centre' who govern the world on behalf of the Creator. In everything that Gurdjieff wrote and said, he left us in no doubt that he believed in the real existence of superhuman but limited and fallible beings. The picture is painted in vivid colours in *Beelzebub's Tales*, most sharply so in describing the 'unforseeingness' which has landed mankind in the predicament of blindness to the essential reality.

Much that has been written in this book turns upon the proposition that a demiurgic action on a global scale is now in progress. Mankind is once again endangering the evolution of the Solar System. Steps are being taken to ensure that this danger is averted. Our most urgent obligation is to aid this action by our own work. We need for this to be in a right relationship with the animal kingdom. Many feel this; but no one understands the deep reason for it. Energies are required that mankind is failing to produce. They can be produced extensively by massive destruction of life or intensively by the conscious labour and intentional suffering of individuals and communities. We must, as a race, be brought to understand that the creative purpose must prevail. If it is not with our consent and co-operation, it will be realised at our expense. If once we accept our destiny we ally ourselves to the power that creates the world. We enter the field of Demiurgic action and can help the Demiurgic Intelligences to perform their difficult task while there is still time. Their destiny is to unite with the *Trogoautoegocrat* by which the cosmic harmony is sustained. In this sense, Beelzebub refers to the *All-quarters Maintainer Peshtvogner* who is one of the sacred Individuals 'nearest to our Endlessness'.

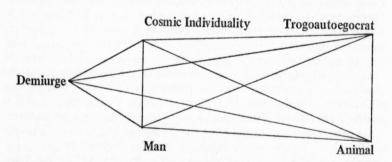

The diagram shows how the higher nature of the Demiurgic Essence merges into the Cosmic Individuality.

The ninth and final pentad is that which shows the Cosmic Individuality as the link between the Creator and the entire world process. Beelzebub

uses the term *Theomertmalogos* which he interprets as 'Word-God' to
stand for the Cosmic Individuality. The 'Sacred Individuals incarnated
from Above' are manifestations of the Word-God. We are here in the realm
of theology where further speculation might seem to have no bearing upon
the Making of a New World. Gurdjieff, on the contrary, was emphatic
that mankind needs to have a new understanding of God and the Creation,
without which the question of the sense and purpose of life on the earth
can have no really satisfying answer. If we recognize that everything that
exists is needed; that there is nothing arbitrary or without purpose, we
can, by that recognition alone, come to a new and solid foundation for
Faith, Love and Hope; and we can see why Gurdjieff says that he who
has Conscience can truly be called the Son of God.

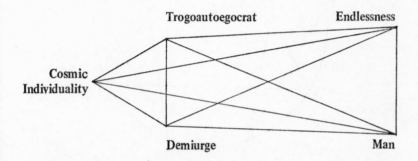

To find man in this highest pentad—albeit as the humblest member,
should remind us of the dignity of human nature.

The *Trogoautoegocrat* is Gurdjieff's major contribution to a new cosmology for it offers an answer to the question "Why is the world structured as it is?" It allows us to connect the functions and purpose of all
the essence classes. It gives a reason for our existence and shows us what
true evolution means. It does not, however, tell us how evolution is to be
maintained in a world of uncertainty and hazard. In order to understand how the world works we must turn from the idea of essence
classes to that of cosmoses. A cosmos is a world. We have the
principle that all cosmoses have the same basic pattern. This pattern is
given by the combination of the cosmic laws of three- and seven-foldness.

This brings us to an entirely different symbol which Gurdjieff called the
Enneagram. I concluded in Chapter 3 that this symbol and the ideas for
which it stands, originated with the Sarmān society about 2,500 years ago
and was revised when the power of the Arabic numeral system was
developed in Samarkand in the fifteenth century.

The enneagram is the symbol of self-sustained evolution or transformation. The essence of this symbol is to portray three independent processes

mutually supporting one another at the precise points where—lacking such support—others would lose their direction and become their own opposite : The enneagram is a triple symbol : triangle and hexagon inscribed in a circle. The hexagon is twisted so that the lines cross three times :

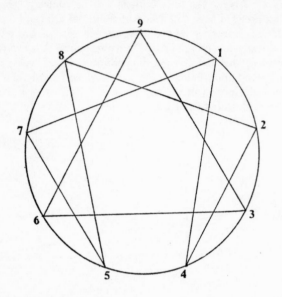

There are endless possibilities of interpretation of this remarkable symbol. The simplest is given by numbering the points on the circumference from 1–9 which gives the triangle numbers 3, 6 and 9, and the hexagon 1–4–2–8–5–7 which is the well-known recurrent sequence that gives the remainder when any integer is divided by seven. This property arises only in a decimal number system, which suggests that it was discovered only after the mathematicians of Central Asia had founded the modern theory of numbers by giving zero a separate symbol. Whereas the belief that the number seven is sacred probably goes back to Sumerian times, the form of the enneagram is likely to have been developed in Samarkand in the fourteenth century. This would account for its absence from Indian or European literature. However, Gurdjieff asserted that it was far more ancient and attributed it to the Sarmān Brotherhood. Both versions may be true. The Sarmāni were custodians of the secrets of Reciprocal Maintenance and no doubt embodied them in sacred dances and symbols. These could have been given a new form when the discoveries of the 'learned men' of Samarkand became known.

In order to understand and make use of the enneagram one must grasp that each of the three processes initiated at the points 0, 3 and 6 must be different in nature and yet compatible with the other two. Generally speaking it can be said that the first is functional, the second concerns being and the third will. Otherwise, one could say that the first is situated in the materal or sensible world, the second is the *kesdjanian* or psychic world and the third in the spiritual or unconditional world. Since we cannot directly perceive the psychic and spiritual realities, we are aware of the second and third processes only at second hand through their manifestations. They are concerned with the transformation of qualities and states.

As all this is very abstract, I shall give my favourite illustration: that of the working of a kitchen in which the meals of a community are prepared. Three processes are involved: the changes in the kitchen, those in the food and those in the eaters. These are different in character but they interpenetrate at every point. The kitchen is the functional element. The food is the being content of the process. The will is embodied in the life of the community, which must eat in order to fulfil its purpose.

We can suppose that there is a chief cook who stands for the law by which the entire event is governed.

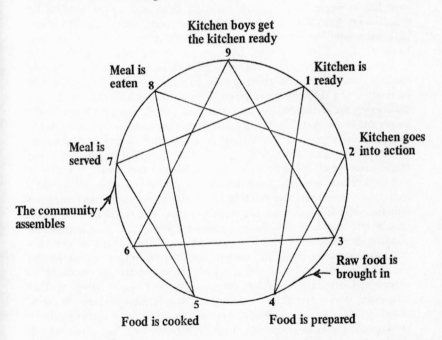

The visible process goes round the circumference in the order 0–1–2–3–4–5–6–7–8–9. The interaction and intergration of the event as a whole requires influences travelling along the path 1-4-2-8-5-7. The basic triad Kitchen–Food–Community is given by the points 3–6–9.

The participation of the kitchen is cyclic : it starts clean, empty and with all its equipment and tools in their resting places, it ends in the same state. It goes from zero round the circle. At the point 5 it is in the maximum state of tension : this is called by Gurdjieff (*Beelzebub's Tales*, pp. 754, 758) 'Harnel Aoot'. It is the 'place of transformation'. The kitchen returns to its primitive state after the meal is eaten and is ready for the next meal.

Similarly the food passes through successive stages of being brought from the store (point 3) prepared (4) cooked (5) served (7) and eaten (8). There is no return. The food now enters the life of the community as its source of energy for the next day.

The community enters at point 6 where the 'dinner bell goes'. The meal is served, eaten and digested. The food and the community have coalesced and their further transformation requires another enneagram.

The interest and indeed, fascination of the symbol lies in the recurrent figure 1-4-2-8-5-7. This expresses with amazing aptness the way the chief cook has to work. In allocating work, he must look to the food to be prepared i.e. from 1 to 4. This shows all the cooks, assistants and kitchen boys what equipment, utensils and tools will have to brought into use (4 to 2). The chief cook must have his eye on the meal. The menu, the timing of all the operations, the entire plan of campaign is directed along the line 2 to 8. The actual cooking must be regulated so that each dish will be ready at the right time and place (8 to 5). The sauces and garnishing, the serving up of the dishes goes by way of 5 to 7. The chef himself will be present to see that this step is perfectly carried through. It is remarkable that here alone in the entire symbol do the lines of action and of supervision—both going from 5 to 7—coincide. The chef retires from the kitchen relying on his subordinate to see that the line 7 to 1 is followed and the kitchen cleaned and put in order for the next meal.

It might seem that the exact fitting is too theoretical. The reader has only to try for himself. The only warning I must give is to be sure that you take a self-contained process or event that really works and that you identify the three lines of transformation on the principle that one concerns the external set-up, one concerns the material to be transformed and the third is connected with the aim and purpose of the operation. Many years ago Clarence King, Chief Engineer at the General Motors British subsidiary, demonstrated that the working of a factory producing a mechanical article like an automobile must be structured according to the enneagram if it is to operate successfully' (*Systematics*, Vol. I, p. 111). It can be shown that a well-ordered school must embody the three processes. The human organism and indeed any living organism, is built on the same model. I hope I have said enough to arouse the reader's interest and encourage him to study the enneagram for his own benefit.

The two symbols—the pentad and the enneagram represent the entire system of the universe scene of the energy transformation (*Ansanbaluiazar*) and reciprocal maintenance (*trogoautoegocrat*). As Gurdjieff 'detested explanations', I will go no further into this scheme. I can assure the reader who sets himself to penetrate into the significances of these symbols that his time will not be wasted.

Gurdjieff's attitude to initiation was firmly stated in the earliest account of his ideas, written in 1915 and called *Glimpses of Truth*. This is the account of a meeting of a cultured Russian with Gurdjieff. After Gurdjieff had given a brilliant exposition of the transformation of energies in man and the universe, making use of various diagrams, the visitor said: "This knowledge you have surprises me, why has it been hidden?" Gurdjieff explained that he could be told because he had previously worked and studied, adding: "Thanks to this work, or your own work, you are able to understand something of what I have told you. Let us suppose that in a year's time we should speak again on this subject, during this year you will not have waited for roast pigeon to fly into your mouth. You will have worked and your understanding will have changed. You will be more 'initiated'. You said that 'knowledge' was 'hidden'" This is not so : it is simply that people are incapable of understanding. Personally, for instance, I should be very glad if I could talk to anyone of the subjects that interest me without having to put myself on a level with their understanding and intelligence. People have too few words for the expression of certain ideas. Where it is not the words that are important but the source from which they came, in the absence of understanding, it is simply impossible to speak.

"What you call 'hiding' is in truth, the 'impossibility of giving what people cannot receive."

Gurdjieff's elaborate symbolism, uncouth neologisms and changes of terminology were not employed to mislead and obstruct his followers, but to ensure that they would make the effort to discover the meanings for themselves. Explanation is often a fictitious help. Initiation is real enough, but it does not consist in making things easy for the seeker.

General Index

Note: (BT) refers to topics in "Beelzebub's Tales"

"Witness" (Bennett), 91
Word-God, *see* Theomertmalogos
work, 55, 115, 119, 120, 121, 126,
139, 141, 153, 154, 156, 158,
162, 166, 167, 168, 169, 170,
172, 173, 175, 182, 190, 204,
205, 214, 216, 218, 230, 231,
232, 234, 235, 238, 241, 242,
249, 254, 258, 269, 278, 297;
and death, 191; and suffering,
195; three lines, 219
World Council of Churches, 267
World Creation and World
Maintenance, Laws of, 66, 67,
107, 277, 280
World Health Organization, 267
worlds, doctrine of, 277; and
cosmoses, 197, 200, 293

Yangi Hissar, 97, 100
Yesi, *see* Tashkent

Yesevi Brotherhood, *see* Dervishes
Yezidis, 15, 17, 83, 87; and ancient
traditions, 63, 71
Younghusband Expedition, 90, 262

Zen Buddhism, 33, 219, 220
Zend, 113f
Zervan, time, 280
zikr, invocation, 30-1, 33, 34, 38, 41,
44, 48, 93, 274; and Gurdjieff,
219, 221; and dance, 223
Zoroatrianism, 12, 30, 45, 58, 59,
60, 62, 185; and aim of existence,
265; Saoshyant, Divine Saviour,
70; and Yezidis, 63, 71; and
hazard, 197; dualism, 199; and
Reciprocal Maintenance, 61;
and Sarmān, 197, 198; love
feast, 291
Zvarnoharno, *see* Avestan hvareno

Name Index

Abdulhalik ,Khwaja of Gujduvan, 34, 35, 38, 104
Abdullah, Khwaja Hasan of Berk, and 'eye of the heart', 31
Abdullah of Gujduvan, 47
Abdulmelik Ata, 34
Agha, Osman, 14
Ahrar, Khwaja Ubeydullah, 46, 47; learning to serve, 48; mission, 49, 58
Alexander, Miss Gladys, 5, 162, 163, 233; extensively quoted: on life at the Prieuré, 139–41, 145–7, 166–7; on American trip, 159–60
Alexander the Great, 69, 224
Alexandra Feodorovna, Tsarina, 116, 117
Alexis, Crown Prince of Russia, 116
Ali, Khwaja Nessadj Azizan of Raymitin, 37, 38, 40, 41, 42, 43
Alsop, Dr., 136
Amtranik, General, 127
Anastasieff, Feodor, 16
Anastasieff, Sophie Ivanovna, 16, 162, 217; see also Gurdjieff, G. I.
Anastasieff, Valentin, 162, 217; see also Gurdjieff, G. I.
Anderson, Margaret, 6, 232
Anderson, Naomi, 182; and publication of Beelzebub's Tales, 176
Anderson, Paul, 182; and publication of Beelzebub's Tales, 175–6; on Beelzebub's Tales, 180

Arabi, Muhiddin ibn, 29, 31
Arif, Mevlana of Dikkeran, 44, 46
Arif, Khwaja of Ringerve, 39, 40
Asoka, King of India, 75
Assurbanipal, 63
Ataturk, Mustafa Kemal, 34
Attar, Sufi poet, 29, 37
Attar, Khwaja Alaeddin, 47

Bailey, Alice, 31
Bartold, Wilhelm, 27, 72
Battuta, Ibn, 29
Bayazid the Thunderer, 33
Beaumont, Mrs., 129, 147
Beg, Maghrib, 30
Bektash, Hadji Veli, 25, 35
Bell, Dr., 137, 156
Bennett, John G., 3–7, 9, 16, 17, 19, 20, 24, 26, 47, 125, 126, 135, 136, 169, 176, 180, 222, 230f, 231, 232, 246; and Gurdjieff, 65, 77, 78, 86, 90, 91, 108, 111, 119, 127, 129, 130, 131, 147, 148, 159, 197, 236, 237, 275; and Naq'shbandis, 27, 79; and Sarmān, 73; and Hidden Directorate, 53; and Yezidis, 63; Inner Circle, 79; at Prieuré, 141, 147, 148, 152, 157, 159; and higher emotional energy, 154; writings, 261, 262–3, 266; and Demiurges, 205, 212, 263; on Beelzebub, 274, 277–8, 280;